THE BATTLE FOR THE SOUL

Books by Robert Crawford

Can We Ever Kill?
Journey into Apartheid
Making Sense of the Study of Religion
A Portrait of the Ulster Protestants
The Saga of God Incarnate
The God/Man/World Triangle
What Is Religion?
Is God a Scientist?
A Dialogue between Science and Religion

THE BATTLE FOR THE SOUL

A COMPARATIVE ANALYSIS IN AN AGE OF DOUBT

Robert Crawford

First published in 2011 by
PALGRAVE MACMILLAN®
in the United States—a division of St. Martin's Press LLC,
175 Fifth Avenue, New York, NY 10010.

Where this book is distributed in the UK, Europe and the rest of the world,
this is by Palgrave Macmillan, a division of Macmillan Publishers Limited,
registered in England, company number 785998, of Houndmills,
Basingstoke, Hampshire RG21 6XS.

Palgrave Macmillan is the global academic imprint of the above companies
and has companies and representatives throughout the world.

Palgrave® and Macmillan® are registered trademarks in the United States,
the United Kingdom, Europe and other countries.

ISBN: 978–0–230–60944–0

Library of Congress Cataloging-in-Publication Data

Crawford, Robert G. (Robert George), 1927–
    The battle for the soul : a comparative analysis in an age of doubt /
    Robert Crawford.
        p. cm.
    Includes bibliographical references.
    ISBN 978–0–230–60944–0
    1. Soul. 2. Resurrection. 3. Future life. 4. Religions. 5. Religion and science.
    6. Science—History—21st century. 7. Technology—History—21st century.
    I. Title.

BL290.C73 2011
202′.2—dc22   2010036206

A catalogue record of the book is available from the British Library.

Design by Newgen Imaging Systems (P) Ltd., Chennai, India.

First edition: March 2011

10 9 8 7 6 5 4 3 2 1

Printed in the United States of America.

To the memory of John Girvan with whom
I shared many hours of study and fellowship
during our undergraduate years.

CONTENTS

INTRODUCTION

When Christopher Marlowe's *Doctor Faustus* was performed in London in 1594 it produced a shock reaction in many quarters. The shock was not only because Faustus was depicted as wanting to acquire power and the control of nature through magic but that he was willing to sell his soul to get it.

One wonders what the reaction of the audience would be today. Is the soul still regarded as precious? Surveys of public opinion are not totally reliable but those carried out by the BBC in the "Soul of Britain" series in 2000 do give an idea of the views of many.

Respondents were asked: "Do you consider yourself solely to be a biological organism that ceases to exist at death?" 52 per cent replied "No," but 31 per cent answered "Yes," and 17 per cent said that they did not know. Further questions revealed a range of opinion regarding belief in the soul, God, and life after death. Many of these respondents did not belong to any traditional religion though they realized the importance of the issues.[1]

How are we to define the soul? The dictionary states that it is the spiritual part of a person regarded as the centre of personality, intellect, will, emotions, and believed by many to survive bodily death. It is the essential part of something; thus we speak of "the soul of the nation," and if we meet a person who displays little feeling we say, "You have no soul."

Mr. Gordon Brown, prior to his becoming Prime Minister of Britain, promised that he would bring the soul back to the party, which meant that he would get rid of sleaze, policy failures, and inculcate duty, honesty, hard work, family values, and respect for others. In the event the promise was marred by the glaring example of greed in his party and others. Misuse of expenses resulted in loss of confidence in the leaders of the nation and they were called to search their souls. Many people believe that Brown's failure to keep his promise was one of the reasons that lost him the election in 2010.

The soul is the centre of the moral and intellectual life, the personification or pattern of a person. It is interchangeable with mind, and demands duty, responsibility, sensitivity, and care for others. After death it is expected to receive a new body suitable for life in different conditions. Some people try not to think about death but are forced to as they stand beside the grave of their loved ones. Is it the final end or is there something more? Is the soul immortal or will the body be resurrected without the soul surviving? What about the reincarnation of the soul? Will we have a second chance of earthly life before a final judgment? Is there such a place as purgatory or some intermediate state where we will be purified in order to live the higher life? What can we say about heaven and hell?

An attempt is made in this book to answer some of these questions. It argues that there is life after death and that both soul and the resurrection of the body are linked. The claim is disputed that we must choose between the survival of the soul and the bodily resurrection and contends that there is need for both. Death is seen not as something final but the gateway to a new life that will be more wonderful than we can ever imagine.

Materialists, of course, have always denied any spiritual part of our nature saying that it is wishful thinking. Their position has been taken seriously in Christian circles and some theologians now think that the best defense of life after death is to dispense with the soul and stress the resurrection of the body. But it is hardly likely that materialists will be impressed with such a resurrection belief since it requires, as far as they are concerned, an unbelievable miracle. How, if we dispense with the soul, is our identity to be preserved in the after life? In order to answer this question it is necessary, as we proceed, to seek a clear definition of the term and understand its relation with mind and spirit.

Philosophers today are occupied with the task of understanding mind and consciousness. J. R. Searle says that it is no abstract problem, as shown by the passionate response to his writing and lectures. Traditionally mind has often been equated with soul and we will argue that it is not "the ghost in the machine" but intimately related to consciousness and spirit.

We live in a multiculture society so the discussion takes note of what six major world religions teach about the soul and ask if their teaching has any agreement with the teaching of science and philosophy. The Semitic religions are considered first: Judaism, Christianity, and Islam; then follow the Indian: Hinduism, Buddhism, and Sikhism. Since the focus will be on the soul in the context of the beliefs and practices of these religions the book is also an introduction to them. It will be argued that we have two basic trends, one that stresses that all possess a soul and it is immortal, not by natural right but a gift of God, and the other that we can place no dependence on this and must rely on the resurrection of the body. The Indian religions except Buddhism emphasise the immortal soul and assert its reincarnation. We also consider the question of whether there are not hints of reincarnation in the Judaic/Christian scriptures.

Of course, it is difficult to accept that we will not see our loved ones again and that all the saints and martyrs who died with the hope of a better existence were deluded. If all those who have given us great music, art, government, philosophy, and science are simply cast as rubbish to the void, can we ever think that life is meaningful? Surely we have not exhausted our possibilities at death?

James Murdoch Ewing poetically reminds us of the greatness of the issue:

> A battle for my soul
> The devil within
> Delights in the serpent
> Entwining my feet
> Pulling me deeper into the pit
> …A battle
> God shall win
> But I want to fight Him
> For as long as I can

God does not have a gender but it is impossible to write about the concept without using gender-specific terminology. I use the masculine pronoun with reference to the deity but recognize that female models do exist both in the religions and in contemporary writing. Concerning the human I have tried to alternate between "she" and "he," and "man" includes male and female.

Throughout I have tried to find the references to the various writers whom I have consulted but if anyone has been omitted I would apologize in advance.

I would like to thank those who took an interest in the project and helped in various ways. In particular, I am grateful to two scientists Professors John Polkinghorne and Russell Stannard who responded to my correspondence quickly and helpfully. My son Paul was very constructive not only in reading the manuscript but also in attending to the technical problems of the computer. I would like to thank Mr Burke Gerstenschlager, editor of Palgrave Macmillan, for his encouragement to continue the work and Ms Ciara Vincent, production editor for supervising the process. Rohini Krishnan of Newgen India has been responsible for the typesetting and has kept in touch with me by phone. She excels in overcoming every difficulty. Finally, the staff of Worthing and Goring libraries UK have been very helpful in finding books which I needed to consult.

CHAPTER 1

THE JEWISH SOUL

You shall love the Lord thy God with all thy heart and with all thy soul and with all thy might.

(Deut. 6.5)

In this and subsequent chapters in order to understand what the soul means for a religion we will place it in the context of the main beliefs.

The Jews are among the greatest people in the world and have excelled in science, music, finance, and their religion has attracted and benefited mankind. Judaism has three pillars: belief in God, the Torah, and Israel the people of God. The faith is straightforward but becomes complicated because members have various attitudes toward the pillars.[1]

Albert Einstein was a Jew but he did not practice the religion. It was a matter of race not faith. The Orthodox Jews, however, stress both and follow the Torah, which is the first five books of Moses. These books point to the tradition and history of their religion, which can be divided into periods: ancient Israel from the beginnings to 586 BCE when the Temple was destroyed; the beginning of Judaism until the fall of the second Temple in 70 CE; the continuance with diverse Judaism from the American and French revolutions of 1776 and 1789 to the present.[2]

THE DIVISIONS

The Orthodox Jews are prominent today in the United States and follow Rabbinic Judaism as it developed through the ages. They are suspicious of converts to Jewry because no one would want to join a religion that has been so oppressed and scorned. They make little concession to the modern world, obeying the Talmud, which, among other things, demands observing dietary laws and the Sabbath.[3]

The Talmud is the major source of Jewish law. It consists of the Mishnah (ca. 200 CE) that is the oral law collected by the second century CE and the Gemara: Rabbinic commentaries on the Mishnah dating from 200 to 500 CE. It exists in two recessions, the Palestinian and the Babylonian.[4] The Orthodox synagogue services are in Hebrew, male and female are separated for worship, women are not ordained, and there is tension between the Orthodox and other forms of Judaism. The neoorthodox make some concession to the changing conditions of the modern world enabling its members to be more acceptable to those of other religions and the secularists.

Hasidim can be mentioned here for it is a mystical movement and part of Orthodoxy. It developed in the second century BCE and opposed the Hellenising of Jewish life and practice. It stressed the practical aspects of life rather than the intellectual, and in the Hasidim (Chasidim) sayings of the eighteenth and nineteenth century meditation is recommended because it brings forth the holy spark in man and strengthens his soul. Once the mystical is recognized as prominent the cultivation of the soul becomes important. The Rabbis are called Rebbes and they stress that God is present everywhere and in a practical sense pay much attention to what they eat.

The Reform was founded in 1840 in Britain and sits more lightly to the Torah than the Orthodox believing that though it was inspired it is still a human writing.[5] They argue that the laws concerning ritual and purity are outdated. Some of them value tradition saying that it is the animating soul of Judaism but others are prepared to abandon all the obligations. Their services resemble that of Christians with sermons in the vernacular, instrumental music and choirs, omission of sacrifice and women ordained as Rabbis. The sexes are not segragated for worship.

In 1885 the Pittsburgh Platform under Kohler viewed the Bible as containing only the moral code of Judaism and abandoned dietary laws, the doctrine of the resurrection of the dead, and reward and punishment in the hereafter. The immortality of the soul was accepted. It is the biggest group in America since 1937.[6]

The Platform was succeeded by a more positive attitude to ceremonial observances at Ohio in 1937. Then in 1999 another Pittsburgh statement opened the doors to Jewish life for all people everywhere by declaring the Mosaic law to be obsolete and no longer valid except for the moral laws.

The Conservative is the via media between Orthodoxy and Reform and though stressing the Torah accepts that it is open to critical scholarship. Thus it modifies strict observance of the Sabbath, dietary laws and has admitted women to train as Rabbis in its seminaries.

The Reconstructionists refuse to think of God as a person. Mordecai Kaplan who founded the group argued that it was to commit the anthropomorphic fallacy, that is, thinking of God as a man. His work led to depersonalising God and doubting a supernatural revealed religion. The concepts of a chosen people and a personal Messiah were denied and Judaism called upon to accept the modern world and change accordingly.

It provoked the reaction of the Orthodox who continued to believe in the coming of a personal Messiah. But the Conservative, Liberal (sometimes called Progressive) and Reform have replaced it with a messianic or perfect age to which history is directed.

The Zionists (1897 CE) are divided into the secular and religious. Gush Emunim is a Zionist movement founded in 1974 that stressed the nation of Israel and were encouraged by its victories over the Arabs and the development of settlements in the occupied territories.

WORSHIP

The morning service in the Authorised Daily Prayer Book states that the soul that God gives is pure, being formed and breathed into the human by Him: "thou preserves it within me; and thou will take it from me, but wilt restore it unto me hereafter";

"Blessed are thou, O Lord who restores souls unto the dead."[7] During evening prayer Orthodox men wear a tallith or shawl and say: "I am here wrapping myself around with a tallith to which fringes are attached in order to carry out the command of my Creator...And just as I cover myself with the tallith in this world, so may my soul deserve to be clothed with a beautiful spiritual robe in the world to come, in the Garden of Eden." The denial of the proper needs of the soul is also seen in prayers of penitence: "For not listening to your voice within us, For denying the needs of our soul, For making this world a god, Forgive us, pardon us and grant us atonement..."[8]

Scripture

The Torah or the first five books of the Hebrew scripture traditionally regarded as coming from Moses is not the same today as what was current in ancient Israel. Variant readings in the Syrian and Greek versions exist from the Massoretic text and the one now in use is not free from error. It has often been pointed out that there are parallel stories in the literature of the Near East but Orthodoxy still holds that Moses wrote the Pentateuch whereas other divisions say it is a combination of divinely inspired writing and the result of human reflection.

Historical criticism of the Bible started in the nineteenth century with the lower historical criticism dealing with the text and the higher analyzing the content. The Orthodox reject the approach but the Reform accept a great deal of it. The ritual precepts (the P or priestly strand in the Pentateuch) could not have applied to the early Hebrews and there are queries about the nature of God. Jewish scholars think that revelation is an encounter between the human and the divine but in the understanding of it mistakes will occur.

A literal interpretation of the Genesis Creation stories is not possible but there are parallels with evolution in that the whole of Creation in Genesis, chapter 1, slowly rises to the human and it is stated, "let the earth bring forth living creatures..."

It is difficult to deal with Leviticus for some of the commands are impossible to implement. God does not command disobedient children to be stoned to death and regulations concerning women slaves need to be excluded. Theologians argued that theology must be progressive and dispense with old traditions and commands.

Concerning God there is a need to recognize the value of metaphor. He is depicted through images and imaginative language. A metaphor is understanding one thing by likening it to something else. We must not mix up the image with the reality to which it points hence care is needed not to confuse something human with God.[9]

With regard to the Hebrew view of the cosmos, the earth is flat and the sun circles it rather than vice versa: we get the thought patterns of the age but despite this the beauty of the message is not affected. The Bible does not teach science. As Galileo said, it shows the way to go to heaven not the way the heavens go.

But there are moral difficulties about the Hebrew scripture. How can it be a guide when we consider the wars conducted by the Israelites in their conquest of Canaan? One answer is that there are higher (God is transcendent) and lower (God depicted as a man) views of God and a gradual revelation. We know what is higher and lower not only because of the developed revelation but because the first finds an echo in our souls and the oral Torah (commentary) helps us to distinguish what is permanent and temporary. It is the moral sense, something recognized by Darwin, as we will see.

Reading the Torah is a way of disciplining the soul or restoring it. No doubt the message was helpful but as time went on the oral law became a burden. It meant that in addition to the five books of Moses there was received an elaboration of the laws and beliefs contained in them. It was transmitted in memory down through the ages until written down in the Mishnah and the Talmud resulting in many rules and regulations making religion a burden rather than a blessing.[10]

GOD

God in traditional Judaism is the supreme Being who was known through His acts and is more than personal. He is holy and cannot be comprehended as He is in Himself, yet can be

found by those who seek Him.[11] Metaphors as we said are helpful especially in trying to understand the divine. Such language
is compared to a map that is not a picture but a symbolic representation, for example, two curved lines for a bridge. The more
we know about what God is not, the more positive we can be
about what He is.

It is the experience of God that convinces of His existence
rather than an intellectual demonstration: "Taste and see that
the Lord is good" (Ps. 38.8). You cannot explain what is taste;
it must be experienced. But there is an ebb and flow in the
religious life so the Hasidim spoke of the various states of the
greatness of soul and the diminution of it. The fluctuating
nature of faith is essential but the experience of the greatness of
soul gives us strength to deal with despair.[12]

It has been said that to believe in God is an illusion springing
from a child's desire to have a father but having desires does not
necessarily mean that their objects do not exist. Judaism is a
historical religion, not one created to fill a need or a desire and
the Jews are still here despite the colossal persecution that they
have experienced. Napoleon may have been right when he said
that the strongest argument for belief in God is their continued
existence. The religion runs contrary to our desires for it is stern
demanding duties and care for others. Men do not usually make
laws that are difficult for them to keep and then be prepared to
die rather than break them.

Traditionally God is considered to be transcendent (Isa.
40.21–22) and beyond our comprehension (Isa. 55.8–9) but
also immanent (Ps. 139.7–12). Thus the Shekhinah, the divine
presence, was formulated during the Rabbinic period and is the
glory of the Lord, an intermediary between the human and
divine. God is everlasting (olam) (Gn. 21.33). Maimonides
(1134–1204 CE) the Jewish scholar said that time was created
so when we think of God existing before the universe we do not
use it in its normal sense. He exists eternally.

The Spirit of God is the agent of creation (Gn. 1), of proph-
ecy (Ezek. 37.7–14) and special powers in man (Num. 11.26).
He functions in different ways: brooding over the creation in
Genesis 1 and bringing the cosmos out of chaos. This ruah
also means wind by which God fulfils His purposes: the breath

by which man becomes alive, bestows intellectual and spiritual gifts and grants powers that seem supernatural (1 Sam. 10.6). The Spirit will anoint the Messiah with inspiration (Isa. 11.1–9) and grant him intellectual gifts and practical powers. Ruah is used as a synonym for God (Zech. 4, 6).[13]

CREATOR

God as creator is central to Judaism and He is purposive in His creation. He works through natural causes and establishes the laws that regulate the natural order. There is interaction with us, not interfering with our free will but revealing what accords with His will.

Adam was created nephesh, a living being, who is composed of body and soul. The word nephesh occurs over seven hundred times and is usually translated as soul but H. W. Robinson argues that it is not a spiritual entity that enters the body at birth and leaves it at death but a principle of life that animates the body. It is the basis of personality. He states that nephesh is not used in the scripture of a disembodied soul or spirit, and the inhabitants of Sheol, place of dead, are not called souls.[14]

We are essentially dust and will return to it again for there is no immortal soul. He is afraid that to postulate an incarnate soul would give the human an independence from God; of course, it might be objected that the soul has come to us as a gift from Him. The question also arises: Was there not something special about the act of breathing into the human since it did not occur with the animals? He does admit that the Hebrew in his primitive psychology made the soul the center of the emotions and that spirit, ruah, became a synonym with nephesh breath-soul (Gn. 7.22) from the exile onward. He repeats that the Hebrew thought of man as an animated body and not an incarnate soul. But this raises a further problem for if ruah is something that man possesses and is equivalent to the soul then it would seem to rise above the simple animation of the body. It is the point of contact for God.

Nancey Murphy notes that certain Psalms speak of the soul being killed (7.1–2, 22.20, 35.7) and accepts the view of Robinson that nephesh meant the whole person. But she says that Robinson believed that in the Christian scripture while thinking of the person as a unity the essential personality, the psyche (soul) or the pneuma (spirit), survived bodily death. It is not because of a natural endowment but its dependence on God. Robinson then has a modified dualism because he was an idealist which governed his view of human nature.[15]

What we know is that Adam comes from the earth. He is flesh (basar), a part of nature, but he interferes with it and seeks to bring it under his control. There is good in him for he has the divine spirit and the divine likeness, but he can yield to the bad by thinking of his superiority and failing to obey his creator.

Was the soul affected by the Fall of man? The Jews do not accept the Christian doctrine of the Fall of humanity but it is in their apocalyptic writings. It indirectly affected Christianity with sin traced back to Adam (2 Esd. 3.21–2) and the evil heart of man but this was balanced in 2 Baruch, "each has become his own Adam."[16] Some Jewish writers postulate a cosmic fall before man came on the scene. It is speculation but there is the belief that human beings have the impulse for good and for evil, yetzer hatov and yetzer hara. According to the Rabbis the soul participates in both and needs purification through study, worship and good deeds. It is the soul that regulates what we do.[17]

Man is unique, knowing good and evil and possessing free will. The School of Hillel and the School of Shammai in the context of the evil prevalent in their day debated whether or not creation should have taken place. The latter said No and the former Yes. After two years of debate the Shammai won, which shows the upper hand of pessimism.

IMAGE OF GOD

Creation does not mean fashioning (yatzar) something out of existing matter but creatio ex nihilio (bara). By using bara the writer is implying that we can explain the emergence of matter, of life, and of the human spirit only by the work of God.

Animals as well as men have souls; this can be proved by the use of the same Hebrew word in Genesis 2.7 and 1.30. Perhaps we should look then for the difference between the human and the animals in the relationship with God, that is, being made in the divine image. To have nephesh is to have life that is given by God and murder is forbidden. Jonathan Sacks, the chief Rabbi, says that to be made in the imago means that life belongs to God and not to us and that we are capable of knowing God. It rules out any killing of the neighbour or relative. We have a moral sense for the scripture assumes that we know when we do wrong, and that was the reason why Cain was guilty. He did not know the rule against murder but should have known the difference between good and evil. Hence we can conclude that we have something that is intrinsic: the moral sense or conscience given by God that has an affinity with the soul.[18]

Some hold that the image is the imparting of God's life giving spirit; man is made a little less than divine and is master of the creation with morality demanded of him. Others define the image in terms of mind or reason and Philo (20 BCE–50 CE), the Jew of Alexandria, believed that the human mind is related to the body as the divine mind to the world since both are invisible and incomprehensible. Such likeness creates in the human a longing to return to the divine mind that is its pattern and origin.

The development of the imago took place in the Judaism of the Hellenistic period where there is the dual origin from the ground and from the divine. The latter is reflected in the recognition of the Creator in His works and the offering of praise to Him. It stands in contrast with the views of Philo whose emphasis is on mind and who does not advocate the theory of the physical resemblance to God. But the Hebrew scriptures have anthropomorphisms, the depiction of God as a man. Thus Ezekiel 1.26–28 has a form of God similar to the human even though He is manifest in fire and brightness. The Rabbis did not like it and insisted that such passages should not be read in the synagogues since Yahweh was incomparable.[19]

It is amazing that the Jews after all that they have suffered, especially the holocaust, can still believe that there is good in man rather than being totally depraved. Each day the Jew gives thanks to God with the words: "Bless the Lord O my soul" (Ps. 103.1). It is understood that the soul responding to the desire to put away evil and attempting to attain goodness recreates itself.[20]

Scholars however are determined to avoid any dualism between body and soul and argue that the Hebrews did not separate form and matter hence basar means that man does not have a body, he is a body: a total unity including the soul. Soul (nephesh) , self or consciousness or the life principle is the inner aspect with the body the outward form.

COVENANT

The word diatheke means an agreement between two; the one made between Israel and God entailed obedience to His commands that were enshrined in the Torah (Exod. 24.1–8). It meant a special relationship with God for which, according to some, the Israelites were chosen. But it did not make them favorites but responsible for carrying out His will. The Israelites failed to keep the covenant and a new one was offered to them in which God would put His laws in their minds and inscribe them upon their hearts (Jer. 31.31–34). The external would be replaced by the internal.

However, according to the first covenant, the sacrifice and the shedding of blood is a necessity. Leviticus 17.11 states: "The life of the flesh is in the blood; and I have given it to you upon the altar to make an atonement for your souls; for it is the blood that makes an atonement for the soul." The soul is very precious and requires the shedding of blood or sacrifice otherwise there is no atonement for sin. The Christian who wrote the letter to the Hebrews, however, sought to demonstrate that the atonement of Christ was superior to the first covenant since it involved not the sacrifices of animals but the giving of his life.

THE KABBALAH

The Kabbalah movement has become known to the general public in recent times because of celebrities like Madonna, Jerry

Hall, Mick Jagger, Goldie Hawn and Diane Keaton who are devotees. The movement emphasizes meditation and rituals rather than self-discipline and claims that the Hebrew scriptures are a blueprint of our destiny and can be deciphered using numerology and astrology. It was criticized by the Orthodox but today there are temples and centers everywhere and usually the wares are overpriced!

There is the belief in the gradations of the soul. The lowest part of the nephesh is common to all while only Jews have a neshamah, the higher soul. It must be cultivated by following the Torah and its ultimate goal is God. The higher soul is a reason for the election of Israel but the majority of Jews would reject this with its implication of favoritism and hold that God loves and guides all His creatures. Yet we will see that the higher and lower soul exists in Hinduism but it relates to reincarnation and does not have such implications.

The Kabbalah mystics in Spain thought that they had a secret tradition concerning the meaning of the Torah. Among them was Isaac Luria (1534–1572) who was born in Safed and put forward the daring idea that the universe is the result of an inherent flaw within the Godhead and the purpose of creation is to correct it. God withdraws into Himself in order that creation might take place. There are five strata in the soul and each travels from body to body from generation to generation independent of the other parts. Each soul is the meeting of these parts.[21]

The soul comes from God and returns to Him: it is the essence of the human. There is the belief that man has a shadow that is his astral body and on death the shadow disappears. We are unable to detect the shadow since it is non-physical. There are the ten Sefirot, a series of emanations in the Godhead. Each soul is a spark of Adam's soul and the individual is responsible for releasing the holy sparks in accordance with his soul root. Adam's soul was shattered by his disobedience and consequently the spark is trapped within us and we must seek to repair or heal it by avoiding evil. The result will be a world of cosmic harmony and modern Jews apply tikkun or healing to ecological and social reform in a secular way.

THE PSALMS AND THE SOUL

Some of the psalms were written at a later period than the one during which David lived but the extreme view that a number were written as late as the Maccabbean era has been rejected as improbable by critics. The Jewish scholar A. Cohen says that it is a disputed question whether the doctrine of immortality is explicitly taught in the Psalms but he believes that it is there though not stressed since they were concerned for this life.[22]

The soul has to struggle to reach the heights and frequently it is used as an idiom for "me" or the person (3.2, 6.5). Though there are hints of immortality there is no remembrance of God in the nether-world that is Sheol (6.6). It is a region beneath the world and corresponds to the Greek Hades to which the spirit descends after leaving the body and continues a shadowy existence of silence, darkness and oblivion. These shades or weak ones (rephaim) still exist despite some verses of scripture that in the preexilic period denied it.

Sheol is envisaged as a walled-in area with gates (Isa. 38.10) that create a feeling of horror and dismay. Yet the righteous thought that their stay would be limited for God would not leave them there but bring them up again to enjoy His presence. In later literature, Sheol is the place where the wicked are punished after death.

Cohen points out that Genesis 2.7 is translated in the Targum, an Aramaic paraphrase of parts of the Hebrew Bible, as man becoming a living soul, a rational being with the power of expressing thought.[23] This is significant since many modern scholars translate not soul but living being. Man is frail, enosh, a mortal being and derived from the dust of the earth, adamah, but distinctive, being made a little lower than the angels.

The soul is the glory of the body and there are intimations of immortality (16.10, 11): "For Thou wilt not abandon my soul to the nether-world; neither wilt thou suffer Thy godly one to see the pit. Thou makes me to know the path of life; In Thy presence is fullness of joy, In Thy right hand bliss for evermore." These verses, though debated by some scholars, have been traditionally interpreted as references to the immortality of the righteous and are used in liturgy with the thought of the deathlessness of the soul.[24] The Psalmist does not see his soul abandoned to the nether-world (17.15): "As for me, I shall behold thy face in righteousness; I shall be satisfied when I awake with Thy likeness."

There is a debate about the famous twenty-third psalm. It can be maintained that the valley of the shadow of death is a deep gloom hence not thinking of the departure from this world and dwelling in the House of the Lord is to be a guest of God. Yet it is forever and it is stated that goodness and mercy shall follow us all the days of our lives. The plain meaning is that it is the end of life when we will dwell in the House of the Lord forever and in any case God can bring the soul up from Sheol.[25]

Suffering affects the soul (31.7) but it can open its eyes to the truth. Sin is a burden on the soul (32.1) yet it continually thirsts for God. Cohen laments that modern criticism tends to deny anything that is traditional. For example, Psalm 51 is considered late and thought to apply to the nation and having nothing to do with David and the crisis over Bathsheba.[26]

The soul is the divine element in man and woman (57.9): "Awake my glory," and the Psalmist calls on it to sing of deliverance. God delivers the soul from the nethermost parts of the earth (86.13). The soul can be tested. God sent leanness into the soul of the Israelites in the wilderness because of their unlawful desires. The soul is the whole being and God strengthens it. God is in the nether-world for He is everywhere and must be in Sheol.

The Psalms testify to the supremacy of man over all things but also his depravity (8 and 14). Attending to the Torah will convert the soul (19.7) that longs after God and waits patiently for Him who will deliver it from death (33.19–20). God will deliver us from trouble and receive us with glory and be our strength forever (Ps. 73.14). The only hope is in God (Ps. 103) who will save the soul from destruction and show His merciful goodness forever.

It would appear then that the Psalms realise the importance of the soul and it is the whole being of man without any dualism of body and soul, a psychosomatic unity. There are intimations of immortality without specifically stating that the soul is immortal. There is a balance between pessimism and optimism.

We are mortal (Ps. 6.5) and in death there is no remembrance of God and in the grave who shall give Him thanks (cf. Eccles. 9.10) but on the other hand there is deliverance from Sheol (Ps. 49.14–15; Job 19.25–27)

DEATH

There were elaborate customs and practices when a death occurred (Gn. 23.2; 11 Sam. 3.31–34) and it continued among Christians. The mourning could last for a long time with loud crying. Sackcloth was worn and ashes smeared on the head (Gn. 37.34; Lev. 10.6). Women played a prominent part with their eulogy and words of consolation. Death is the greatest enemy but accepted calmly as a procedure before going to sleep with ancestors.[27]

It is as natural as birth for it was believed that the soul returns to God. The relatives stay at home wearing no leather shoes, sit on low stools and are given the support of the community. The dead are buried fully clothed in an open tomb that usually takes place immediately on death. Personal objects and a memorial are placed in or near the tomb, mourners cover their faces with ashes, hair and beards are shaved, and no cosmetics are worn. Usually a person is buried with his deceased relatives but there is no ancestor worship or prayer for the dead. It is burial rather than cremation.

Every effort is made to achieve equality in death by using a simple coffin, and during the mourning a candle or a lamp is kept burning for the departed soul especially when prayers are offered. At funerals among the Eastern European Jews the prayer is: "O God full of compassion...May his or her resting place be the Garden of Eden. May the Compassionate One shelter him or her forever in His protective wings and may his or her soul be bound up in the bond of eternal life."[28]

The Jews have their own cemeteries, and earth from the Holy Land can be thrown into the grave. Traditionally death was signified by a cessation of breathing but keeping a body alive on a ventilator meant that organs could be transplanted and Jews when they are assured of brain death are likely to accept it.

In Orthodoxy the body is not left alone before the funeral. It is prepared for burial by a group who bathe and clean it and a prayer shawl may be placed around a man's shoulders. The funeral takes place as soon as possible after death but not on the Sabbath or the first and last day of festivals. The Orthodox do not agree with cremation and there is a belief in the physical resurrection in the Messianic Age. Flowers are not customary. The orthodox belief does not mean that a physical resurrection is an identification with the material of the old body but the sum-total of the deeds, thoughts, habits and character. The soul is the personality that will continue in the after life.[29]

IMMORTALITY

Immortality had been hoped for by humans from the Neanderthals onward. Israel was surrounded by people who believed in the survival of the soul hence food, drink and weapons were buried with the dead throughout the Fertile Crescent. It was thought that contact with the spirits of those who had died could be made (Saul [11 Kings 21.6] and the Witch of Endor) but such a practice was generally condemned because it showed lack of trust in Yahweh and interference with His control of the dead.

In Leviticus (20.6) there is the command, "Do not turn to ghosts and do not inquire of familiar spirits." Witches and "mediums" were banned or burned and those who resorted to them were accursed. There was to be no trafficking with spiritualism, black magic and ouija boards. The book of Deuteronomy (18. 9–12) condemns divination: a soothsayer, an enchanter, a sorcerer or the consultation of a ghost.

We have seen that there are intimations of immortality in the Psalms and it is reflected in current daily prayers: "The soul You have given me is pure, my God. You created, You formed it, You breathed it, I acknowledge You Lord my God and God of my fathers, Master of all creation, Lord of all souls. Praised are You Lord who restores the soul to the lifeless, exhausted body."

The hope has remained despite the holocaust. Leo Baeck, a Rabbi and leader of German Jewry survived a concentration camp and emerged to serve progressive Judaism. He published a prayer that was prohibited by the Nazis but still read in many synagogues in 1935. This prayer advocated the belief that

Judaism is a history of the nobility of the soul and of human dignity.

Josephus believed in the immortality of the soul and pointed to Eleazar, leader of the last defenders of Masada, who said that it is death that gives liberty to the soul and allows it to depart to its pure abode. It was thought that there was transmigration of the soul but it applied only to those who deserved punishment and gave them a second chance to change. Jews refused to fight on the Sabbath during the war with Antiochus Epiphanies (Mac. 2.20–38) and were annihilated. But such just men must be rewarded with an after life. It is said in the book of Wisdom: "…the souls of the just are in God's hand, and torment shall not touch them. In the eyes of foolish men they seem to be dead…but they are at peace…they have a sure hope of immortality" (3.1–6). Yet there appears to be the need of correction after which they will receive their reward.

This book written about 50 BCE–50 CE embraces the pre-existence of the soul, immortality and the evil nature of the body. It agrees with Philo and Rabbinic Judaism about the immortality of the soul and it was needed to justify the belief that Yahweh was a moral God.

But in 2 and 4 Maccabees we also find the resurrection of the body in connection with the righteous and the belief that the living can assist the dead through prayer and sacrifice (11 Mac. 12.38–45). It is the only passage that justifies purgatory and masses for the dead.[30]

Hope in immortality sprang from the problem of suffering. Job knew that the good man did experience suffering but he rejected the accusation that he was paying for his sins. He is being tested as the introduction of the book shows with Satan used as the instrument of God. It is an example of the innocent suffering as vividly portrayed by Isaiah. But Job's faith scaled the heights: "I know that my redeemer lives" (Job 19.25–27; cf. Ps. 16.11, 73.24, 139.24).

It is true that suffering can be a punishment for sin: David lost the child of Bathsheba and suffered greatly for his sin. Ahab was killed because he stole the vineyard from Naboth. Suffering can refine character but the Jews could not accept this when they experienced the holocaust.

Various explanations were put forward. Did God withdraw as the Kabbalists insist? Or did Jews suffer in order to hasten the rule of God over the world or did they die for the sins of humanity as God's suffering servant? Some writers are silent about it while others stress free will that requires a limitation of divine power. Some speak of the absence of God but the rise and power of the state of Israel shows that Hitler did not win the ultimate victory.

There is the example of resignation by Job when he said, "Even if He slay me yet will I trust Him" and the acceptance that the ways of God are incomprehensible: "If I knew Him I would be Him."[31] Job was reinstated and all the things he lost were given back to him whereas those who died in the holocaust have no recompense if there is no after life. Some assert that if the holocaust points to the absence of God then the state of Israel shows His presence, but despite all the attempted explanations such suffering is and will remain a mystery.[32]

The belief in the immortal soul was introduced into Judaism from Greek thought in the Hellenistic period and it appears in the liturgy: "My God, the soul You have given me is pure. You formed it and breathed it into me; You preserve it within me, and You will take it from me to life everlasting." Some scholars say that it is a clear allusion to Genesis 2.7 and a fine example of the fusion of biblical and Greek elements in Judaism. It is confirmed in Ecclesiastes 12.7: "The dust shall return to the earth as it was and the spirit shall return to God who gave it."

RESURRECTION

Robinson writes about the hope of a resurrection from the dead as in Isaiah 26.19 dated about 300 BCE:

> Thy dead shall live,
> Their corpses shall arise,
> They that dwell in the dust
> Shall awake and give a ringing cry.
> For the dew of lights is Thy dew
> And the earth shall cast forth or give birth to the dead or the
>   shades.

He does not accept Ezekiel 37 as a vision of the resurrection of the dead but as an image of national revival and return from exile in Babylon. It may be so but there seems to be some connection with a resurrection since it is stated that graves will be opened and that they will live (37.11–14).

He does not believe that Isa. 53 is a belief in individual resurrection of ancient origin but this can be questioned since it speaks of the servant offering his soul as an atonement for sin and his reward will be with the great. How, if he does not have an after life? He says that Job 14 dismisses individual restoration but this is the beginning of Job's reflection on what has happened to him and even here he poses the question: "If a man dies shall he live again?"[33]

But it may be that the resurrection was for the righteous only until Daniel 12.2 when it included the wicked:

> Many of them that sleep in the dust of the earth shall awake, some to everlasting life, and some to shame and everlasting contempt.

Such a hope transformed Judaism, Robinson thinks, from a non-belief in life after death in 350 BCE to belief in a resurrection in 50 CE. Certain passages point to it, namely in Psalm 73 where though his body is dying he believes that he is of value and matters to God. Death could not be the end (73.24). Hence in Isaiah we read,

> All shall pass before Yahweh who has swallowed up death for ever; and the Lord God will wipe away tears from all faces. (Isa. 25.7, 8)

Robinson does admit that while each part of the body was thought of as a self-contained entity there was a unity of consciousness through the idea of the breath-soul nephesh, indicated by its use as a personal pronoun.[34]

It was held that God dwelt in heaven beyond the sky (Isa. 66.1) and that the righteous would go there after death. The Rabbis suggested that the souls of scholars were rewarded after death by admission to a higher institute of learning! They condemned those who did not believe in the resurrection or the divine origin of the Torah.[35] In the Rabbinic literature the idea of the immortal soul is combined with the resurrection of the body, but in the modern period belief in bodily resurrection has declined though not the immortality of the soul. David Goldstein states that mankind possesses a soul that is a part of the divine spirit within everyone and it needs to be cultivated if the ways of God are to be imitated.[36] The soul is a spark of the Godhead or an element of the divine within humanity and is immortal.

What then happens to the soul after death? Some think that it survives in an individualistic recognizable form, and some believe that it is subsumed into a world soul and a smaller group affirms the transmigration of souls.

MESSIAH

The concept of the resurrection of the body developed in the second century BCE together with the hope of a Messiah. There are different views regarding its origin as we noted with Orthodoxy believing in a personal one who will come to lead all to God. Reform look for the establishment of the kingdom of truth, justice and peace but the hope of the Messiah is also in neo-Hasidic and neo-Kabbalistic groups. The Zionists speak of the beginnings of the messianic age and the religious groups among them think of the creation of the state of Israel as the first step toward redemption.

In the Hellenistic and Roman periods we have the presence of the concept of both the immortality of the soul (The Testament of Abraham) and the resurrection of the body (Dan. 12.2). The Rabbinic view may have been that at death the soul leaves the body but may return to it from time to time until it disintegrates. Such an idea could have sprung from an ancient Jewish belief that after death the departed soul does not wish to abandon the body and is anxious to rejoin it hence for three days it continues to hover over it or keeps revisiting the grave.[37]

Maimonides believed in the resurrection of the dead, the coming of the Messiah, and that only in solitude could the soul soar to union with God. In the world to come there is nothing corporeal so the souls of the righteous are without bodies. They do not experience fatigue and have a knowledge of God that is unobtainable while living.

The soul belongs to an order of existence higher than that of the angels. Eternity is outside of time and space so heaven is not an extension of our time or place but rather a state of the soul. The Messiah would come as King and restore the kingdom of David, building the sanctuary and gathering the dispersed Jews. The soul will continue to exist as pure mind contemplating God.

Maimonides' ideas caused much controversy and were considered by many as a distortion of Jewish belief. But many Jews today would agree with him since they do not accept the resurrection of the body that would require a miracle not acceptable to science. The Orthodox envisage the Messiah as a normal man without supernatural trappings and embrace the ideas of Maimonides that he will be a descendant of King David and bring all Jews back to the orthodox way of life. When he comes, the Temple will be rebuilt and the sacrifices renewed and deep study of the Torah will determine conduct. But for progressive Jews the whole idea is doubtful and they seem to prefer a messianic state rather than the coming of an individual and all are called not only to look forward to such a state but also build it.[38]

The Messiah is usually Jehovah in Hebrew scripture (Isa. 65.17) who creates a new heaven and a new earth but this alternates with his anointed one who is both divine and human (9.6–7). In the English Bible, it is Immanuel and in Isaiah 11.1–5 it is a human ruler, a descendant of Jesse. Hence there continues to be uncertainty about the status of the Messiah. In the past there have been those who claimed to be the Messiah particularly Shabbatai Tzevi in the seventeenth century who aroused much fervour and excitement but eventually disappointed his followers with conversion to Islam. The focus now is to create the Kingdom of God on earth, and thus Zionism with its advocacy of the state of Israel has gained prominence. There are also Jews who are converts to Christianity and accept that Jesus was the Messiah being the son of God, a supernatural and spiritual figure, who is part of a divine trinity.[39]

APOCALYPTIC (SECRET) LITERATURE

Though not in the Hebrew canon Apocalyptic literature influenced the Jews regarding the end of time. The writings contain material about a judgment, resurrection of the dead, a new heaven and new earth and punishment of enemies in hell (2 Esd. 7.33–38). The Kingdom of God will be established on this earth with the Gentiles gathered (Isa. 2.2–4) and all nations entering the Lord's house. The Day of the Lord will be preceded by signs in nature with darkness, sorrow and anguish, enmity among friends and relations and break up of society. Jehovah is central to the Day since He will be judge and set up His kingdom on Mount Zion but sometimes the central figure is the Messiah the representative of God and Elijah is the forerunner. Only the remnant of Israel will be saved.

These apocalyptic views were popular but were regarded with suspicion by the Pharisaic party. They developed in the two centuries before Christ and the people appeared to be familiar with its Messianic ideas. Some of the literature included the Book of Enoch, The Testaments of the 12 Patriarchs, the Psalms of Solomon, the Book of Jubilees and the Ascension of Isaiah. Other literature developed after the Christian era.

Enoch describes the coming and punishment of the wicked in the pains of Sheol but the Ascension of Isaiah (4.18) states the final punishment will be annihilation and it is also in The Testament of Hezekiah, which is incorporated into the Isaiah book and the Assumption of Moses. Throughout these books it is the soul that is mentioned whether to experience condemnation or blessedness.

A general resurrection is envisaged in Enoch but there is uncertainty in other books where the focus is on the righteous (Book of Similitudes). The 12 Patriarchs are definite about the resurrection of the righteous but other books fluctuate regarding the fate of the wicked. The Son of man is the Messiah in the Book of Enoch and He has a throne of glory at Jerusalem, the center of the new kingdom. In the Rabbinical literature the Messiah is the central figure who existed before creation but not eternal for He is a human, born of a woman of the seed of David. He will be majestic and destroy His enemies who do not believe in Him.

Resurrection would be in the Holy land (Ps. 72.16). Those who had died before were to be gathered in Sheol and brought up with the mark of circumcision but it precluded the Gentiles from resurrection. There would be a messianic banquet.[40]

HELL

This has always been a debatable issue. In the apocalyptic writings there is a development of the understanding of heaven and hell (Enoch. 21, 22.10ff. 27) but there is no explicit reference to it in the Hebrew scripture. There is the pit (Ps. 28.1), and in Rabbinic literature, Gehinnom or Ghenna, a valley associated with fire and death. A hot place in some accounts, cold in others and many tortures take place, which match that of Islam and Christianity.

Many today view hell figuratively, not literally, since it is thought that a moral God would not create such a place and in any case such suffering must be terminable since it is for finite sins. The whole matter is controversial not only in Judaism but also in other religions as we will see.[41]

REINCARNATION

It is not thought that the Jews held the doctrine of reincarnation, something we will see in the Indian religions, but E. P. Sanders points out that there are hints of the transmigration of the soul with the Pharisees and Josephus due to Greek influence. Today most Jews consider that the soul is the center or core of the person in a nonphysical sense and some believe in reincarnation. Gilgul means rolling reincarnation, souls roll from body to body, and the belief emerged in the tenth century. The Kabbalah took it seriously believing that there is migration up to three bodies.[42]

An orthodox Jew when interviewed said that the soul can return to earth a maximum of seven times until it fulfils the set of conditions required of it. A reform Jew asserted that the soul never gets lost but goes through to the next generation.[43]

CONCLUSION

The religion does not define the soul but in general it is regarded as the core of personality and there is a psychosomatic unity of soul and body. It seems that eventually the immortality of the soul rather than the resurrection of the body was preferred because the latter would require a miracle. The Reform, the largest group in America, believe in the immortality of the soul but the Orthodox continue to believe in a physical resurrection when the Messiah comes.

Jonathan Sacks points out that for the Hasidic movements the source of the soul is in God, that is, a part of God. As bodies we are separate but as souls there are no divisions, implying that at the level of the soul loving your neighbour is loving yourself. There is a unity of the people, a larger self, the collective soul. We think of this when we speak of "the soul of the nation."

Sacks believes that we are a body conjoined with soul, the dust of the earth joined to the breath of God so in each of us there is a moral spark that requires nurturing. To defeat evil and find God, quiet contemplation in the soul is needed. Here mysticism that is part of all religions seeks to satisfy the soul.

The soul that is the basis of personality does seem to be intrinsic in Jewish thought, not something that simply functions in various ways. If this is so it is important for our future discussion as many today argue for the functional position. The same applies to conscience and the moral sense. We will see Darwin contending for a social development with regard to them but not the soul that he considered a hard problem and did not deal with it!

There were intimations of the soul's immortality as we have seen in the Psalms and the mystical writings of the Kabbalah. But the real development occurred in the apocalyptic writings and these, though not part of the Hebrew canon, were to influence the Faith. It appears at times that the soul and spirit are synonymous or at least go together and at death return to God. The image of God distinguishes us from the animals hence we are able to relate to God and have conscience and morality. We will find that these ideas reappear in Christianity that has its roots in Judaism.

CHAPTER 2

THE CHRISTIAN EXPERIENCE OF THE SOUL

What shall it profit a man if he gain the whole world and lose his soul?

Mt. 16.26

In the history of Christianity, poets, philosophers, and hymn writers have extolled the soul (psyche), which can mean person, life, personality or self. But what do people think of the soul today?

Prior to the "Soul of Britain" survey of public opinion that we mentioned in the introduction, John Bowker investigated the concept of belief in the after life and discovered that many people were worried about their soul at the end of earthly life. Some thought it would be purified in purgatory while others believed it would enter heaven or hell. But there was debate about whether or not these places existed and if the soul slept after death before facing some kind of judgment? Others showed an insight into the meaning of eternal life by contending that they possessed it now in association with the resurrection of Christ and did not need to wait for death.[1] Clearly this view had emerged after a reading of the Gospel of John.

In this chapter we consider first the Christian view of creation and then go on to other beliefs that deal with the soul.

CREATION

Traditionally it was thought that God had created man directly, but the theory of evolution put forward in the nineteenth century by Charles Darwin changed this view and challenged the belief that a soul was implanted by God at the creation.[2] It depends on how we interpret scripture as we noted in chapter 1 for there can be allegorical, mythical, or literal interpretations. The early Church Fathers treated Genesis in a poetic way and Augustine has an allegorical interpretation of the early chapters with the darkness representing the soul.[3]

The human is the pinnacle of creation but disobeys God, seeks autonomy, and separation from Him hence the doctrine of the Fall and original sin, which meant that the sins of the first humans were passed on to their children. Today the story of Adam and Eve is regarded as the story of everyone repeated in each generation for "every man is the Adam of his own soul."

Concerning creation the Hebrew verb, bara, can be used for secondary creation but it usually means bringing creation out of nothing. It is divine, not human work. Other verbs are to make, asah, and to form, yatsar. Asah is for making things and yatsar for fashioning out of preexistent materials.[4] "Create" in a primary sense is used of God in Genesis chapter 1 but it can also refer to the making of the sun, moon, stars, animals and man from preexisting materials. Evolution presupposes something that must evolve and could mean secondary creation by which the substance already in existence is given form.

Creatio ex nihilio is not found in the scripture except in 11 Maccabees 7.28 . It cannot mean that the world came into being without a cause for it is stated that it was by the will of God and the word of His power (Ps. 33.6.9; Heb. 11.3, 5). Creation is distinct from God but dependent on Him. He is not the soul of the world or it emanates from Him or is identical with Him but He is present in all and through all (Eph. 4.6).

SCRIPTURE AND THE SOUL

What is puzzling today is that translators of the New Testament often translate soul by life but at other times retain it. Psyche or psuche can mean physical life and it is possessed by animals as well as humans. If the soul is the principle of life it is very important but the argument means that it is part of our physical make up and is different from the spirit of man that is pneuma.[5] The latter holds the key to the spiritual not the soul.

But there are difficulties here. First, it is not always possible to translate soul by life hence the word is retained. Second, it opposes the tradition of the church that placed a high value on the soul and in funeral services it is the soul that is committed to God. Third, if the writers of the New Testament meant life they could have used bios or zoe. The first refers to biological life, the second to the eternal life that Christ can give. Fourth, soul and spirit often go together as we saw in the last chapter. In Matthew 10.28 we see that the body can be killed but man cannot kill the soul and in Luke 8.55, the young girl receives her spirit again and lives. Soul and spirit are the carriers of salvation and are to be cared for throughout life.

In Gethsemane the soul of Jesus is grieved unto death (Mk 14.34; John 12.27) so the soul is the center of the emotional life. Mary puts soul and spirit together in her song that magnifies the Lord (Lk 1.47.). Later it is stated that "A sword will pierce her soul" (Lk 2.35). In Matthew 16.26 there is no profit in gaining the whole world and losing the soul but again in modern translations soul is translated as life. In Luke the soul is the inner self (Lk 12.19) and it will be demanded of us by the Judge at the end of life. We are to love the Lord our God with all our soul (Lk 10.27). Soul and spirit are united (Hebs. 4.12–16) but can be divided by God. In Thessalonians Paul prays that they may be kept sound in spirit, soul, and body (1.5.23).

Evolution teaches a natural process with a continuity between animals and man but many Christians think that it was only the body that evolved in this way not the soul that comes from God. However, whether evolved naturally or coming directly from God, the theist believes that God is behind the process and uses evolution as His method of creation. We know now that the animals are close to us and in a later chapter we will raise the question of how the human is distinct from them, and if they are the same as us on the basis of having a soul why is it that we engage in worship of God and they do not.

As we have seen, in Hebrew thought the soul, nephesh, describes man as a whole, but it together with spirit is the higher element of the body. Both designate the immaterial element of the dead. Texts such as Revelation 6.9 and 20.4 point to the existence of souls in heaven. In the first passage the writer sees the souls of those who had been slain for their witness to Christ, and in the second, souls will live and reign with Christ for a thousand years. These are disembodied and both passages indicate that the soul survives death, but there appears to be a period perhaps of soul sleep. The passage says that they lived again and ruled with Christ for a thousand years. In the bringing of soul and spirit together perhaps we might talk of the spiritual soul.

The Greek soma is usually translated as body, psyche, the soul and nous the mind. Jacob and his kindred are called souls and Paul says that every soul must be subject to the higher powers (Rom. 13.1). Peter describes the joy of seeing Jesus whom they have loved and states that they will receive the end of their faith namely the salvation of their souls (1 Pt 1.9) but warns of fleshy lusts that war against the soul (1 Pt 2.11). They were going astray but now are returned to the Bishop and Shepherd of their souls (1 Pt 2.23), and when they suffer they are to commit their souls unto their creator (1 Pt 4.19). They have purified their souls by obedience to the truth (1 Pt 1.22). Soul is used in the sense of person when he refers to the flood: "In the ark a few people, eight souls in all, were brought safely through the water" (1 Pt 3.20).

Lot was distressed by the behavior of those around him: what "he saw and the things he heard made their lawless conduct a daily agony to his law-abiding soul" (2 Pt 2.8). In Hebrews 10.39, faith will save the soul and this is repeated in James 1.21: "you must receive...the word which is able to save your souls." Again in James 5.19, "A man who turns a sinner from his wandering way will save that sinner's soul from death." All of this makes clear that it is hard to dispense with the term. Even those scholars like H. Wheeler Robinson who we noted in the last chapter contended for an animated body not an incarnated soul saw an advance in the New Testament that the essential personality, psyche or pneuma, survives death.[6] The soul or spirit being disembodied is not complete without the body.

The importance of the soul is shown when the New Testament quotes Isaiah who applies the soul to God: "Behold my servant whom I have chosen, My Beloved and Only One in whom my soul has found delight…" (Mt 12.18) and to come to Jesus is to find rest for the soul (Mt 11.28).

THE IMPACT OF GREEK THOUGHT

The Greek philosophers had an influence on Christianity, which is evident in the New Testament, for example, in the Gospel of John and the Letter to the Hebrews. In particular Plato (ca. 429–347 BCE) and Aristotle (384–322 BCE). Plato taught that the soul can fall from the reality of beauty and goodness, which is its true home and pursue possessions and pleasure. It is on a journey of passion and the proper destiny of each soul is to return, passion exhausted, to the world of the real. He distinguished between appearance and reality so he would have endorsed what the Hindu Upanishads say, "Lead me from the unreal to the real," to the One beyond all finite reality. Death is a migration of the soul from this place to another.

The Greeks viewed matter as evil and the need for the soul to escape from it but Hellenistic Christians mainly held to the resurrection of the body, which was a well-established Judaic doctrine, and thought that it expressed the immortality of the soul. Hence we have the two ideas and they are confused in later thinking. We will see this in considering Paul's problem with the Corinthians concerning the resurrection of the body.

Plato put forward the world of forms that were transcendent and apprehended only by the intellect. They are universals with an objective existence, a hierarchy crowned by the Form of Good. Our world of becoming is founded upon them but is not stable like they are. Only the soul is permanent belonging to the forms and not affected by change because it is preexistent, immortal, and immaterial. We recognize the forms by a process of recollection, indeed knowledge is remembering. The soul, psyche, being preexistent recollects the knowledge that it had prior to embodiment.

Man is tripartite: reason, spirited element or emotion, and has an appetitive element or carnal desires. The soul is the supreme principle and there was a World Soul directing and animating the universe. Since the Form of the Good that could be equated with God cannot be defiled by corrupt matter there is in the Timaeus a demiurge or craftsman who shapes the world out of preexistent material according to the pattern of the forms. The forms do not "come to be" as happens to things or objects here, which are subject to change. Forms are like mathematical ideas, the objects of pure thought.

The soul causes things to be alive, it animates our bodies and is of different kind than the body and carries on after death. I am my soul not my body. Socrates, thinking about his death, reminds his friends that they will not be burying him, only his body, "when I drink the poison I shall no longer remain here with you but will go away to some kind of happiness of the blessed."[7]

Opinions differ as to whether Plato believed that the soul was trapped in the body or the ruler of it as its rational part. He does have the picture of a two-horse chariot whose driver, reason, tries to control the force of the two horses, one (spirit) cooperative and one (desire) that seeks to rebel and drag the whole chariot in the wrong direction.

Plato whose concentration was on maths knew that squares and triangles do not change hence he believed that there is the changeless area beyond our material world and the possession of the soul ensures our immortality. The question does arise: Is there a better chance of the soul surviving as a substance as Plato believed or as the form of the body as in Aristotle? A substance would mean duality with the body and that was the problem that confronted Descartes later.

Aristotle (384–322 BCE) argued that the forms exist in the real world in substances or particulars not as abstract universals, not men but individual men. Body and soul are a unity, body is matter, soul is form, and it moves the body. God is the eternal soul or eternal mind, unmoved yet moves all things, and the soul is on a journey from the sensual to the vision of the deity.

It is useful to reflect on the soul as the form of the body. What did form mean in the New Testament? There are two Greek words involved here: morphe and schema (Phil. 2.1–11). Jesus was in the form of God, morphe, but found in fashion, schema, as a man. What is the difference between morphe and schema? A person's morphe does not change, it is what he always is but the schema is the outward form and varies from place to place and from time to time. We know it as we look at pictures of ourselves from youth to old age that shock when we see the change that has taken place! But we know we are the same person for the morphe is our unchanging essence.[8] We will see that the Buddhist denies it since he rejects the soul and stresses change rather than permanence.

Philo the Jewish philosopher writing in the first century CE saw the soul surviving death and he represented the kind of Greek thought that argued for its immortality.

IMAGE OF GOD

We noted the image of God in the last chapter and here consider the New Testament view. It is confirmed by Paul when he speaks to the philosophers of Athens on Mars Hill saying that all are the offspring of God (Acts 17.28). The Church fathers thought that the image meant our rational and moral characteristics and capacity for religion but the Reformers disagreed and restricted the image to original righteousness which was lost in the fall. John Calvin argued that Adam had true knowledge, righteousness and holiness, with the primary seat of the image in the soul so he had natural endowments and spiritual qualities that were original righteousness. Only the spiritual qualities were completely lost.

Modern theology followed Schleiermacher in rejecting the original state of righteousness and insisted that the image is a certain receptivity to respond and grow into God likeness. He held that whatever the Fall did to mankind it did not mean the loss of reason though it has been affected by sin (Gen. 9.6; 1 Cor. 11.7; Jas. 3.9). Modern theology tends to reject a primitive state of holiness and contends that man was created in a state of innocence with free will so that he could choose the moral standard.

Evolutionists think that man began in a state of barbarism and slowly developed amidst the struggle between good and evil. Man was not created immortal and death was natural: Adam died because of the original constitution of his nature. Karl Barth argued that the Fall was not a historical event but belongs to super-history (Urgeschichte) but he could not escape the historical criticism of the documents and those who speak of history have to take note of symbols, metaphors and myth.

The Eastern view of man was that he was created perfect, incorruptible, immortal and passionless but these powers were lost at the Fall. Free will remained so the image of God was damaged but not effaced entirely. Christ restored that nature to its perfection and showed that man could be raised up and deified. The emphasis is on the incarnation as the saving grace though the West looks to the Cross and the resurrection but these differences are not clear cut. What we can say is that original sin is not a prominent belief in the East as in the West. Both, however, realized the value of mysticism that paved the way for the soul's union with God.

Some scholars take a radical view of the New Testament but admit that Jesus reflected the image of God. How the early people interpreted and what they thought of Jesus is important. Even those who date the Gospel of John as late as 120 CE admit that some of the ideas parallel the synoptic Gospels being developed more abstractly. We know that the Church fathers did develop the Logos of John and Paul with his high Christology wrote only a few decades after the death of Jesus. Critics have debated about his knowledge of the historical Jesus but concede that much of what he said was based on the values that Jesus put forward.

LIFE AFTER DEATH

There are parables in the Gospels that give some indication of what life after death is like. Lazarus and Dives is one in Luke 16.19–31. The parable teaches that after death we preserve our identity so there is no merging with God and we retain our memory for without it we could not be judged. There is also recognition of loved ones. The sin of Dives or the rich man was that while he did no harm to Lazarus he did nothing for him. He simply ignored him. But scripture says that to him who knows to do good and does it not to him it is sin (James 4.17).

However, he developed a concern for his brothers asking that they be told of his agony so that they would not come to where he was but he is told that even if one rose from the dead they would not listen. Lazarus was in paradise but what does it mean? In the Septuagint it means Eden (Gen. 2; Isa. 51.3), a Persian word for a walled garden and its loss meant the loss of God. It symbolizes heaven or the presence of God and points to the new heavens and new earth (Rev. 2.7). There is no indication that Lazarus was in purgatory suffering some form of purification.

Paul experienced paradise in the third heaven (2 Cor. 12.1–4). It raises a point: If both Jesus and the dying thief went immediately to Paradise it implies the immortality of spirit/soul for it was before the physical resurrection of Christ. Jesus asked God to receive his spirit. Another question is related to this. In 2 Corinthians 5.1–10 Paul speaks of being found naked. Does it mean the freeing of the body for a higher destiny or is he referring to the Greek idea of the immortal soul or of the body as the prison of the soul or is he simply pointing to the frailty of human existence since he has mentioned suffering before it. Commentators differ in their explanations.

When Jesus faced the Sadducees he knew that they disbelieved in the after life for they did not accept the prophets and the writings. The Gospels record an encounter between the Sadducees and Jesus in which they tell the curious story about the woman who had seven husbands and they wanted to know which one she would have in the hereafter. Jesus replied that when we rise from the dead there is neither marriage nor giving in marriage. Some are cautious about accepting the story but nevertheless conclude that the ideas expressed correspond to the eschatological thought of Jesus.[9] It implies that we will be bodiless and resemble the angels of God, reflecting what Paul said about flesh and blood not inheriting the kingdom of God. But on the other hand he contended for a spiritual body.

Sarx or flesh is difficult to interpret and has various meanings. It could be understood as our lower nature that is liable to temptation (Rom. 7.18) but it is also used in the sense of man or humanity (Rom. 3.20) and of the body (Rom. 2.28). The flesh is seen as the opposite of the spirit (Rom. 8.9).[10]

Can we gain any clue by the reference to our being like the angels? An angel is a messenger, a spiritual being that does not exclude a body but is also not of flesh or bones. Angels are invisible, immortal (Lk 20.36), and have a moral nature so can be punished for wrong doing. There are good and bad angels and Satan is the head of the latter. While critics dismiss them, liberal theologians often think of angels as symbolic representations of the protecting care and helpfulness of God. Reflection about them does give us some indication as to our condition in the next life.

Unlike the Sadducees the Pharisees did believe in the resurrection of the body, the immortality of the soul, future retribution, angels, spirits, divine providence and man's free will. Though they got a "bad press" in the Gospels it is thought that they saved the faith of Israel after the Sadducees vanished from the scene with the destruction of the Temple in AD 70. The Essenes may be thought of as extreme Pharisees but denied their legal moralism and their casuistry. They were not happy about animal sacrifices and stressed a devout mind and spirit, accepted the prophets and apocalyptic literature. They were a monastic brotherhood and supported themselves. Some think that they believed in the resurrection of the body and strictly observed the Torah but others say they emphasized the immortality of the soul believing that it was preexistent. Death was the liberation of the soul and end of the body. Hence they held a dualism of the body and soul. It is believed that John the Baptist came from this group and left them to preach the message of repentance. The discoveries at Qumran have increased the knowledge of the Essenes.

Also, there was a variety of beliefs among the Jews and others at this time: no resurrection, immortality of the soul, resurrection but not of this present body, corporeal resuscitation at the end of time, transmigration, and so on.

MIRACLES

It is necessary at this point to discuss miracles since the resurrection of the body is connected with the greatest miracle in the New Testament, the resurrection of Christ, which we will discuss shortly.

There are many miracles in the Gospels and three Greek words are used to refer to these. The first is teras, which means an astonishing event and the reaction to it is one of wonder and amazement. The second is dunamis from which we get the word dynamite and is a deed of power. When Jesus performed a miracle the question raised was from whom he got such power. The third is semeion that is often used in the Fourth Gospel and means a "sign" giving us insight into the mind of the person who performs it. It also demonstrates the power of God.[11]

The question is: Do miracles violate the laws of nature? David Hume contended that the belief in the resurrection of the dead was contrary to nature's laws; yet he did accept that the laws of nature were just summaries of what had so far been experienced. He was reaching forward to the modern view of probability rather than certainty.

Today we know that nature is no longer looked upon as mechanical particles determined by fixed laws but as governed by statistical laws that do not determine occurrences of single events but proportions in the larger classes of events. The original law might have been incomplete and needed widening to incorporate the new happening or a law might have been incorrect. How can we know that a law has been broken since it simply describes what might happen given certain initial conditions? And a miracle might involve the suspension of the usual course of events. Laws require a law giver and He could suspend these when a necessity such as healing was required. A scientist cannot prove that the laws operate in all conditions.

Hume seems to think that God would need to intervene from "the outside" but the theologian argues that He is immanent in nature. Miracles point beyond the event: they are signs. But why does God not perform miracles more often such as to intervene at Auschwitz or some other dreadful torture place?

Of course, at times He does seem to intervene. An example is a boy playing with a toy car on a railway. As the train approaches, his mother is filled with horror but cannot do anything and it seems that his death is inevitable but suddenly the train slows down and comes to a stop a few metres away from the body. "It is a miracle," cries the mother but later it is revealed that the reason for the train stopping was due to the driver having had a heavy meal, suffered a heart attack, and passed out. Immediately the automatic braking system came into play and stopped the train. Was it divine providence that the boy was saved, with God working through the natural? But why on this occasion and not others when His action is needed?

God can use the natural that is an earthquake as in the case of opening the doors of the prison for the apostles (Acts 5.19) or is this just a supernatural interpretation of a natural event? Hume said it is better to believe in the regularity of nature than the breaking of its laws and no miracles occurred in his lifetime as those narrated in scripture. We like to recount stories of wonders and they are accepted usually by ignorant people. But if this was the case why were miracles not accepted readily by the pagan world whom Hume regarded as ignorant? The fact is that every time apostle Paul preached the resurrection there was a riot or he was treated with scorn (Acts 17.32). Scorn was the reaction of the Greeks considered the most intelligent people in the world at that time. Indeed they would have treated Hume as a barbarian since he did not speak Greek!

Having said that, it is recognized that what appeared to be a miracle in one age would not be recognized as the same by another. Modern technology has produced such marvels as aesthetics, surgical operations, TV, travel to the moon, and so on that would have been considered miraculous in the first century. On this basis our modern age excludes God's actions. But it may be that it is not supernatural versus natural in many cases of healing but God working through the natural that is modern medicine. The Hebrew did tend to make God responsible for everything and did not have the concept of secondary causes.

To see the miracles as signs (semeia) is to concentrate on the spiritual meaning. In this case a miracle must be examined in order to see whether we can take it literally or as embodying some eternal truth.

Hume thinks that the writers of the Gospels had a vested interest and were biased particularly regarding the resurrection of Christ. They were deceivers but if so why did they not deny the belief when ordered to worship Caesar? They were Jews who believed that worship was for God only yet dedicated it to Christ as well. They would not give it to Caesar even if the refusal meant death.

Laws of nature are based upon observation, experiment and experience. On the basis of experience and observation, we expect that when A appears B will follow but this is not always so. Better weather can normally be expected in England in June rather than in December but then the unusual happens in a certain year: a mild December and a bitterly cold June. The uniformity is broken sometimes. The meteorologist can give us reasons as to how it happened and that on the basis of past observation it is unlikely to occur again but since he cannot observe the future he cannot say for certain. As one forecaster said recently, "what I am giving you now is a forecast not certainty." All we know is that A is normally followed by B but there may be exceptions to this regularity.

Science is based upon experiments that take place under controlled conditions and they are repeatable. In order to prove or falsify something, experiments are performed again and again. It requires only one exception to arise to disprove a law provided that the experiment can be repeated. But miracles are not repeatable. They are particular and peculiar events in human situations; consequently they do not destroy large-scale laws.[12]

Moreover, the biblical record indicates they are not random or arbitrary without rhyme or reason but are an answer to need and relate to the self-disclosure of God. An event such as the resurrection of Christ is unique and unrepeatable. But it is not sufficient reason to abandon natural law for to do that it would need an experimentally repeatable exception: "the miracle does not fall into this category, otherwise it would itself be a new small scale law, and a violation of regularity."

In sum, if acceptable this argument means that miracle has the peculiar power of violating but not destroying a law of nature.[13]

Whether or not a miracle occurs depends, of course, on the evidence. David Hume said we need to proportion our belief to it. It is somewhat different from saying that miracles do not happen because of an a priori ruling that they just cannot happen. The evidence for each occurrence must be carefully sifted and reasons given for the supernatural, mythical, or naturalistic explanations. W. Heisenberg did see indeterminacy as a real feature in nature that falls outside the state of affairs to which causal and necessary laws apply; hence the novel, unusual, unexpected event may not appear so improbable as in the Newtonian machine-like universe.

Healing miracles are not as suspect as natural but they need to be related to a wider conceptual scheme that makes sense of their occurrence. They are not magical tricks or random events but occur in a sequence and are related to the self-disclosure of God. The world was disordered by sin, disease and death, and the miracles of Jesus brought the new order of healing and life. Even a naturalistic explanation of the miracles of Jesus credits him with amazing insight and compassion. It was in connection with the healing miracles that Jesus came into conflict with the Pharisees. They recognized that he could do them but objected when he healed on the Sabbath day (Mt 12.9–14).

It is interesting to note that Hume had his problems about causation. He denied causation in his first *Inquiry concerning Human Understanding* contending that what we had was constant conjunctions, that is, events of this sort are regularly followed by events of that sort. But when he comes to miracles in his later *Inquiry concerning the Principles of Morals* there is no indication that causal connections and necessities are nothing but false projections onto nature.[14] He seems to have forgotten what he had previously said about cause and effect.

We may conclude that there is no necessity that what has always happened must happen and what happens today may happen tomorrow. On this basis, Augustine's definition of miracle has force: "Miracle is not contrary to nature but what is known about nature." Miracles do not always create faith but those who have faith can create miracles. In the Gospels Jesus seems to be dependent on the faith of the one who asks for a miracle of healing. Indeed where there was no belief in him in Nazareth he did not perform any miracles. Hume, of course, ruled out faith in God.

The test of miracles is their effects. If they are sensational and bizarre, and Jesus refused to do such in the account of his temptation, they do not accomplish any good. When a miracle results in righting wrongs, saving lives, healing or relieving the oppressed, it deserves examination.

DEATH AND RESURRECTION OF JESUS

Tacitus, the Roman historian, and Celsus, who was an opponent of Christianity, confirm the Crucifixion. The Talmud states that Jesus was executed on the eve of the Passover while the Qur'an mentions the event but gives it a docetic interpretation: it only seemed that they crucified him.

Resurrection was expected at the end time when a judgment would be administered and the dead restored to life but the resurrection of Christ was totally unexpected as occurring in history at a specific time. Jesus died on the Cross with his followers scattered. He was cursed (Dt. 21.23) and forsaken by God (Mt 27.46), just another failure, but a few weeks after his death his disciples who had left him to die were proclaiming that he was alive and was the Lord and Messiah. Such a transformation requires a remarkable cause (Acts 2.24).

There are inconsistencies in the reports of the resurrection but it is to be expected in the case of a unique event. What is clear is that the early Church was certain that he had risen from the dead. Some critics, however, think that he did not expect an individual resurrection for himself since what he said had the background of the corporate resurrection of Israel (Dan. 12.2). Any predictions of Jesus regarding his resurrection were the creation of the post-Christian community but it does not rule out that he foresaw the corporate resurrection of Christians as lying beyond his own death. Paul, however, claimed that Christ's resurrection was the guarantee of ours.

The appearances of the risen Christ are accepted by form critics as pronouncement stories and have a good historical reliability. Paul's first letter to the Corinthians is very near these events, written about 55 CE, with Crucifixion either in 30 CE or 33 CE and he refers to appearances (ophthe). It is said that he had a vision of Christ that differed from the other apostles but the same verb, ophthe, is used to describe the appearance to Peter, James, and other followers (1 Cor. 15.9). It means plain seeing and differs from epiphanie, the appearance of Christ in his second coming. Horao meaning mental insight is normally used of seeing a vision like the one he had of paradise (2 Cor. 12.3–5; cf. Acts 7.31).

Just like the followers and disciples, Christ was physically seen (theoreo) by Mary as well, but the different form of his body made her think he was the gardener. It was not like the appearance of a spirit, pneuma. Thomas demanded plain seeing and was allowed to touch the wounds (John 20.24–25). Yet some still contend that they were hallucinations or subjective visions sent by God but it is unlikely that the disciples being demoralized would have been convinced by these. They knew that their witness to such an event meant persecution and even death.

When there was a doubt Jesus reassured them that he was not a spirit. There is a difference between seeing and recognition as in the case of the travelers on the road to Emmaus. His followers did not recognize him until he broke the bread. We often identify people by their characteristics, the way they walk, speak, make decisions, and use their hands. It was the manner in which Jesus broke the bread that brought recognition. The Gospels report that he did appear to them in another form. We sometimes recognize a person when he calls us by name. It happened to Mary Magdalene. Why? Mary was a prostitute and the men who used her did not care what name she had. It was Jesus who called her by name and she never forgot that it meant he was recognizing her value as a person.

Where did the appearances take place? Mark does not have them but foretells one in Galilee (14.28; 16.7). Matthew and

Luke insist that they were in Jerusalem. A common feature is the difficulty of recognizing Jesus; some doubted (Mt 28.17). There is no attempt to agree about appearances or recognition so they were not copying from one another.

The appearing and disappearing meant there was the presence in a different mode or form. We have seen earlier that form, morphe, means the essence of a person and in Mark 16.2 it is used: "he appeared in another form to them." It was the same Jesus whom they had known but the schema had changed, varying from place to place and from time to time.

It was difficult for them to believe in a suffering Messiah until they searched the scriptures. They looked again at the suffering servant of Isaiah and saw that it meant more than the nation of Israel. It pointed to an individual and his suffering. Hence they gave him the worship due to God (Mt 28.9) for Jesus had risen from the dead and was not tied to space and time. (Lk 24.31; John 20.19, 26).

THE EMPTY TOMB

The story of the empty tomb is very early and the disciples verified the discovery of the women that it was empty. They did not go to the wrong one on Easter morning (Mark 15.47). Though Paul does not mention it he says that he was buried and the story of Joseph asking for the body is quite plausible to prevent it being cast into a common grave. Rudolf Bultmann, however, thinks we are dealing with an apologetic legend for the identity and number of the witnesses differ in the various Gospels as does their testimony. But if the writers had wanted to convince, why did they not refer to more reliable witnesses than the women whose testimony in those days did not carry the same weight as that of men?

Another question is this: Did Nicodemus or Joseph of Arimathea in the absence of the disciples remove the body to another tomb? Not likely since they could have given this explanation to the authorities. Nor is it possible if the disciples returned that they removed the body. They would have hardly dared to preach the resurrection if they had a dead body on their hands and it is difficult to accept that the women went to the wrong tomb since the authorities must have conducted an exhaustive search of the tombs to find the body.

THE NATURE OF THE RESURRECTED BODY

What kind of body did the disciples see in the tomb? The Gospel of John records the visits to it. The clothes in it had collapsed as if the body had slipped through them.[15] It was like a glove when the hand is withdrawn, the glove remains but the hand has gone. But does the physical reality of the body of Jesus in some of the appearances not oppose what Paul says about the nature of the postresurrection existence (1 Cor. 15.35–50)? One answer is that Jesus did not leave his earthly body behind but took it with him so that the incarnate and the crucified one with all the saving benefits is present for us.[16] But how does the explanation fit in with Paul's declaration that flesh and blood will not inherit the kingdom of God?

Paul was a Jew and knew the apocalyptic literature and the writings of Philo and Stoicism that were prominent at the time. He shows this in his speech on the Areopagus: "God who dwells not in temples made with hands…who gives to all life, and breath, and all things…in whom we live and move and have our being" (Acts 17.22ff.). But he differed in preaching a personal God not a world soul or a spirit that pervaded creation like a physical substance with the souls of men as its particles.[17] He appears to hold a dualism of body and spirit without the degradation of the Greek view of the body (Phil. 3.21). It belongs to our low estate yet is the temple of the Holy Spirit and there is a need to glorify God in our bodies.

There was the Jewish belief in resurrection but it tended to be materialistic, the same body that died was to rise again. It would be reassembled by the act of God. Paul rejected this and takes up the via media: Christ had appeared in his resurrected body and he could be identified but there was a difference for the body of humiliation had become the body of glory. The Greek Corinthians asked about the bodies of those who would be resurrected and his answer was that they would have one like that of Christ: "The Greek view of immortality safeguarded spirituality but endangered personal identity. The Jewish view safeguarded identity but endangered spirituality. Paul's view preserves both spirituality and personal identity."[18]

In dealing with the nature of the resurrection in 1 Corinthians 15.36–41 Paul compares it to a plant, to fleshy being, and to celestial and earthly physical bodies. The seed sown is related to the new plant that appears but it has a different body. The seed sown results in an animal body for we are of the dust but it is raised as a spiritual body. He goes on to say that while there is much that is similar in the flesh of man and animals there is that which is different. God can take our natural and perishable bodies and make a new spiritual body, not a nonmaterial but one organized in a similar way yet radically different in that it will not perish and is glorious. A new body will be appropriate for the new age but will retain its individuality. Adam had a natural body with a soul but the new body will also have the life giving Spirit.[19]

Paul is pointing out in the seed analogy that there will be a difference but continuity. What is the continuity? It cannot be the body that like the seed dies so it must be the soul that follows the pattern of what we are. The natural man has psyche and the word means soul, life, breath, or spirit that is the activity of self-conscious reflection. For Paul psyche means life, a living man, or soul (2 Cor. 1.23, 12.15; 1 Thess. 5.23). Flesh and blood cannot inherit the kingdom of God or the perishable inherit the imperishable. But the seed analogy fails for the plant is another form of the same seed but we will be transformed.

Soul and Body

There is no sharp distinction in Hebrew thought between soul and body. James Moffatt quotes J. Pedersen: "The soul is more than the body but the body is a perfectly valid manifestation of the soul indeed the body is the soul in its outward form."[20] It is the resurrection of the body not the immortality of the soul that is central to Paul's thought but it does not mean lack of interest in the continuity of the soul or personality.

Soul is mentioned by Paul on various occasions: "Moreover I call God for a record on my soul...." (11 Cor. 1.23); "He will be spent for their souls" (11 Cor. 12.15); and he prays that spirit, soul and body be preserved blameless until the coming of Christ (1 Thess. 5.23). The soul for him is the source of action in doing the will of God (Eph. 6.6) and they are to stand in one spirit with one soul (Phil. 1.27). In Colossians 3.13 he writes: "Whatsoever you do from the soul, work as to the Lord and not to man."

Soul and spirit go together and are not in opposition to one another but likely to be the same thing under different aspects. Spirit is energy, power, and soul is the seat of feeling, thought, will. In the passage from 1 Thessalonians mentioned above there is no antithesis between soul and spirit and both are likely to figure in the new dispensation and made capable of so doing. The body too will be changed as Paul maintains. In other words the whole nature of the redeemed person will be present in the after life.

CONCLUSION

The importance of the soul is clear in the New Testament and is used to designate the person. There is a unity of body, soul and spirit. The soul could be seen as the form of the body and the center of activity. Spirit and soul are close together and man cannot destroy the soul. It can be seen as the coded pattern of what we are and could be given a new body in the after life. Soul is the essence of what we are, the inner self, the person. We could think of a spiritual soul.

Morphe as we have seen means that the essence of something does not change but the schema does. In his resurrection Jesus was the same one that they had known but the form of his appearance changed.

In the first century there were a variety of interpretations of immortality, some contending for the immortality of the soul while others argued for the resurrection of the body. Paul stressed the latter and believed that we would receive a spiritual body.

We will now go on to see in the next chapter how the soul was understood in the developing doctrine of the Church.

CHAPTER 3

THE SOUL AND THE DEVELOPMENT
OF CHRISTIAN BELIEF

In this chapter we consider the view of the soul as the Faith developed and the problems posed today.

The Apostles' creed encompasses belief in the resurrection and ascension of Jesus, the resurrection of the flesh and the everlasting life. The Nicene creed believes in the resurrection of the dead and the life of the world to come and final judgment. The Athanasian creed recognized by the Catholic Church is not thought to be by Athanasius and its date is disputed. It mentions the union of soul and flesh to make a man.

Origen believed in the preexistence of the soul and a pretemporal Fall. Jerome and Hiliary contended that God creates a new soul at each birth which was accepted by the Eastern and Western Church but Tertullian and Luther preferred traducianism meaning that the soul is transmitted by parents to children. The belief went well with the transmission of sin but the East did not like it and Aquinas denied it.

Augustine (354–430) found it difficult to choose between the theories but Calvin accepted creationism. Both, however, recognized that we must care for the soul in the war against the flesh. Augustine believed in the unity of soul but was a substance dualist. The soul is the better part of man: scripture speaks of the inner man and the outer. The inner soul has reason and will and personal identity is secured by memory. The image of God means that the soul is immaterial and immortal, it is not limited spatially, permeates the body, and does not die. As an imperfect spirit, marked at the outset by the sin of Adam and Eve, it hankers for sin even after conversion and is the center of mental and brain activity. Augustine did not make any decision regarding the origin of the soul's union with the body and on the possibility of preexistence he does not affirm the Platonic doctrine.[1]

Augustine has a soul-deciding theodicy in contrast to Irenaeus who advocated soul-making. John Hick accepts the latter view and sees God making man in His image as the culmination of the evolutionary process. Since we are in epistemic distance from God we do not know directly His presence, and suffering is necessary for the development of the soul.[2]

Thomas Aquinas (1225–1274) saw individual immortality of the soul as a natural conclusion to be drawn about the human body. The soul was bestowed by God at the appropriate point in the development of the human embryo. He asserted that soul could exist on its own and after death continue in an intermediate state before being reunited with the body.[3] The soul was reason and emotion and would eventually get a new spiritual body at resurrection. He relies on Aristotle's distinction between form and matter, which means that the soul is the form of the body not in the sense that the soul is the shape of the body but in that it organizes and activates it.[4]

The Reformation in the sixteenth century was concerned with the salvation of the soul. Did it happen by faith or works? The medieval Church believed that God created body and soul and salvation was mediated through the sacraments. After death the just would enter heaven where their souls would experience the direct vision of God. Those who had died in grace but were not yet ready for heaven were purified and paid their debt of temporal punishment in the fire of purgatory but their release could be hastened by the prayers of the living and by the offering and sacrifice of the Mass. Those who were not Christians went to hell. On the final day of Judgment, Christ would be the judge and there would be a general resurrection of the dead and the body of each person would be reunited with his soul to share its reward or punishment.

The Reformers doctrine of justification by faith and free pardon by God's grace opposed any idea of being right with Him through good works. The Council of Trent (1563) replied with its doctrines of purgatory, prayers and masses for the dead, sacramental penance, ascetical practices and indulgences. The Reformers denied all of it insisting that the debt had been paid by Christ so the sinner was clean and nothing further was needed. Calvin and other Reformers rejected the Catholic doctrine of baptism which meant that the sacrament had an efficacy to cleanse from original sin and to infuse divine life into the soul. The infusing was not just favor but grace which meant a new state of supernatural life.

The Anabaptists accepted the belief in the vigil of the soul, that is, that the souls of the dead did not survive in any conscious state before the Last Judgment that traditional theology had asserted. It insisted that there was a particular judgment after death with the saved going to heaven either directly or via purgatory but the damned to hell. At the general resurrection the body would be raised to share the eternal life already experienced by the soul. Luther rejected purgatory and apparently for a time doubted the natural immortality of the soul. Calvin wrote a treatise against the Anabaptists.[5]

Indulgences could remit temporal punishments that were due for sins after death. A spiritual treasury had been amassed from the merits of Christ and Mary and the saints, and an indulgence for the release of the souls of the dead in purgatory was also obtainable. Indulgences cost money but as the Vatican salesman Tetzel cried: "The moment the coin rattles in the box, the soul leaps out of purgatory"![6] Luther thought that the soul slept prior to resurrection and judgment in an unconscious state. Calvin on the other hand spoke of the "wake of the soul" and this was accepted by Catholicism in the Fifth Lateran council (1513).[7] The Council of Trent defended purgatory and argued that the souls being detained there are helped by the intercessions of the faithful and the sacrifice at the altar. It also commended the use of images, intercession and invocation of saints and honor due to relics and so on.

In the subsequent Confessions of Faith, the Westminster (1643) reveals the Protestantism that emerged from the

Reformation. It teaches that when the body dies the soul passes immediately to God who gave it. Eventually at the last judgment soul and body will be reunited; but the criticism is that this is the Greek belief in the immortality of the soul.[8] However, as we pointed out, Greek influence is already seen in the New Testament and we cannot simply write it off.

In the Articles of the Church of England (1563) there is the belief in the resurrection of the flesh that appears to mean that the old body will be reassembled. The fourth article says that Christ took again his body with flesh, bone, and all pertaining to the perfection of our nature and he ascended into heaven hence the particles composing our flesh will be collected and the identical structure restored. It opposes Paul's view that an entirely new body will be created by God.

Currently, advances in doctrine have been made in the dialogue between Catholics, Anglicans, Lutheran, Reformed and Methodist Churches. Discussions have been going on from 1967. As a result it is stated that agreement has been reached on justification by faith. But further dialogue is needed on indulgences, penance, human cooperation with God, the Church, and the ministry. The ministry has become a central issue but the polemics and controversies over the years have been left behind. The teaching of scripture has been given priority and tradition has been recognized but the nature of ministry, the question of the ordination of women, and the place of the Pope continue to be difficult issues. Clarification is also required on the sacrificial character of the Mass, the nature of the change wrought in the bread and wine and the real presence of Christ. What does transubstantiation mean and can nonordained persons celebrate the rite?[9]

The soul is prominent in the services conducted at the burial of the dead. The priest on the authority of the Church says: "Forasmuch as it hath pleased Almighty God of his great mercy to take unto Himself the soul of our dear brother here departed we therefore commit his/her body to the ground; earth to earth, ashes to ashes, dust to dust; in sure and certain hope of the resurrection to eternal life through our Lord Jesus Christ…"[10] And/or: "We humbly commend the soul of this thy servant…into thy hands…Wash it, we pray thee, in the blood of that immaculate Lamb, that was slain to take away the sins of the world...that it may be presented pure and without spot before thee...”[11]

In brief, the history of the doctrine of the Church shows clearly the belief in the soul and its passing into the after life.

MYSTICISM

Mysticism impressed both Catholic and Protestant and meant an immediate awareness of God. Thomas a Kempis in the fifteenth century was a well known practitioner and earlier, Bernard of Clairvaux (1090–1153), believed that the soul of the mystic is emptied of self and lost wholly in God without actually achieving an actual union. It was St. Francis, however, who reached the heights of mysticism believing it to be an extension of normal consciousness that plumbed aspects of truth not revealed by the intellect. There is the immanence of the divine within us giving a direct experience of God.

The cultivation of the soul continues in the Order of St. Francis. There is conversion, purgation with the threefold vow, austerity of life, humility, obedience and poverty. Then illumination leading to holiness, brotherly relation to all creatures, compassion, desire for martyrdom for Christ, power in prayer. This was continued with union or perfection, loyalty and understanding of scripture, inspiration in preaching, gifts of healing and sanctification, culminating in the sacred stigma and from it deepening holiness and awareness of God.

If the soul responds to God it becomes unified with Him and more and more withdraws from the world-system with its illusory quest for money, status, ambition, and power. It becomes active in the service of others as shown by St. Teresa, St. John of the Cross, the great Carmelites and others. The soul lives in God and God in the soul, a mutual indwelling that restores and heals the Imago Dei.[12]

Nature mysticism, person mysticism, and soul mysticism are all found in Shelley and Wordsworth. The point is to reach a union with God but it can result in a declared identification with Him, which had unfortunate consequences for the Muslim mystic the Sufi Mansur al-Hallaj who said that he was the truth.

The Muslims could not accept it since the truth was one of the words used for Allah and al-Hallaj who was executed in March 922.[13] It seems more likely that he was speaking metaphorically rather than literally in a numerical sense, an awareness of the divine, a unity of will, with the soul being transformed but remaining distinct from the being of God.

Identity after Death

John Hick points out that there are various ways of identity: somatic, seminal principle, form, flame, substance, organizing principle, or the same code. The body is capable of being coded, transmitted and then translated back into its original form. He says that today there is belief only in the empirical self and a psychophysical unity. Soul is simply the way we behave or function. God resurrects or recreates us as a spiritual body that embodies our characteristics and memories. He then proceeds to his replica theory, a divine creation in another space of a person's replica. I am in a certain space now but there could be another space that is invisible. It exists though I cannot see it just as someone in that space cannot observe me if I am elsewhere.

He favors considering the individuality of the body as more like a flame than a substance. It is a pattern of change or a message and as Hick said capable of being coded, transmitted and then translated back into its original form, so we could transmit the whole pattern of the body with its memories and a receiving instrument could reembody these messages in matter. It would contain the same information of the original body even though not the same matter; hence we can conclude that identity depends upon the codes.

He advocates replicas. We can imagine someone dying in London and then reappearing in New York in that we reappear in a different space with same memories and so on. We could have bodies that are the outward reflection of our inner nature.

He is thinking of creation in another space, a spatial heaven that would not be related to ours. But is this conceivable for a physical replica requires a physical world in which time and distance matter and energy interact in the same way as in our own. Paul Badham wants to replace Hick's suggestion with a planet or some other star in another galaxy. The examples given by Hick indicate that the replica has the same memory and awareness of his former life but what would the replica be of? Childhood, youth, middle age, old age? Hick answers that resurrection body created at the last moment would involve healing and repair. We return to this question in a later chapter.

Paul Badham thinks that the exact replica should be replaced by a substantial or somatically identical body so that the recreated person is of the same substance of the deceased. In this case the deceased body and soul would function perfectly in this new life, that is, the complete man conquers death. John Hick contends that we are incomplete at death so process toward perfection is needed. He does not believe in sudden change for how would we be the same persons and why could God not have done this in the first place and saved us all our trial here? An intermediate state would enable us to respond freely to being changed and it could have sex and marriage. It would not be heaven where we are to be like the angels.

Badham, however, rejects Hick's reinterpretation of bodily resurrection as an untenable hypothesis.[14] He holds that the resurrection does not provide the sole justification for belief in life after death because from the second century, the majority of believers affirmed the immortality of the soul. It was defined as a dogma by the Lateran council (1512–1517) and held by the Reformers. Today the belief continues in spiritual bodies with the soul expressing itself through them as it has done with the earthly body. The important thing is not viewing the body simply as a physicochemical constitution but in relation to a person. The same personality will have a body in the after life as in this. Identity will be personality and we retain our intelligence, memory traces, dispositions, and soul or spirit. So I will still be I and you will still be you.[15] Badham thinks that individual personalities might receive new and quite different bodies in another mode of being but it depends on the validity of some concept of the soul. It would ensure personal continuity between the two types of existence so belief in the soul is defended.

REINCARNATION

The concept of reincarnation is ruled out by Hebrew 9.27, which states that we die once and after that the judgment. Hick would agree saying that he cannot find definite evidence for reincarnation in the New Testament and rejects Leslie Weatherhead's interpretation of the story of the blind man in John 9.2–3. Weatherhead thought it confirmed reincarnation. But Hick has to take into account other passages such as Matthew 16.13–14 where people identify Jesus as John the Baptist, Eligah, Jeremias, or one of the prophets. Herod suspected that Jesus might be John whom he had recently beheaded (Mt 14.2).

Jesus said that the coming of the Messiah would be preceded by the reappearance of Eligah but added: "Eligah is come already, and they know him not...Then the disciples understood that he spoke to them of John the Baptist" (Mt 17.21–13). Reference to the identity of Eligah also appears in the saying: "Among them that are born of women there hath not risen a greater than John the Baptist...And if ye will receive it this is Eligah" (Mt 11.14). Tertullian and Irenaeus rejected reincarnation because of lack of memories of former lives and the problem of personal identity.

An investigation of people who remember at least one past experience shows that children recall better a previous life but it soon fades; examples are normally drawn from Eastern culture where reincarnation is accepted. Remembering requires inheritance of acquired characteristics but genetics denies this. After a long discussion Hick cannot reach a conclusion regarding whether or not reincarnation is true or false but continues to argue that Weatherhead was wrong in saying that the early Church accepted reincarnation for the first five hundred years and only in 553 CE did the Council of Constantinople reject it. He says it was taught by the Gnostics whom the Church opposed.[16]

Dr. Ian Stevenson in his investigation of reincarnation mentions twenty of two hundred cases. Typical is someone who early in life remembers a former life but gradually forgets it in manhood. David Hume conceded that reincarnation was possible and that it was the only form of survival. Reviewers of Stevenson's work argued that they knew of no conclusive argument on the basis of which we could rule out reincarnation on a priori grounds as conceptually meaningless or self-contradictory.

New Age religious movements stressing the spirit or soul believe in reincarnation. They think that it takes many lives to reach moral maturity but there are differences on how long the cycle continues. Yet the belief does help to explain the trouble and frustration of this life as an inheritance of a past life and asks how a single life has eternal consequences. But since we are fulfilling the consequences of another life we should not interfere or indeed help others when they get into difficulty. It is a defect since it opposes moral responsibility and the indignation we feel when we see someone being hurt.[17]

ESCHATOLOGY

Parousia means arrival or presence. The word is found in the eschatological parables of Matthew 24 and in the epistles (1 Thess. 4.16). It is possible that Paul did change his mind as to the immediacy of it but all his epistles are in the one decade so he reminds both the Romans and the Philippians that they were waiting for the savior from heaven (Rom. 13.11–12; Phil. 3.20). Maranatha was an Aramaic phrase found in 1 Corinthians 16.22 and could mean "Our Lord come" recited in worship by the early Christians.

Did Jesus believe in what has been called consistent eschatology, meaning the end of the world or realized eschatology holding that the Kingdom had arrived with him? Or is the best view inaugurated eschatology, which means that he brought some of the elements of the Kingdom but not all (Mt 24–25). The Gospels assert that Jesus did speak of his Second Coming and the Christians expected it but various interpretations have been applied. Some think that he did not say what the Gospels report or he meant that it was a symbol of God's final triumph rather than a promise of an actual future coming. The Church misunderstood what he was saying if he did say it. Others believe that Jesus comes to help them while making decisions. What can be said positively is that the sayings affirm the Christian hope of

God's final fulfillment so there is no need to commit oneself to its nature or the time.[18]

But speculation continues. Will it occur after the calling of the Gentiles, the conversion of Israel, the apostasy of the anti-christ and much tribulation? Then there is the belief in a millennium either before or after his return. Those who hold this position rely basically on Revelation 20.4–6 and see the resurrection, final judgment, end of the world, separated by such a time factor. Opponents argue that there is no separation but that the events coincide (Mt 13.37–43; 47–50; John 5.25–29; 1 Cor. 15.22–26).

A later form of postmillennialism does not pay a great deal of attention to scripture but argues that divine intervention is unnecessary for evolution will happen in the millennium and it is we who must bring in the new age. But this is to repeat the arguments of the nineteenth century and the stress on social progress and belief in the ability of mankind to act in a more civilized way. It is always a hope but the wars of the twentieth century and the continued inability of mankind to live in harmony does not promise much unless there is divine help. The scripture seems to point to a new creation rather than simply a renewal of the old.[19]

We are united with Christ in life and we will be united with him in resurrection (Rom. 6.4–5). It all depends on the faithfulness of God in changing the cosmos with the first things having passed away. Judgment will be imposed upon evil doers but in the Fourth Gospel it is self-imposed (3.19).

The antichrist (1 John 2.18, 22; and 11 John 7) has often been discussed. Is a person meant or a principle of evil? Nero was seen as the antichrist, the man of sin, but if it is a principle, it will reach its height at the end of the world. Some see judgment as symbolic of the separation of the world and the Church or unnecessary since our destiny is determined at death by our acceptance or rejection of Christ.[20]

John Hick writes about a possible steady progress toward a future perfection. He holds that the self-conscious ego will continue to exist after bodily death but only saints, and arhats or buddhas, will be perfect enough to attain the "heavenly" state. What will happen to the rest of us? He believes that the purpose of our lives is gradual perfection, which cannot happen with most of us here. There may be an intermediate state as described in the *Tibetan Book of the Dead* but it would be subjective and dream like before embodiment in another world. This gradual perfection could be accomplished in purgatory.

PURGATORY

The concept of purgatory was opposed by the Reformers as we have noted but reaffirmed by the Council of Trent, a time of purification for those who have been saved. Belief in a second chance for those who have not professed faith in Christ is ruled out. Augustine believed in purgatory on the basis of 1 Corinthians 3.11–15 and Matthew 12.31–32. In the second century Judas the hero of the Maccabees prays for those who have died and makes atonement for them (11 Mac. 12.39–46). This is used by the Catholic Church to justify the practice of saying prayers, making offerings, and masses for the dead but the Articles of the Church of England deny that belief in purgatory has warrant in scripture.

Current defense of the doctrine argues that Matthew 12.32 implies that there is forgiveness in the age to come and 1 Corinthians 3.15 states that Christians who have been less than faithful will be saved through fire that is the purification of purgatory. Since nothing unclean will enter heaven the soul will need to be purified.[21]

IMMORTALITY OF THE SOUL

In the absolute sense only God has immortality and He confers it on us (1 Tim. 6.15, 16). The scripture does not speak explicitly of the immortality of the soul but rather that Jesus brought life and immortality to light (11 Tim. 1.10). But it is asserted that some passages such as Matthew 10.28 confirm the immortality of the soul for only God can kill it.

If the materialist grants that the soul exists, he can go on to say that it and the mind are just a product or function of brain activity and die with the brain. The response to this takes the form of asserting that the brain merely transmits just as colored glass transmits light. Light exists independent of such glass and so does thought. In any case the Christian belief is that the soul will be united to a new body that will operate on a much higher level than the earthly one and will have a brain suitable to it.[22]

Some hold that the soul sleeps but there are scriptural passages that point to a conscious life after death (Lk 16.19–31, 23.43; 11 Cor. 5.8; Phil. 1.23; Rev. 6.9–11, 7.9, 20.4; 1 Thess. 5.10). There is debate about immortality but generally it is thought that we will receive it from God and do not possess it inherently.

Wolfhart Pannenberg argues that it is not possible to maintain that the soul has a natural immortality because of the intimate connection of body and soul but Allan Galloway who has given a clear exposition of Pannenberg questions this. Pannenberg says that we think now of processes in the world rather than a changeless substratum and physiology, and allied sciences have made the idea of a life existing apart from the body inconceivable. His argument is limited for the Greek concept of soul must be rejected if necessary, neither on sociological or scientific grounds but philosophical and that means reckoning with Descartes as we will see in chapter 8.[23]

HELL

Evangelicals note that today eternal punishment is denied and hell is a subjective condition, which we can experience here on earth. Hell is an absence of God, disturbance of life, sufferings in body and soul, pangs of conscience and so on. They agree that much of the language about hell is figurative and eternal may be an age or period of time. Yet they hold on to thinking of heaven and hell as places not simply conditions.[24]

The Church of England doctrine Commission 1995 states that there has been a shift away from everlasting punishment to alternatives like annihilation, which C. S. Lewis embraced. It is a state of being that we choose and is not parallel to heaven. Lewis goes as far as to say that God is committed to reconcile everyone to Himself.[25]

It is contended that aionios (eternal) does not mean endless and kolasis (punishment) means pruning for growth hence it is corrective. Purification will take place in purgatory. F. D. Maurice suggested punishment was being without God and was dismissed from his chair at King's College, London, but the Evangelical Alliance omitted any direct reference to eternal punishment from its basis in 1970. It was recognized that there is a disproportion between it and finite sin. Their current basis of faith allows both traditionalist and conditional interpretations of hell and there are prominent evangelicals like the Revd. John Stott who are of the latter. The World's Evangelical Alliance recognized the immortality of the soul and resurrection of the body in 1846.

Hades should not be translated as hell for it was regarded as the land of the dead and in early Jewish belief there was no punishment for the "shades" or those that had a weak existence there. But Gehenna was called hell and located in the Valley of Hinnom outside Jerusalem. In pagan worship infants were sacrificed but it eventually became the public refuse dump. It was the place of waste and evil and eventually came symbolically to stand for hell, where the wicked were destroyed.

Concerning heaven it is noted that the word occurs sparingly in the Gospels and "eternal life," "glory," "my Father's house," are substituted. But unlike hell it is a place of rejoicing, singing, closeness to God and bliss of every kind.

UNIVERSAL SALVATION

Universal salvation was possible according to some of the Greek fathers but Augustine opposed and it was condemned along with Origen at the second council of Constantinople. During the Reformation the radicals affirmed it but they were denounced by the main stream Reformers. Some liberal theologians approve universalism on the basis of Romans 5.18 and 11.32 but generally evangelicals deny it.

CONCLUSION

The importance of the soul is clear in the New Testament and is used to designate the person. There is a unity of body, soul and spirit. The soul could be seen as the form of the body and the center of activity. Spirit and soul are close together and man cannot destroy the soul. It can be seen as the coded pattern of what we are and could be given a new body in the after life.

With Augustine the soul is the inner essence and is the center of reasoning and will. It is immortal. Purgatory was denied by the Reformers but the Catholic Church still believes in it as a place where the soul is purified. The concept requires the presence of the soul in the after life.

In drawing attention to the soul as the form of the body we mentioned in the last chapter morphe and schema (Phil. 2.1–11). A person's morphe does not change, it is what he always is but the schema is the outward form and varies from place to place and from time to time. We know we are the same person for the morphe is our unchanging essence but the Buddhists deny it as we will see. Their stress is on the impermanence of everything.

Mysticism is one way to cultivate the soul but the flesh lusts against both spirit and soul. There is also the question of whether or not the soul evolved naturally or was given by God. Salvation of the soul has been stressed in the Bible and Christian doctrine but there are different views of the method.

The soul is needed for the continuity of our identity after death but there is tension between the immortality of the soul and the resurrection of the body. The latter requires a miracle and we have contended that there is good evidence for it. If spirit and soul are close together as we have suggested then we can speak of a spiritual soul that could take a new body.

But we need to discuss in later chapters the view that mind and soul are just products or functions of brain activity and die with the brain.

There are various speculations about the end of the world, heaven and hell, purgatory and the judgment. The debate continues but Christians need to heed the warning of Rheinhold Neibuhr who cautions them not to pay too much attention to the furniture of heaven or the temperature of hell!

CHAPTER 4

THE MUSLIM CLAIM

In the name of Allah the Compassionate the Merciful.[1]

Every surah or chapter of the holy Qur'an begins with the above declaration of faith and enshrines what the Muslims think of Allah or God. Muhammad is the prophet of God. He was born in Mecca about the year 570 CE and may have been influenced by Judaism and Christianity. The claim of the Muslim is that he is the final prophet and the Qur'an was given to him in stages by Allah.

Reacting against the tribalism and the many gods of his people he desired a unifying force but was unprepared for the vision that came to him in a cave. He was petrified and did not know what to do until he returned in a collapsed state to his wife Khadijah who assured him that God had enfolded his soul. She told him that she dared to hope that he had been chosen as the prophet of his people.

Muslims assert that the Faith did not begin with Muhammad but was in the world from the beginning and is the only religion that has preserved the scripture in pure form. They refer to the promise in Deuteronomy of the prophet who was to come and believe it was fulfilled by Muhammad. He was unlettered but God put His words in his mouth.

During the course of his life while he was often victorious against his enemies he suffered ridicule from unbelievers who considered him mad, a charge often levelled against prophets in every religion. Unbelievers said that he had invented the

Qur'an. It was forged with the help of others and consisted of fables, dictated to him morning and evening. In short he was bewitched. The Qur'an records this (surah 25.3) and justifies the prophet stating that unbelievers are lying and will pay the penalty on the last day.

GOD

There is belief in the one God and the Last day:

> Believers have faith in God and His apostle, in the Book He has revealed to His apostle and in the Scriptures He formerly revealed. He that denies God, His angels, His Scriptures, His apostles, and the Last Day has strayed far. (surah 4.136)

There are ninety-nine names given to God who does not resemble us and is not begotten being eternal with all power and knowledge. But He is also personal and is closer to the human than the jugular vein (surah 30.15).

Commentators on Islam stress that it is difficult to speak of God because our words fail to capture what He is really like. The language used is not scientific, which is committed to facts, but expresses an attitude. The danger is subjectivism.[2]

THE QUR'AN

It provides evidence of the compassion of Allah and His promises to mankind but it also contains dire warnings for unbelievers. The sacred book was communicated by Allah to the prophet:

> And this Qur'an is not something
> That could be manufactured without God;
> Rather it is a confirmation of what came before
> And a clear explanation of the (eternal) Book
> There is no doubt in it—from the Lord of all creation.
>
> Do they say that He has forged it?
> Say: let them bring a chapter like it,
> And call on anyone whom you can besides God.
> If you are truthful. (surah 10:35)

It can be interpreted allegorically but also historically with an understanding of the times and conditions of the events. There are essential verses that state the core of the faith but others are symbolic and have multiple interpretations. Ta'wil is the allegorical interpretation of the Qur'an imparting new meaning and explaining ambiguous passages.[3]

The soul often referring to the person is mentioned. It reveals the human potential for good:

> By the soul and Him who moulded it
> And inspired it with knowledge of sin and piety;
> Blessed be the man who has kept it pure,
> And ruined he that has corrupted it. (surah 91.6)

We need to care for the soul by good deeds since it is prone to evil. Bad deeds will incur punishment at the Last Day while goodness will be rewarded. Predestination is evident and much debated by scholars in connection with free will. Every soul will answer for itself at the Day of Resurrection, no soul will bear another's burden (surah 39.7).

HUMAN NATURE

The human is the vice gerent of God and falls into sin when Satan or Iblis tempts him/her. We are made of clay and the spirit breathed into us:

> Recite in the name of your Lord who created-
> Created man from clots of blood
> Recite! Your Lord is the bountiful One,
> Who by the pen taught man
> What he did not know. (surah 96.1)

Yet he has also been moulded in a noble image and there will be a boundless recompense for the believers who do good works. On the day of resurrection it will be seen that evil doers have forfeited their souls and will suffer much. Allah "takes away mens' souls upon their death and the souls of the living during their sleep. Those that are doomed He keeps with Him and restores the others for a time ordained" (surah 39.42).

Nevertheless He forgives all sins for He is the forgiving and merciful One and if we turn in repentance and surrender to Him His scourge will not operate. But there does not seem to be any second chance after this life.

The image of God was the possibility of our reflecting divine traits but within limits, which are not to be confused with the divine essence that remains hidden. There is the divine potential in the human for God is immanent as well as transcendent.[4] This life for many is only a sport and a diversion but others withdraw from the world and enter a monastery. These views and behavior are not acceptable (surah 57.25).

EVIL

Satan was condemned because he refused to prostrate himself before Adam who had been created by Allah (surah 2.32). He said that he was nobler than Adam since he had been created from fire whereas Adam was from clay. It was pride that led to his fall and expulsion from Paradise. Human beings have been created from a single soul and from that soul the female species was created (surah 4.1). Adam and Eve confessed that they had wronged their souls and were driven out of the garden.

BEHAVIOR

Killing is allowed if done in a just cause but manslaughter is forbidden. The soul can motivate a person to kill as in the case of Cain who killed his brother. To kill someone except as a punishment for murder or other wicked crimes is considered to be the killing of all mankind but those who fight for the cause of Allah will be pleased with His gifts and richly rewarded. The difficulty is to know what the cause of Allah is and whether He intends that we should use force.

Adultery is forbidden and must be punished (one hundred lashes usually commuted now to a fine) but the accusation must have the support of four witnesses. Women are to preserve their chastity and draw veils over their bosoms which prevents them being molested. Divorce among the pagan Arabs was by the formula: "Be to me as my mother's back" and the Qur'an issues penalties against this:

> Those that divorce their wives by so saying shall free a slave before they touch each other again...He that has no slave shall fast two successive months...if he cannot he shall feed sixty of the destitute. (surah 58.1)

Divorce is allowed and the women who get it are not to be harmed. They are to be treated with kindness but a man has a higher status and can marry two, three and even four women (surah 4.1). On one occasion, I talked to a group of Muslim women about it and they laughingly pointed out that the man must be able to keep them in separate quarters or houses. A rather expensive business which few could afford! But the law regarding inheritance is unfair since a male inherits twice as much as a female (surah 4.10).

Alms given to the poor can earn forgiveness (surah 2.267); fasting is meritorious but drinking and gambling do more harm than good.

THE PILLARS

Islam has five pillars. The first is the Shahadah, the belief that there is only one God and that Muhammad is His messenger. Other pillars are Salah; to pray five times each day; Zakah—giving money to the poor; Sawm—fasting during the month of Ramadan and Hajj, the pilgrimage to Makkah, the holy city.

The Shahadah is a statement of belief and must be repeated many times daily. In particular it must be said first thing in the morning and last thing at night, whispered into the ear of every newborn baby and the last words repeated before death. It opposes the Christian Trinity that is regarded as polytheism. The call to prayer is

> God is great, I bear witness that there is no god but God, I bear witness that Muhammad is the Prophet of God, Come to pray, come to success, God is great, There is no god but God.

At public prayer in the Mosque (Friday) the Muslim turns in the direction of the qiblah, that is, toward the Ka'bah in Mecca, which is the mother city (surah 62.8).

In the care of the soul the festivals contribute with the practical seen in zakah, which is the giving of money to the poor in order that they can buy food at the end of Ramadan. One festival is called Id-ul-Fitr and the fasting unites all Muslims rich or poor in the effort to deal with worldly desires and to purify their souls.

The Hajj or pilgrimage to Makkah (Mecca) is a spiritual experience and all except the old, sick, disabled or poor are expected to go on it at least once in their lifetime. Just before they enter the city, they take off their normal clothing and put on special ones. The male wears two white, unsewn cotton sheets and the females put on a long, plain dress and a head covering. They enter a holy state called ihram. Many of them keep these clothes and are buried in them.[5]

JIHAD

The militants say it means war and complete sacrifice in defense of the faith but most Muslims interpret this as being the moral struggle against evil and they only fight war in self-defense:

> Permission to take up arms is hereby given to those who are attacked, because they have been wronged. God has power to grant them victory: those who have been driven from their homes, only because they said: "Our Lord is God." Had God not defended some men by the might of others, monasteries and churches, synagogues and mosques in which His praise is daily celebrated, would have been utterly destroyed. But whoever helps God shall be helped by Him. (surah 22.37)

But fighting in the holy month of Ramadan is forbidden and when the Muslims did it against the orders of Muhammad they were defeated for such disobedience. But a greater sin is oppression, which is worse than killing. And those who turn their backs on the Faith and will not fight will enter hell. Muhammad it is said had help from angels at the battle of Badr.

Jihad is self-defense but Osama bin Laden carried out offensive warfare and killed nominal Muslims by quoting verses from the Qur'an that suited him. His suicide bombers have shocked the world and caused many innocent deaths. Fighting must be in the cause of God and He does not love aggressors (surah 2.189). Those slain in the cause of God are not dead, we are just unaware of them. They are alive and well provided for by their Lord. Those who are left behind will eventually join them (surah 2.149, 3.169).

THE NIGHT JOURNEY

Muhammad had this dream or experience, which, was real and he discovered that there were levels in heaven. At the first, angels and the prophet Adam greeted him, at the second other prophets such as Jesus and John the Baptist, at the third Joseph and Solomon, and at the fourth he met Moses and his sister, Miriam. At the fifth he saw Ishmael, Isaac, Elijah and Noah, at the sixth another group of angels, and at the seventh he met the greatest of the prophets, Abraham. Then on to Gabriel who made him promise to pray five times a day, a duty followed by all Muslims. The night journey is interpreted by some as an inner spiritual journey that each must experience into God and then from God. One way to understand the divine within us is by repeating prayerfully the Names of Allah that are many.

SALVATION

The Muslim must obey the Pillars of the Faith and forgive his enemies as Muhammad did when he entered Makkah in 630 CE. He threw out all of the idols in the Ka'bah (cube), the shrine set in the courtyard of the great Mosque. The only pictures left were those of Mary and Jesus or Isa that shows the Muslim acknowledgment of the greatness of the prophet Jesus though there is no acceptance of the Christian belief that he was the Son of God. Hence salvation rests upon obedience, not any divine grace as in Christianity. But we can qualify this when we discuss the Shi'ah.

DIVISIONS

There are a number of divisions but the three important ones are the Sunni, the Shi'ah and the Sufi. The Sunni are the majority but the Shi'ah has always been prominent especially in Iran. In Islam when the prophet died, division ensued as to who should be the successor and two groups emerged. The Shi'ah thought the successor should be Ali, cousin of the Prophet and husband of his daughter Fatimah and after him his grandsons Hasan and Husain. But Abu Bakr, father-in-law of the Prophet and one of his closest friends, was elected. He in turn named Umar Khattab as his successor to be followed by Uthman.

Under these Caliphs, Islamic conquest was very successful but the Shi'ah remained dissatisfied until Ali at last became the fourth Caliph. Unfortunately he and his grandsons were killed: Husain at the battle of Karbala in 680 CE, a place forever sacred to the Shi'ah, and Hasan by poison. The hatred and strife generated continues between these divisions until the present time.

The Sunni are followers of the sunnah: the right path or the path of tradition. They profess to follow the example of the Prophet, hold to the consensus of the community and believe that the imam should have no authority except to lead public worship. They reject temporary marriages but have a much more tolerant attitude toward customs and tradition.

The Shi'ites differ from the Sunni in contracting temporary marriages for short periods and in their worship and ablutions. They also have an interesting idea about the resurrection body: it is the astral body that will not experience death but will be joined with the spirit or soul to form the resurrected person.

Karbala for them is more important than Mecca and the battle that took place there is commemorated annually in the Passion of Husain. His sorrow was redemptive, a vicarious merit that is remembered when pilgrims go to Karbala. They believe that their leaders, the Imams, are descendants of the Prophet

through his daugher Fatimah and possess infallible authority
and superhuman powers. Hence what they say is more important than the consensus of the community. If there is vicarious
merit in the sacrifice of Husain then we need to modify what
we said about the nature of salvation as dependent on good
works or self-help for it could mean that he is looked upon as a
savior who would help them.

One particular revolt against the Sunni was led by Muhammad
ibn-al-Hanafiya, a son of Ali by a wife other than Fatimah.
He died in the battle, but afterward a rumour circulated that
he had simply disappeared or concealed himself and that he
would return to restore justice and peace. He is now thought
of as the Madhi, the rightly guided, and regarded as divine. It
resembles the Messiah idea of other religions and as usual has
led to a number of pretenders proclaiming that they are the
expected one. But the two groups of Muslims have in common
the Qur'an and some traditions.

The Shi'ah has split into various sects about doctrine and
who should be the Imam. There are the Isma'ilis in Egypt,
the Assassins (Persia and Syria), the Zaydis (Yemen) and the
Twelvers, who accept a line of twelve Imams as distinct from
the Isma'ilis who believe in only seven. The Aga Khans belong
to the Isma'ilis. The Sunni have persecuted these over the years
and in response the Shi'ah have ritually cursed Abu Bakr, Umar
and others, and celebrated the murder of Umar.[6] There is a
need to heal these divisions if peace is to come to regions where
they exist.

Sufism for its part stresses the inward mystical side of the
soul. It signifies that God is everywhere and within us (surah
41.54), fasting, pilgrimage and tithing are done for the good of
the self or soul. Sufism seeks a direct and personal experience
of God:

> Awhile, as wont may be, self I did claim;
> True self I did not see, but heard its name
> I being self confined, self did not merit,
> Till, leaving self behind, did self inherit.[7]

We are all self-centered and fail to realise our true personality.
To achieve the true self requires union with God or denial of

it. It has parallels with Hinduism, Sikhism and Christianity but it does not mean that the self no longer has a place or is just an awareness of unity from which one returns to normal selfhood. It warns against the selfishness of the self and the need for it to experience the inner transformation of God. Salvation then is self-transformation.

But this mysticism was criticized by the Sunni since it stressed the inner life and not the external behavior laid down by the law. Thus if God is everywhere as the Sufis believed then why is there need to go on pilgrimage to Mecca? The group developed communal ritual accompanied by music and it gained more importance than other aspects of the law or sunnah. Suspicion was aroused among the Sunni for the power of the Sufi teachers threatened their jurists and rulers, and at times it must be admitted that the Sufis went to excesses in their emotional experiences.

Human beings in the image of God is interpreted as our duty to actualise the divine character traits latent in our souls. Special teaching is needed to do this and recognition of the stations of ascent on the path to God. By this ascent there is a spiritual transformation hence there is a departure from the intellect and rational approach (kalam) to the Qur'an. The accusation was that they were paying attention to the immanence of Allah but not His transcendence. Sufism focussed on the personal and the nearness of God seen in the imaginative qualities of the soul, as the Qur'an teaches, for wherever you turn there is the face of God (surah 2.115). It is the soul that can bridge the gap between God and us.

They were intoxicated with God stressing His compassion, love and kindness, teaching that His unveiling can be brought about by poetry and recognition of His nearness. Reason only dissects and reaches an agnostic position but the Sufi (word derived from the white woollen garments that the mystic wears) although intoxicated with God does return to the sober consideration of the world. The unity must be carefully stated, however, not like Hallaj whom we mentioned who said: "I am the Real."[8]

It is pointed out that nafs in the Qur'an can sometimes mean soul and at other times self. We should not talk about it as a thing. We look in a mirror and see a physical form but the fact that we recognize it shows that there is more to self than a physical form. The soul refers to everything that we are including our awareness of ourselves and others. If we say that the soul is not there because we are unaware of it then we would have to admit that the unconscious mind is not there on the same grounds. Sufism holds that the resurrection will be spiritual in contrast to the main groups who argue that there will be a body but a different one from the present.

Moral purification of the soul is necessary so that bad habits are left behind and concentration on God needed. To refer again to the helpful analogy of the mirror, "The soul is like a mirror; with reason only part of it is polished and only part of the universe is reflected in it; but when it is wholly polished it reflects everything."[9]

Sufism has influenced modern European intellectuals in France and Switzerland but has had to contend with secularism and fundamentalism. It is popular with the masses since it avoids the abstractions of philosophers but the intellectuals consider it to be outmoded or a form of escapism into the inner recesses of the soul.

PHILOSOPHY

There have been many philosophers in Islam with debates about the existence of God but we need to restrict our thinking to the question of the soul. Philosophy in Islam stemmed from neo-Platonism which was influenced by Aristotle so the soul was important and is damaged by the qualities of the body. It must free itself from them before experiencing bliss. The Greek Plotinus influenced many with his account of the process of emanation starting with the mind (nous) and from it the soul (psyche), which after incarnations returns to God.

But a reaction was led by al-Kindi (d. 866) who sought to defend the worldview of the Qur'an. He argued that the soul is a substance derived from God by emanation and is different from the body that it tries to control. He accepted Plato's tripartite division of the soul and at death it will join the higher world but some souls will require purification. Al-Kindi held

firmly to the creation ex nihilio, the resurrection of the body
and the universal providence of God—all of which are fundamental Islamic tenets.[10]

Abu Bakr al-Razi (d. 925/935) is also worth a mention being
regarded as the chief Platonist of Islam. He believed that the
soul was originally separated from matter but became beset by
erotic passion and could only be satisfied when it was joined to
a body. Man also received the gift of reason that aroused the
soul from its slumber and passion but if it did not happen then it
is reincarnated. Such teaching together with his disparagement
of revelation did not endear him to the orthodox Muslim.

Free thought continued particularly with al-Rawandi (d.
911) who rejected revelation in favor of the primacy of reason
and went as far as to deny the miraculous nature of the Qur'an
and the claims of Muhammad to be the apostle of God.[11]
Others that followed continued the denial. Best known is Omar
al-Khayyam (d. 1123) who was overwhelmed by the power of
fate:

> The moving finger writes and having writ,
> Moves on; nor all your piety and wit
> Shall lure it back to cancel half a line,
> Nor all your tears wash out a word of it.
>
> There was a door to which I found no key;
> There was the veil through which I could not see;
> Some little talk awhile of me and thee
> There was, and then no more of thee and me.[12]

The Mu'tazilah rejected such pessimism derived from a belief
in fate and rigid predestination (jabr) and advocated free will
(qadar). They stressed the justice of God, the reward for good
deeds, and the importance of revelation in the Qur'an.

The leader of antiphilosophical dissent was Al-Ghazali (d.
1111) one of the greatest Sufi teachers who thought the soul
was a spiritual substance. The intellect is abstract, different from
the soul that is the motive power that causes life and growth,
it is the form of the body and remains after its death.[13] He is
against the philosophers who he accuses of denying the resurrection of the body and believing in the immortality of the

soul. Immortality cannot be proved by philosophy but is guaranteed by revelation (surah 3.169). He holds firmly to an after life and quotes the verse we have mentioned: "Do not suppose that those who have died in the path of God are dead; they are rather alive with their Lord."[14]

On the Day of Judgment the soul will be united to a body made up of the same matter as its original body or of different matter. His reaction to philosophy led him into a mystic union with God, but not identifying the Creator and the creature.

Two other philosophers have made contributions to the understanding of the soul. The first is Ibn Sina (Latin name was Avicenna 980–1037). The soul emanates from God and is the first perfection of the human body for unlike reason it is able to apprehend truth intuitively. With him soul and body are separate substances and personality resides in the soul. It rules the body and at death continues to exist but there is no bodily resurrection. Pure souls enter into bliss while the others are subject to eternal torment. The common people cannot obtain the bliss of heaven because of stupor or ineptitude or being unprepared by nature![15] They need to cling to religious truth that he regards as inferior to philosophy.

He was criticized, of course, notably by al-Shirazi (1572–1641) who held that a person's first or natural birth will be followed by a second birth on the day of resurrection. With the latter birth, soul and body become identical, that is, with the habits or traits acquired here. He affirms the identity of soul and body by the resurrection of the individual. It is possible because the resuscitated body assumes a spiritual form and is then identical with the soul. However speculative we may consider this to be, it does show his opposition to Ibn Sina's lack of belief in the resurrection.

The second philosopher Ibn Rushd (Latin name was Averroes 1126–1198) admired Aristotle and concentrated on the intellect. He rebuked Al-Ghazali for his attack on philosophy and pointed out that the Qur'an distinguished between verses that were "sound" and those that were "ambiguous" and that only philosophers could interpret the holy book properly. Al-Ghazali had accused the philosophers of denying the eternity of the world, God's knowledge of particulars and the resurrection of the body but Averroes points out that the conflict over these in philosophy and theology is purely verbal or semantic.[16] To insist on the immortality of the soul rather than bodily resurrection is not a denial of the after life but a reflection on the mode of it, something that occurs in other religions. And the only reason the Qur'an represents the resurrection in terms of sensuous images, punishments and rewards is to make the truth more intelligible to the masses who cannot comprehend abstract spiritual language.

Concerning the soul he thinks that the ultimate destiny is in its liberation from the bondage of the body whereby it is able to rejoin the intelligible world. Subsequently he and his followers were vilified and it was contended, erroneously according to Fakhyr, that he had held the thesis of double truth, according to which a proposition may be true in philosophy but false in theology or vice versa. In 1277 his books were burned but the Latin translation of his commentaries on Aristotle has survived.

DEATH RITUAL

Cleanliness is important for the Muslims; so at death the body is washed, the mourning clothes put on, and burial follows quickly. Coffins are not used but the earth does not press against the body for there is either a trench in the floor of the pit or a niche at the side. The face of the corpse is turned toward Mecca and when a tomb is covered with a slab of stone a hole is left in the middle for the soul to breathe. It is odd for the general belief is that the soul leaves the body at death. Since Allah created he can raise the dead:

> Thus shall God recompense the righteous whom the angels will reclaim, in all their virtue, saying, Peace be on you, Come into Paradise the reward of your labours. (surah 16.31)

The soul is ruh that is the spirit from God and will return to Him. The Qur'an is read throughout the mourning period but crying is frowned upon since Allah has received the soul of the departed. All, rich or poor, once they are dead are treated in the same way for everyone is equal in the sight of Allah. The body is taken to the mosque or an open space for the funeral prayer: "O God, pardon this dead person; lo, Thou are the Most Forgiving, the Most Merciful."

Then handfuls of earth are dropped into the grave and there is the belief that the grave is visited by two angels who question the dead person to see whether he/she is fit to enter paradise. It is thought that the soul goes to a separate place after it leaves the body that should be buried in order that the bones will be reassembled. Hence cremation is not acceptable.

Like most religions there is difficulty in defining the soul. The Muslim says: "we can't feel the soul, we can't see it, but we can't see electricity either. But we know, because there is a bulb here which tells us that is electricity running there."[17] The soul is a form of spiritual energy. Some confirm this by pointing to the Buddhists who explain the process of reappearance by energy, though denying a soul, and the Sikhs who use the analogy of electricity.

ANGELS

Angels were created by Allah and are His messengers helping Muslims to pray properly. Everyone has two guardian angels and they keep records of the deeds done by the individual. There are four special angels: Jibril who gave God's word to the prophets, Israfil in charge of the final destruction of the universe, Azra'il the angel of death who is present at every deathbed to receive the soul and Mika'il the guardian of believers who guards every Mosque.

HEAVEN AND HELL

Hell has physical punishment and with seven levels for different persons according to their deeds. Paradise has seven levels with a journey needed to reach the highest level. Though Allah is compassionate and merciful tortures in hell are bountiful; there are also beautiful pictures of heaven where those who trusted in Allah and followed His commandments will recline upon soft couches and feel neither scorching heat nor biting cold. They

shall be served with silver dishes and beakers as large as gob-
lets and attended by boys graced with eternal youth who will
look like pearls and bashful virgins whom no man has touched.
Marriage is not ruled out (surah 76.9. 2.23). The question
at the judgment will be whether the person believes in Allah
and Muhammad His prophet. The result of such belief will be
announced on the Final Day that is a long way off but the judgment will also concentrate on deeds.

Life for the Muslim is a kind of "testing ground" and there
will be no second chance after death. The souls of those who
die before the Judgment Day will be taken by Azra'il to a
waiting place that is called barzakh or barrier before they face
judgment on the Last Day (surah 82.19). Some take heaven
and hell literally, others symbolically. In a literal interpretation
it is forever (surah 39.71, 64.8). Believers enter eternal life and
are reunited with those they have loved. The Qur'an is full of
judgment and such a day will be ushered in with apocalyptic
signs and all who have died recover their bodies and stand
before the Judge. To each a book is given, if placed in the
right hand it is a passport to Paradise, if in the left it means
hell. The decision is based on holding the Faith of Islam and
performing the acts required of the believer. The resurrection
is physical.

Allah has created man with a peculiar innate permanent judge,
which is his conscience or reproachful soul, and the importance
is seen in a surah entitled, The Resurrection:

> I swear by the Day of Resurrection and by the reproachful soul.
> Does man think We shall never put his bones together again?
> We can remould his very fingers. (surah 75.1)

The reproachful soul foreshadows the judgment but how can
the scattered bones of dead people be resurrected? The answer
is that He has created and can do it again and a second creation
will be easier than the first. It is necessary to remember that
Allah can do what we cannot (surah 36.77). At the judgment
the soul will act as a reckoner against us and the payment for
misdeeds and good deeds will be in full. The after life is not
tagged on at the end but seen as a stage that follows from this

one. Concerning the judgment Muhammad said:

> No person will leave the judgment place before being asked about four things; his life span and how he spent it, his knowledge and what he did with it, his body and in which things he wore it out and his wealth—from where he collected it and how he spent it.[18]

Some Muslim commentators on the Qur'an are willing to accept evolution and that Adam was not the first human being but was the one whose intellect was capable of accepting revelation. They go further and assert that the soul is created and is not eternal and its birth is not a process distinct from the birth of the body. It does not enter the body from some source outside but is a distillation from the substance that is being developed in the mother's womb. It is distinct from the substance and gives it animal characteristics, reason and intelligence. An illustration is that of a chemical process whereby certain substances combine to form a new substance possessing distinct qualities of its own. Alcohol is distilled from beet, wheat, corn, yet it has qualities different from those of the basic substance from which it is manufactured. The raw material rots but alcohol is preserved. The soul is the ultimate stage of the evolution of the human body in the course of its creation. It possesses faculties but can express itself only through the body, just as various other things.

One writer contends that at death the soul enters a spiritual body and perfect souls will be admitted to Paradise but the imperfect will enter hell, which is a state of healing for spiritual ills, so a kind of purgatory. When healing is completed each will enter paradise hence a universalism in that all souls will have attained paradise and hell is terminated. The writer who puts forward the above views accepts the appearance of a holy prophet the Messiah,[19] which in this case is he! It renders him suspect and while his opinions are different they would not be acceptable to the majority of Muslims.

There are seven heavens as we noted and all souls will parade before Adam in the first but the idea of the heavens conflicts with the belief that the blessed pass into paradise, which is beyond the heavens and is the garden of Allah.

Man has been formed in a noble image but will be reduced to the lowest level if unfaithful whereas there will be a boundless recompense for the believers who do good works. The soul has been moulded by Allah who gave it knowledge of sin and piety so happy is the man who has kept it pure but woe to those who have ruined it. On the day of resurrection it will be seen that they have forfeited their souls and they will suffer much. Nevertheless God forgives all sins for He is the forgiving one, the merciful, and if we turn in repentance to Him and surrender ourselves to Him His scourge will not operate (surah 39.49).

OTHER RELIGIONS

Judaism and Christianity are respected and it is significant how often the prophets of both are mentioned and stories from the Hebrew scripture highlighted. God has revealed the Torah and the Gospels for the guidance of mankind (surah 3.4). Jesus is given special status with the virgin birth confirmed and as Messiah could raise the dead (surah 3.40.110). In the light of this it is odd that the Qur'an claims that Islam has been exalted by Allah above all religions (surah 61.9) and religions prior to Islam were only partial statements of the truth.[20] The only true Faith is Islam (surah 3.19) for the Qur'an gives us the full and complete truth. Muhammad is the final prophet yet it is admitted that he is no more than an apostle (3.140) and the people of the Book (scriptures) will be admitted to Paradise if they do what is right (surah 5.65).

It is quite legitimate to make war on unbelievers (surah 9.73), but there is no compulsion in religion. While Christians and Jews who believe in Allah will have nothing to fear on the judgment day, any belief that God has a son or that there is a Trinity in the godhead is condemned. Jesus did not tell his disciples to worship him (surah 5.114). It may be that the Muslims are thinking about sonship in a physical sense rather than spiritual. On the Day of Judgment every soul will need to believe in Muhammad and what has been revealed to him that is the Qur'an.

Conclusion

The soul is referred to many times in the Qur'an and it means the inner core of the person. Some see it as given by God but others paying attention to evolution insist that it has developed naturally. It is taken by Allah at death. The mysticism of Sufism attends to the soul and it is believed that it is the bridging of the gap between God and us.

In the speculations of the philosophers there is either acceptance of bodily resurrection or the immortality of the soul and some were accused of heresy. Sufism sees the resurrection as spiritual and does not envisage a body in the life after death.

How to describe heaven and hell is a problem and the interpretation depends on whether we take the many accounts in the Qur'an literally or symbolically. The discussion of the philosophers shows that some of them preferred the symbolic to the literal and a spiritual resurrection rather than a physical. The general belief of the people is that the old body will be reassembled.

There are traces of the belief in a kind of purgatory for the healing of all before admittance to paradise and there is a division about whether or not hell is eternal or temporary. Some see it as temporary like purgatory but there does not appear to be any second chance though at times among the philosophers there are hints about reincarnation. The Shi'ah have the concept of an astral body or spiritual in connection with the resurrection.

There is a divine element in the soul but it is subject to temptation and needs to be kept pure by the performance of good deeds. It is understood by some philosophers influenced by Aristotle as the form of the body and a dualism of body and soul is not ruled out. Soul is ruh, the spirit from God, so there is the bringing together. The Qur'an lays emphasis on good deeds as the way of salvation but as we saw in the Shi'ah with the passion of Husain there is redemptive suffering and he could be viewed as a savior who would help them. There is also the Messianic concept with the hidden Imam who will eventually return.

CHAPTER 5

THE HINDU AND THE
IMMORTAL SOUL

Hinduism and the immortal soul
Lead me from the unreal to the real;
Lead me from darkness into light;
Lead me from the mortal to the immortal.

The Aryans who invaded India came from what is now Turkey, Russia and Iran, and their scripture and way of life had a profound effect on the people of the land. Hinduism has many gods and believes in the immortality of the atman or soul that seeks to attain oneness with God or Brahman who can be regarded as personal or impersonal. He is transcendent yet immanent within the soul and union with Him is possible only after many births. Practice is more important than theorizing and following the example of holy people who have achieved liberation.

There is acceptance of the authority of the scriptures, the validity of ceremonies performed by Brahmin priests, the eternal reality of Brahman in its various forms and the importance of the soul.

THE SCRIPTURES (SCRUTI)

The scriptures are classified as those inspired directly by God: the *Vedas*, the *Brahmanas*, and the *Upanishads*. The laws of Manu (smrti) are not revelation nor are the sayings of prophets, saints and epics contained in the *Bhagavad Gita* and the *Puranas*. It is just as well that the laws of Manu are not defined as scripture since they classify women as subordinate to men.

The *Gita*, song of the Lord, is the most popular scripture and teaches that the soul cannot die. Reincarnation is like leaving off old clothes and putting on new ones and the god is Krishna who has a higher nature (soul) and a lower one (body). Epics such as the *Ramayana* have been filmed for television and the Tantras feature the goddess Shiva who encourages practices opposed to that of the Brahmins. But these scriptures stem from the upper classes and are of limited importance in understanding what people believe. Hinduism does not have the same problems about history as the Semitic religions and weaves together fact and fiction without much distinction.[1]

Arjuna is the hero of the *Bhagavad Gita* (fourth and third centuries BCE) and is commanded to fight friends and kinsmen who oppose him. How can he do it? If he kills them he will not be able to enjoy his wealth or any other pleasure for he will be cursed with blood guilt. He says that he would much rather spare them and eat the bread of a beggar. He asks: "Is this real compassion that I feel or only a delusion? My mind gropes about in darkness. I cannot see where my duty lies?"

He then appeals to God Krishna who answers that if the time has come for them to pass to their next birth then Arjuna by killing them is helping them on to the next stage of their soul's journey! The wise do not grieve for the living or the dead since there never was a time when they did not exist. In other words, the cycle of birth, death, and rebirth goes on:

> Know this atman (soul)
> Unborn, undying
> Never ceasing
> Never beginning
> Deathless, birthless,
> Unchanging for ever
> How can it die
> The death of the body?
>
> Knowing it birthless
> Knowing it deathless

> Knowing it endless
> For ever unchanging
> Dream not you do
> The deed of the killer
> Dream not the power
> Is yours to command it.[2]

Hence he must do his duty as a warrior and fight this righteous war. It is the way of devotion to his god. Happiness is experienced in the soul by unselfish action, the ceasing of lust, greed, hatred and being free from the delusion of the I and attachment. Interpreted in the spiritual sense it refers to the battle between good and evil and that the atman is eternal so you cannot kill it. In any case what we see around us is transitory; it is the unseen that is real.

GOD AND THE GODS

In Hinduism the main God is Brahman, though there are various manifestations of Him. It is impersonal in the early *Upanishads* (referred to as it) but in the later becomes more personal and we are able to pray for His help and use yoga which involves meditation and asceticism to effect union with Him or Vishnu. Vishnu is prominent in the *Gita* and to some extent replaces Brahman. It was Vishnu with his incarnations in Rama and Krishna and the emphasis on personal devotion that impressed Gandhi.

INCARNATION

God appears in human form when the need is imminent:

> When goodness grows weak
> When evil increases
> I make myself a body
>
> In every age I come back
> To deliver the holy
> To destroy the sin of the sinner
> To establish righteousness.[3]

RITUALS

The physical representation of deities is widespread especially in the temple, which is the residence of the gods. The image is bathed, decorated and wakened in the morning with songs of praise and when the worshippers bring their offerings, a bell is rung to warn the god and a ritual is performed by the Brahmin priest. He offers a prayer in the classical language of Sanskrit and he is in charge of the daily homage/worship to the deity. In the temple there is the recitation of the scriptures, meditation and contemplation, music is played and hymns sung. Gifts include food that is then distributed to the worshippers as prasad. Prayer is individual rather than corporate with the lighting of a lamp (usually earthen) as a token of devotion. The prasad, food remaining from sacrifice dedicated to God, is consumed by the worshippers showing that they have shared in the life of the divine.

The home has a shrine to the god, a separate room, which must be kept scrupulously clean, and the lady of the house makes offerings to it. The family gathers around it for worship in the morning and evening with the women taking a central role. The villages have their own deities, and ceremonies are conducted by the village priest (bhopa). But many Hindus argue that religion is to be equated with the human spirit or soul hence external places such as shrines, temples and places of pilgrimage are not that important. It is the internal not the external that is stressed. Secular art is allowed in the temples with scenes of erotic love because it is believed that sexual desires are to be conquered and nothing in human life must be excluded from religion. There are also wayside shrines, and pilgrimages to sacred places are common. There are a number of sacred rivers, and bathing in the Ganges is believed to wash away life cycle sins.

There are life cycle rites (samskara); birth, initiation, marriage, and death. Marriages are often arranged by the parents. At death the dead body is regarded as unclean and cremated. It is washed, dressed in new clothes, laid on the funeral pyre adorned with flowers and carried to the place of cremation on the bank of a river. The eldest son says the prayers and kindles the firewood and the body is consumed by the flames but the soul is set free. The ashes are then gathered to be deposited in a sacred river. At home ceremonies last for about ten days; during this mourning period, the relatives are considered unclean. Special rice is prepared as an offering to the soul of the dead, prayers are said once a month for a year so that the soul can return to earth as a better being to proceed to the goal of moksha (liberation). In villages, bhut is the term for ghost and anyone who has died by suicide, drowning, fire, violence may become one and cause disaster to the family of the person involved. It is important then that a bhut should not come near the dead body so it is never left alone. Many Hindus believe that we can contact the dead.[4]

The practice of suttee, which is the burning of widows, is condemned today but was common in ancient India. It was the practice of a woman to mount the funeral pyre of her dead husband which meant that she was making the ultimate sacrifice and her husband's family would honor her by building a temple in her memory. She could be sure of a better rebirth.

THE SOUL

The place Hinduism gives to the soul is much greater than any other religion. This atman is related to the Absolute or Ultimate Reality namely Brahman that is the cosmic principle of the universe, the essence that underlies it. Brahman is the self or soul of the universe, the sutra-atman and the inner controller of each being, the atman within each of us. Just as salt mingles with water and cannot be separated from it, Brahman pervades the individual. The atman is a miniature of the universal soul Brahman that is the power, source, and sustenance of all things. It is indescribable, immaterial and is referred to negatively (neti, neti). Yet positive qualities are postulated of it, reality (sat), consciousness (chit), happiness or bliss (ananda).

The phrase "that thou art" (tat twam asi), "you are yourself that very soul," in the *Chandogya Upanishad* is a statement of the identity with Brahman. The distinction between body and soul follows Plato who as we mentioned thought of the individual as a soul (psyche) imprisoned in a body. Svetaketu, a student, wants to know where is the Real or where is God and how is He to be found? His father tells him to put a piece of salt in the water and come to him the following morning. When he returns the father says that he must bring the salt to him but Svetaketu groping in the water could not find it for it had dissolved. Then the father told him to sip the water in the middle and at the end and so on. Always the salt remained the same so his father said it is true that you cannot perceive it here, but it is equally true that it is here. This finest essence—the whole universe—has it as its Self; "That is the real, that is the Self, that you are."[5]

The *Upanishads* refer to the atman as the inner self and it is nothing less than Brahman. A distinction is then made between this real self or atman and the apparent self or jiva that can be observed by the senses. It is subject to time and change, to suffering and sorrow, to decay and death while the true self does not change and does not die. It means that there is an identity between you and me for we both share the atman. What we normally see are outer layers of personality and not the true inner self atman that must obtain unity with God. It is not the atman that is reborn but the jiva or jivatman. The atman is the real essence that will eventually fuse with Brahman but it is not like the Christian idea of the individual soul.

It would appear in all of this that the Hindu is making a distinction between the external and internal with the former changing but the latter remaining the same. We have noted this distinction in other religions.

There is a new temporary empirical self then in each reincarnation and the eternal self observes what is going on; this can be explained with the analogy of two birds sitting on different branches of the same tree. The one observing is the eternal self or atman and the observed the empirical jiva but this makes the eternal self merely an observer not undergoing the incarnations. Hinduism seems to be getting at what has inspired novelists: the divided self or the transcendental self of Immanuel Kant. There is the self that I am conscious of now but there is also a deeper self of which the conscious ego is a temporary vehicle. But it is the jiva that registers and embodies the moral, aesthetic, intellectual, and spiritual dispositions that have been built up during the living of my life or succession of lives. It is this jiva then that is reincarnated until in the last incarnation is united with the atman and Brahman.[6]

Krishna teaches the warrior Arjuna that there is a cycle of birth that continues until the self is liberated. There are various ways by which it is accomplished: jnana-yoga (the discipline of knowledge), or karma-yoga (the discipline of action) or bhakti yoga (the discipline of devotion). What is important is gaining knowledge of the true self or soul, atman, which has the same characteristics as Brahman. Arjuna must do his duty despite his desires and attend to bhakti yoga, and Krishna who is identified with Brahman will help for he is a savior and manifests grace toward him. The emphasis is on the immortality of the soul, not the reunion of body and soul as traditionally taught in the Semitic religions.

There was also a philosophy that was materialistic and denied the soul. The Lokayata philosophy of Charvaka argued that all knowledge is ultimately based on the senses and only what can be perceived is real. But in general Hinduism is aware of an unseen world and believes that empiricism is only one way of getting at the truth.

LIBERATION

Hinduism stresses an intuitive grasp of Brahman leading to duty, action, and devotion to Brahman or Vishnu. God loves the soul and wants its love. Krishna shows with the girls, gopis, how passionate this love can be and reveals Vishnu in the *Gita* as personal, like a father with his son, a friend with his friend, a lover with his beloved.

In the villages there is the desire for survival and betterment in life just as in the Western world but there is also the quest to acquire merit and be reborn well and to find the liberation that will end the cycle of rebirth. There is belief in an after life where there are terrifying hells and pleasant heavens hosting the various gods: Indra, Shiva, Vishnu, and others.

The soul that has attained liberation, moksha, crosses the ocean of existence and reaches the other shore safely. It is united to its source in the Absolute or Brahman just as the drop is absorbed in the ocean. The longings of the soul for union with God is seen in the satsangs or assembles that include hymns, dancing, greeting one another, scattering of flowers and red powder, offering of sweets, and handing round of pipes. Bhakti or devotion popular in the villages is a way of salvation to a unique and personal God, the Lord, Isvara. Questions that arise are similar to those of other religions: Are we united already with God and only need to realize it or is there a gulf between the deity and us requiring an act of divine grace to bridge it or does the truth lie in the via media, He is both in us yet beyond us? We will find answers to these questions later in the classical philosophers.

DIVISIONS

There are no clearly defined divisions as in other religions but the Brahmanical religion present in the *Upanishads* led to the worship of the two great gods, Shiva and Vishnu, and there are followers of each. The Hindus are tolerant and worshippers can alternate between the gods. Vishnu is the god of the *Bhagavad Gita* and Shiva is associated with asceticism, yoga and contemplation. Vishnu has had many incarnations with Krishna as one of the most popular but there is also Kali who will destroy the wicked and bring the age to an end.

Socially there are divisions in the Hindu society. The Brahmans are the highest caste, followed by the Kshatriyas, warriors and rulers, then Vaishyas, the agricultural workers and merchants, and Sudras called the peasants who are often craftsmen or cattle rearers or servants. Outcastes or pariahs or untouchables are not members of this caste system even though their exclusion was declared illegal. Marriage between the castes is forbidden.

REINCARNATION

As leaving aside worn-out garments
A man takes other, new ones,
So leaving aside worn-out bodies
To other, new ones goes the embodied (soul).[7]

The doctrine began with the *Upanishads* that defines the soul as the consciousness in the life powers. It is the light within the heart. Religious rites done when performed with true devotion are believed to produce good results so they have virtue in themselves. Certain acts are appropriate to one class or caste but not to another, that is, a warrior does his duty, a priest performs the rites and the peasant works manually but whether the act is sacred or not depends on good or evil results.[8]

The belief in transmigration or rebirth (samsara) means that we are on a wheel of birth, death, and rebirth. Some thinkers hold that the soul (atman) is reborn into another form of life on earth whereas we have distinguished between the empirical self or soul that is reborn, but not the atman. In any case good actions mean a rebirth in a higher form of life. Hence the stress on nonviolence (ahimsa) and respect for the animal world as the soul may be reborn as one. The goal of life is to escape from the wheel of death and rebirth in order that the soul may be drawn toward Brahman, the world soul, which underlies all creation.

Meditation and contemplation, yoga exercises, renunciation and asceticism will all be of help to find the soul. It is like peeling an onion; meditation strips off the waste layers until the real part emerges, namely the soul. One can achieve this by doing the caste duty, devotion (bhakti yoga) to the god of one's choice, expressed in love and faith by means of righteous living, and the ritual of worship. True knowledge of the relation of soul to Brahman is liberation from samsara the cycle of rebirths. The mind will be prominent here for the body is like a chariot with the senses as the horses and the self or atman the charioteer. The person must control his senses as the charioteer controls his horses. The picture resembles the one presented by Plato.

The Semitic religions find reincarnation difficult to accept for their belief is in linear time rather than cyclical but the doctrine gives some reasons for the good suffering and the bad escaping since there is a balance in the long run. We noted the claim in Christianity, denied by some, that the early Christians believed in reincarnation until the time of Clement of Alexandria and Origen in the third century.

At the end of life the dominant thought governs the next birth. Karma is the link between one life and another. In the *Upanishads* those who have the right knowledge and worship pass into the cremation fire and arrive at the world of the gods and there is no return to earth. But those who believe in sacrifice and merit arrive at the world of the ancestors and as long as there is a residue of their works, eventually they return to earth. Rebirth is determined by karma, which means moral law: the working out of the result of past actions, so there is no need for God as a Judge handing out punishment or reward on the Resurrection Day. Deeds have their consequences to the agent without the need of external punishment; it is a moral law of the universe. There are many hells and heavens but these appear to be temporary. They look like intermediate states where we wait for rebirth. Heaven is beautiful while hell is horrible.

Reincarnation depends on remembering our previous lives, and study of the unconscious shows that memories can be brought to surface that are hidden from us. Each new life must arise, if karma is correct, out of the character of the former. Character dispositions are passed on and memory provides the link from one birth to another.

Those who believe in the doctrine can point to many prominent people who were not Christian believers yet accepted it. Thomas Huxley said: "None but very hasty thinkers will reject it on the grounds of inherent absurdity. Like the doctrine of evolution itself, that of transmigration has its roots in the world of reality."[9] While there is no scientific proof there is empirical evidence from credible sources. Atheists such as Freidrich Nietzsche said: "Live so that thou mayest desire to live again— that is thy duty—for in any case thou wilt live again."[10] People from every walk of life have believed in reincarnation, including General George S. Patton, George Harrison, John Lennon, Sylvester Stallone, John Travolta, Shirley MacLaine, and Elton John.

CLASSICAL PHILOSOPHY

There are six philosophical groups: Sankyha, dualistic and atheistic, Yoga that concentrates on helping the self to liberation,

Mimamsa that stresses the importance of dharma or right action, Vedanta meaning the end of the Veda, Nyaya the logic that leads to liberation and Vaisheshika, analyzing dharma and other elements.

There are three famous philosophers: Sankara, Ramanuja, and Madhva. The first advocated monism (only one Being exists) and taught that we lose our individuality in being united with Brahman. He repeated: "That is the real, that is the soul. That art thou." He was challenged by Ramanuja who insisted that souls retain their individuality and are devoted to Brahman who is a personal God. He maintained the principle of identity-in-difference, that is, we are like Brahman yet unlike Him. Brahman is in us but also beyond us, therefore, not identical, and immortality will not be absorption into Him but an eternal individual existence in communion with Him. It is modified dualism and is more in line with Hindu worship with its bhakti or devotion and appeal to the masses. Madhva, however, maintained a strict dualism, we are not like God.

Since they are very important we look at these philosophers in more detail.

SANKARA (788–820 CE)

According to Sankara atman is pure consciousness that remains even when the mind passes away; but the average person does not know how to distinguish between atman and nonatman. In the Panisads there is the lower and higher Brahman, the higher being immutable and the lower, Isvara, creator, Lord and ruler of the world. Hence Sankara distinguishes between Brahman saguna and Brahman nirguna, one with attributes and the other without.[11]

Followers of Sankara point out that empiricism is not enough for it raises the question: Who is the knower? True knowledge is the knowing of both object and subject. We know by our senses and the use of scientific instruments but how do we know our inner selves? Maths and geometry are beyond empiricism and there are intuitive truths and logic. Knowing a "thou," myself, is different from knowing the world, an "it." The world is an illusion seen through our human perception and time itself is part of this illusion for it has cycles of ages that repeat and each life is determined by karma.

Vedanta, meaning end of Veda, is based on the *Upanishads,* which Sankara interpreted. An interesting point is that Brahman is sometimes identified with the word OM and the world develops from this sound. The name of Brahman as OM would be analogous to the Word of the Gospel of John from whom all things are created. OM is sound and everything is created by sound.[12] Followers repeat the sound in meditation over and over again.

We are one with Brahman but there are differences between us. It is like looking at the ocean where we see that there is no distinction between the waves and yet there are waves that are long and short, waves that come crashing in and those that come in more quietly. We might think of the unity with Brahman in terms of community but Vedanta goes further and incurs the charge that it is diminishing individuality.

The atman is the impersonal part of Brahman present in the individual and the intention is that the soul will escape from the self and be reunited with Him. The empirical self as we mentioned is not immortal but the soul is and manifests Brahman. As from a blazing fire there springs forth thousands of sparks that are like little fires, from God the imperishable diverse life forms are produced and indeed go back again to Him.

There is speculation about consciousness. When we die we lose it. Is it just a subjective effect or an offshoot of the brain or an inner awareness? For Vedanta it is outside of time and it does not end at death. What it does is to act as a substratum or backcloth to all the states of waking and sleeping. It is the universal not the individual self even though it is immanent in all. Like the morning and the evening stars each is recognized by its own criteria though in fact they are the same. The question about consciousness will arise again in chapters 9 and 10.

Evolution is an understanding of the physical but there is also the spiritual and mental. To concentrate on the physical is like paying attention only to ink marks on paper, its size, chemical composition, and atomic structure and forgetting meaning and purpose. Man is more than a being of five senses and cannot be studied by empirical methods alone for reason, insight and traditional teaching contribute to his understanding. Attention confirms that the mind (chitta) exists. I do not hear the clock ticking because I am attending to something else. It is the mind that controls attention or directs consciousness into other channels.

With Sankara all things are identical with Brahman and he expounds the *Upanishads* on that basis. The world itself is a self-realization of Brahman. This is pantheism, everything is divine. Sankara's advaita or nonduality resembles the Absolute idealism of Hegel.

Sankara's view of the soul can be put thus: God is identical with the soul, soul is identical with the world, thus God is identical with the world. His philosophy has been very influential and was embraced by Swami Vivekananda (1863–1902), Mahatma Gandhi (1869–1948), Sri Aurobindo (1870–1950) and Radhakrishnan (1888–1975). The latter philosopher was influenced by Vedanta, which he thought was closely linked to Indian religion and affects the world view of the Hindu of the present day.

RAMANUJA (ELEVENTH–TWELFTH CENTURY)

Theism is represented by Ramanuja who emphasized the grace of God. He rejected Sankara's doctrine of the unreality of the world and the identity of the soul with Brahman. Souls are redeemed from the cycle of rebirth by their devotion to the Lord Isvara and enter into eventual communion with him so there is no merging with the Absolute. He taught the doctrine of identity-in-difference where Brahman is seen as both identical with and different from the atman.[13] We are like God yet unlike Him, something we saw in the discussion of the image of God in Christianity: it meant likeness but unlikeness since marred by sin.

With him the soul is eternal and timeless, spiritual, pure consciousness and of the same substance as God. It is true of Hinduism as a whole but he stresses that souls are distinct from God and only by achieving moksha, liberation or salvation, do they enter into communion with Him. God is the Supreme Soul and all creation forms His "body" but at the same time

He is in a different category. When he said that the world was the body of God he meant it was under His control. There is a higher and lower Brahman, the former not being subject to pleasure or pain but the lower and causal affected by them. He causes the world by entering into matter through the soul. The released soul is disembodied and there is the possibility of personal immortality. It is qualified dualism.

We need the grace of God to achieve salvation; this can be explained through the analogy of the cat and the monkey and their care of the young. The cat when it wants to move its kittens elsewhere picks them up by the scruff of the neck, the monkey carries the young ones on its stomach and the offspring has to cling to it. Similarly, God by His grace is doing all can for our salvation like the cat, but the monkey way shows that we have to put in our efforts too.

MADHVA

Madhva believed that knowledge removes ignorance but it cannot bring release from sin. He was a dualist (dvaita), according to which we and the universe are distinct from God and will retain such separation in the after life. This is more in the Semitic tradition and it is believed that Madhva was influenced by Christianity.[14]

There are three classes of soul: those who are intended for liberation and communion with Vishnu, the majority of souls that are of indifferent quality with many rebirths, and souls that are depraved and can expect hell. He was not very successful in trying to impose this teaching on Hinduism since he insisted that hell was eternal.

In brief our survey shows that we have monism, qualified dualism and dualism. There is a lot to be said for the position of Ramanuja for as we have seen in the Semitic religions there is the image of God that implies some likeness to God and yet there is the difference as shown by the history of mankind.

But Hinduism does raise the question: If all souls are equal why the inequalities of the caste system? The answer might be that every soul has karma attached to it and if it is bad there is a price to be paid in the next life, which could mean inequality.

Sankara saw the inequality in terms of ignorance and the lack of the right kind of knowledge and viewed the worship of the villagers on a lower level than that of the religion of the higher castes. Ramanuja countered by insisting that worship was essential for the salvation of the soul and could not be placed on the lower level. Sankara's position stemmed from distinguishing between higher and lower levels of truth and placing the villagers on the lowest level.

Other philosophies such as Sankhya contended for souls being entangled in nature and the aim must be to gain insight into the difference between soul or spirit and matter and gain release from the latter.[15] Yoga should be taught for it purifies the consciousness and allows the spirit to become evident. Only by such practice can rebirth end. The system was atheistic.

Apart from the theories of these philosophers, which the populace had difficulty in understanding, there is a practical reliance on religious experience. It means a change from selfishness to unselfishness and it must last. Such an experience has been shared by ordinary believers and great saints and enabled them to show compassion and goodness. It cannot be described because it is different from sense perception that forces itself upon us and it does not have public proof. Sankara did believe in religious experience but his abstract reasoning about it failed to impress many people.

ETHICS

Ram Mohan Roy (1772–1833) did a lot to change the superstitious practices of the Hindus. He disliked idol worship, was influenced by Christianity and rejected the concept of the transmigration of souls. Due to his influence the burning of widows was made illegal in 1829. After him Hinduism became different since he challenged many of its assumptions; yet its sacramental and liturgical structure remained largely the same.

The caste system continued but was attacked by Mahatma Gandhi (1869–1948) who opposed it, especially the attitude toward the untouchables. Gandhi was very conscious of the plight of these harijans whom he called angels of the deity and he also protested about the inequality of women. With the efforts of many such as He, Hindu social practices have changed: widows can marry, child marriages are rare, the temples are open to untouchables, devadasi tradition is abolished, and the caste system has eased with barriers breaking down. Intercaste marriage is the exception.

Dharma can mean law, duty, justice, virtue. Santana dharma is eternal law and sadharana dharma is general morality incumbent upon all Hindus. It demands fairness, forgiveness, charity, purity, honesty, sense control, prudence, wisdom, truthfulness and freedom from anger. Conduct rather than creed is stressed with no division between the sacred and the secular. Hindus are not allowed to gamble, engage in illicit sex or get drunk and must realize that a good life will follow if actions in a previous one have not been bad. But there is a radical trend called Tantra that relativizes the usually accepted values. It accepts caste-free sexual intercourse and allows the consumption of meat, fish and alcohol. Sex is seen as a means to union with Lord Shiva. Euthanasia is favored by many Hindus and abortion was legalized in India in 1971. I have discussed these problems elsewhere.[16]

CONCLUSION

There are many gods in Hinduism but they are viewed as various/multiple aspects of a single Brahman who is the Absolute. The soul is more complex in Hinduism than in the other religions. It has both negative and positive qualities and difficult to describe but it is seen as the light within the heart.

Its importance is left in no doubt but there is a dualism between the empirical self or jiva and the real one, atman, and it is jiva that is reincarnated. Jiva is embodied in an individual's present self and it registers the moral, aesthetic, intellectual and spiritual dispositions that have been built up during the living of the current life or succession of lives until finally united with Brahman.

Atman is the eternal soul and Sankara with his monism made it identical with Brahman. He has also the suggestion that atman is equivalent to consciousness and it remains after death. We will see this speculation regarding consciousness in later chapters.

Ramanuja's opposition to Sankara's teaching has been noted and a lot of what he says appears more in line with the Semitic traditions. We are like God yet unlike Him and he holds the two in tension whereas Madhva has no doubt that we and God are distinct. But it is agreed that a good life can earn release from the cycle of rebirth and the soul either merges with Brahman or enters into communion with Him. There is help from Krishna according to Ramanuja who can assist us in gaining liberation.

There are many hells but there is some evidence to suggest that they may be temporary and would depend on the cycles of rebirths coming to an end. The danger of illicit desires is clear and with Buddhism this will be of great importance for it will contend that desire is the root of most of our problems.

Since there is little evidence of bodily resurrection the immortality of the soul is crucial to the Faith. The concept of incarnation is accepted but the avatars are many and temporary and do not have the permanency of the unique incarnation claimed by Christianity.

In Hinduism, much attention is paid to ritual but it is the inner cultivation of the soul that is important rather than the external aspects of religion. The question is: How do we know our inner selves? The Hindu believes that knowing the inward is different from knowing the outward. The Faith draws our attention to the reality of the unseen, something that is generally absent in our modern world.

CHAPTER 6

THE BUDDHIST DENIAL OF THE SOUL

There is no agent, one finds only action,
A way exists, but there is no wayfarer...
Mere suffering exists but no sufferer is found;
The deeds are but no doer is found.

(Visuddhi-Magga XVl)

Unlike other religions, Buddhism denies the soul or any agent; human beings are simply a collection of qualities or characteristics. After considering the enlightenment and teaching of the Buddha we will look at this in detail.

There is difficulty in knowing the exact details of the life of the Buddha and his followers because the sources give us only a religious or spiritual biography, a hagiography, not a historical account. The Buddha means the enlightened one and applies to Gautama Siddhartha. He was reared in luxury but became depressed when confronted by old age, illness, and death, which showed the impermanence of life and the centrality of suffering. Leaving his family and all the wealth that would be his, he practized self-mortification but without success. Enlightenment, the wakening to the delusions of life, came through meditation and he reluctantly decided to preach and formed the sangha or monastic order.

He believed in rebirth but was skeptical of either a permanent soul or annihilationism. According to tradition the Buddha had many lives and his enlightenment went through various stages of jhana, knowledge, until he had memory of them. He saw the rebirth of people according to their karma, and how spiritual faults prevent enlightenment, but it was the third stage that brought him the awakenment.[1]

He knew that he had a miraculous birth and the tempter (mara) could not defeat him.[2] Having acquired the heavenly eye he understood karma and the insubstantial nature of everything. Ignorance makes us unaware of the illusion of the soul or the ego. After much thought he decided not to share his experience with others, which is odd because the experience must have delivered him from selfishness! And even odder, since he did not believe in the gods, was the fact that he was persuaded to preach by Brahma Sahampati, king of the gods. After his enlightenment he said:

> I have overcome all foes; I am all wise; I am free from stains in every way; I have left everything; and have obtained emancipation by the destruction of desire...I have no teacher; no one is equal to me; in the world none of the gods, no being is like me. I am the holy One in this world, I am the highest teacher...I have obtained Nirvana...[3]

Since he denied the ego why is it so prominent in this statement? I suspect that he would say that referring to the I is only using a label, it has no permanent significance. Then he went on to state that his reason for not wanting to share his experience with others was that people would not understand it. What he had achieved was the knowledge of the basic truth of things, seeing them as they really are. Anyone can become a Buddha who has achieved the goal of the path but usually it means a person of great cosmic significance whose appearance is very rare and is achieved after many successive births.

THE PROBLEM

The human being is composed of skandhas or bundles or qualities. First, there is the body and the senses. Second, there is the mind (manas), the sixth sense. Third, there is perception, recognition, or interpretation by which we classify things and experiences. Fourth, there are intentions leading to skillful or unskillful actions resulting in karma, which determines our birth. Finally, the fifth skandha is consciousness, which is a process, not a thing or an abstract concept. There is no core or soul. It is an illusion and from it flows our desires that lead to suffering.[4] An analogy would be the chariot, which is not any one of its parts or the sum of the parts but simply a label given to a group of components structured in a certain way. There is no intrinsic chariotness that we can identify and no self or soul intrinsically in us:

> Just as when the parts are rightly set
> The word "chariot" is spoken
> So when there are the skandha
> It is the convention to say "being."

But is the whole not more important than the parts? We cannot have one without the other but it is the finished product that is useful. And how can we compare living beings with a chariot? The analogy does not hold. But the Buddhist believes that while there is no me or ego there is personality, continuity, and recognition. We exist as a stream of mental and physical processes but if the components are structured in a certain way it must mean that there is a principle of organization. The parts could be organized in a different way and make something else. Someone made the chariot but the Buddha said we do not have a creator. How then did we come into existence?

The Buddhist concentrates on becoming rather than being. He contends that everything is impermanent and that applies to what we call the self. We cannot distinguish it from our experiences. When we introspect our ideas, feelings, consciousness, we never, as the philosopher David Hume pointed out, find a self. But despite this we continue to think of consciousness as an inner subject with which it is identified, and an outer object with which it is not; there is the "self" and the "not-self." It is difficult to accept the Buddhist's position because we think that it is we who are having the experiences.

The skandhas, physical and mental, work according to patterns without any substantiality and build up our character from childhood to old age thus providing continuity that must be present if there is to be morality. But I must be the same person who did that action yesterday or I am not responsible for it. The Buddhist has a problem here. But if there is no self or soul, perhaps consciousness is an integrating factor? The Buddha denied this and thought it was only a name given to the flow of experiences that depend on cause and effect. All things originate in dependence upon this flow. The impersonal lawlike nature of causation is the explanation.[5] Even the mind that plays such an important part in Buddhist meditation and might imply an ego or soul is seen simply as a collection of fortuitous and disconnected thoughts.

The Buddha's teaching has caused much debate. Some scholars take the general view that there is no self or soul but others insist that there is a self beyond the senses and that the Buddha never taught that the self "is not" but only that it cannot be apprehended. It is argued that we do not have a spark of divinity or an immortal soul but there seems to be a higher self that emerges as the lower dies. The soul or self grows, changes, and contains four of the five skandhas, so it is unwise to stress no-self, no-soul for the Buddha was only against an abiding self.[6]

But the no-soul view is confirmed by the second discourse of the Buddha, the suitta pitaka. He addresses former ascetics and says:

> ...understand and remember that whatever feelings, perceptions, mental formations or consciousness, and whatever corporality be it yours or another's, large or small, present, past or future, high or low, far or near, gross or subtle; none of these is yours. These do not belong to you. You are not these, and this is the true wisdom.[7]

Such absence of belief in the soul and in a creator God has conveyed the impression that Buddhism is not a religion but an ethical understanding of the need for renunciation of worldly values, liberation from attachments, and morality. Aid is not sought from the gods in Theravada Buddhism and there is no worship (bhakti).[8]

The Buddhist agrees with Heraclitus that we never step into the same river twice. All is in flux. But is the Buddhist forgetting that the river remains? The Buddha did concede that most of us felt that we had a self. When I review my past life I can think of many experiences and developments, both physical and mental, from childhood. Change, and hopefully improvement, has taken place but the core remains the same so that I cannot say that I am another person. However, when a mental illness occurs such as dementia the past is largely forgotten and there are doubts about the immediate present. Relatives become unrecognizable and they often say it is not the same person.

One can agree with the Buddha when he traces so much suffering (dukkha) to the ego for our desires are often not fulfilled and we feel frustrated and depressed. It is only in recent times that the full effect of clinical depression has been understood leaving a person with little motivation to do anything. But all suffering cannot be traced to the human condition for nature itself behaves in an unpredictable way at times with, for example, earthquakes and hurricanes leaving thousands homeless and many dead. Dukkha, the first of the noble truths that is suffering, misery, pain, may simply mean that things are unsatisfactory.

Suffering arises from desires and these must be eliminated but there are good and bad desires. With regard to the former they have led to improving the conditions of the poor, building places of worship, improving travel, advancing technology, launching into space and so on. Of course, the Buddhist is right about the bad desires of lust, greed, hatred, and the necessity of avoiding extremes of pleasure or mortification and following the middle path.

Most religions recognize the problems associated with concentration on the self and there is a call to deny it. The empirical self must die for the immortal self to be found. It is the mystical tradition but it does not mean that the self and human individuality do not exist. The Buddha seemed to think that we feared nonexistence after death and deluded ourselves with the belief in an ego or soul that would continue.

In Buddhism much is made of the principle of causality. Events flow from causes, one thing exists because another preceded it. There is the chain of becoming and there are twelve dependent originations. There is ignorance deluding us that we have a self or soul and from it desires. When we engage in intentional activities, consciousness arises and it remains after the death of the body. From it comes a new birth unless consciousness is ended with liberation or nirvana at the point of death. The cause of rebirth is the consciousness of self and from it too comes names and forms and sensations of sight, smell, taste, touch, hearing and mental activity. Then there is feeling that creates attachments or aversions to objects. Each quality or effect flows from what went before.

Buddhism rightly opposes too much individualism and points toward interdependence. It fits in with current ideas about community, being influenced by parents, teachers, and friends. Hence we transcend the ego. If we are to develop our personalities we need to be outgoing and realize how dependent on others we are.[9]

There are four Noble Truths and ignorance of them is the problem. The First Truth is about suffering (dukkha) likely to mean dissatisfaction. Pleasure does not last because it, like everything else, is impermanent and ends in frustration. The Second Truth reveals the cause: craving and ignorance leading to rebirth (samsara). The Third Truth is cessation of suffering or nirvana here and hereafter:

> There is brethren an unborn, an unbrought-to-being, an unmade, an unformed. If there were not, there would be no escape for one who is born, brought to being.[10]

The Fourth Truth is the eightfold path, which means right effort, mindfulness, concentration, knowledge, and liberation.

Understanding these Truths will lead to the remedy for suffering.

THE REMEDY

The cure for the disease is to take refuge in the Buddha for he is the doctor. There is continuity in our lives:

> There is neither identity nor difference in a sequence of continuity. For if there were complete identity in a sequence of continuity there would be no curds produced from the milk; if there

were complete difference the owner of the milk would not own the curds. This is the case with all conditioned things.[11]

And when this configuration of events ceases at death another takes its place, which is rebirth. The new will be connected with the old but different for the human may be born as an animal.

Persons are causally connected by physical and mental events rather than enduring substances. It might be thought that consciousness would give us something substantial but it is just a stream, an awareness arising out of matter and sensation. It does not exist independently of them. It is important for rebirth since it establishes a new foothold or support for itself on the death of the body. It is not absolutely the same as the earlier one or completely different from it. But if we are only a stream of consciousness, looking at different people and how they vary implies that there are different streams. How is this variety to be explained? The Buddha knew a lot about the environment in which he moved but nothing about genes and their impact on personality and behavior.

The Puggalavadin and other groups argued that the person or puggala was a subtle skandha among the five and it is reborn. They argued that if the puggala (person) was the same as the five aggregates then when they were destroyed the person would be annihilated. It would oppose the belief that the Buddha still lived but if the puggala was different from the aggregates then it was like the atman and this would be the mistake of eternalism. A via media was sought by asserting that the puggala cannot be defined but is the subject of our experiences and also transmigrates and eventually attains nirvana but opponents were not convinced, arguing that it was the return of the atman.[12]

Perhaps the Puggalavadin were thinking of moral responsibility because it is a person who is morally responsible. He is the agent.[13] P. F. Strawson said that personhood is irreducible and cannot be explained away in terms of construction of arms, legs, feeling, intentions and ever changing mental and physical moments. The Puggalavadin might have been influenced by the Jain belief in an immaterial eternal soul. But it was not the general belief among the thirty groups in the early

centuries of Buddhism,[14] and though they were quite successful at times they do not appear to have had any lasting influence. They were condemned by the third council at Pataliputta
in 427 BCE.

The Buddha did give the impression of body/mind dualism
when he was discussing one of the sutras. He said that the five
aggregates are like a burden and the person is the carrier of that
load, but the Dalai Lama comments this is not the Buddhist
standpoint for in general there is a denial of the atman, there
is no separate eternally abiding soul principle. Yet he admits
there is still a variety of positions with some saying that the
person is among the physical aggregates either as consciousness or the totality of aggregates while others say it is a mere
designation.[15]

The Buddha was sensitive to the receptivity of his audiences
and was loath to answer difficult questions. One was what
we have been discussing: Is there such a thing as a "personal
essence" or self? He did not reply positively or negatively when
such a question was posed by someone who believed in the
atman for if he denied the selfhood of a person, it would lead
to discomfort and nihilism, a total denial of the existence of
persons or agents. If he affirmed the self, it would be seen as
clinging to an egoistic, isolated notion of self; being sensitive to
these needs and being unwilling to impose his views on others,
he did not reply.

But how can a person be simply a material process? Identity
is important since we are concerned about ourselves and what
others think of us. We want to be altruistic and need to deny
ourselves but we do it in order to find ourselves; we do not
believe the self is an illusion. It is wrong simply to identify with
what role we play in life: a working person, father, mother, son,
daughter and so on. Sartre writes of a man who was a waiter
and was foolish enough not to think of himself as having any
other identity.

Buddhism has an affinity with Chinese philosophy, which
stresses change. Yin is the female principle of darkness and pas-
sivity, yang is the male, light and active. They interpenetrate
each other and the world; yet it cannot be light all the time and
everywhere; there are shadows such as suffering. Taoism says

that we do not have a fixed identity, we are what we are through change. If anything is fixed it is change itself.[16]

DIVISIONS

Two forms of Buddhism emerged: the Theravada or tradition of the elders and the Mahayana (150–100 CE) that had new sutras and is called the great vehicle. It stressed the bodhisattva (Being of Awakening), the compassionate one, the Buddha to be, who postpones nirvana in order to help others. While the Buddha was omniscient and an infallible teacher, the bodhisattva is a savior, the embodiment of wisdom. He has the perfections of moral conduct, patience, energy and absorptive meditation.[17] Importantly he combines the social virtues of a righteous householder with the ascetic ideals of a meditating monk, bridging the gap between monastic and popular Buddhism. The bodhisattva is worthy of worship.[18]

Theravada understood the Buddha as neither man nor god, but one who far transcended the nature of both, the teacher of gods and men.[19] The life of the Buddha conforms to the pattern of dharma or dhamma, which means the law of the cosmos. He was infallible and stressed his teaching: "Who sees dharma sees me. Who sees me sees dharma."[20]

In Theravada the remedy was to rely on one's own ability to realize nirvana. It is a form of religious individualism that follows the path laid down by the Buddha and in the context of the Sangha, hence the statement that the only logical Buddhist is the monk. The Sangha is "an association of self-reliant individuals."[21] The arhat (worthy person) was the one who gradually found nirvana by meditation and being obedient to the Buddha precepts. He concentrates on destroying his desires and wrong views about himself and the world and thus escapes the wheel of rebirth. This arhat ideal was challenged by Mahayana and the fact of interdependence is against such individualism.

Some believe that the Buddha's achievement of nirvana was the end of his existence like a flame going out, but his merits and benefits are still there and can be communicated to us. Many other Buddhists including the Tibetans see the Buddha in terms of the three kayas or three embodiments.[22] The three bodies are in Mahayana, three different aspects of the Buddha nature: the eternal teaching or essence (Dharma-kaya), the historical (Nirmana-kaya), and the transcendental (Sambogha-kaya), which is the heavenly body. The transcendental body encourages bhakti or devotion. There are three jewels: the Buddha, the dharma or teaching and the sangha or monastic community. A declaration of faith is this:

> I take refuge in the Buddha.
> I take refuge in the Dhamma or Dharma
> I take refuge in the Sangha.

The Buddha is the refuge because he has shown the way and the Dhamma is the teaching of the Buddha through which we can find the way. The Sangha tell us about the Buddha and his teachings.

The five Precepts come after the Three Jewels: do not destroy life, do not steal, do not commit adultery, do not tell lies and do not drink alcohol. They are the basic rules of life for the lay Buddhist.

The Mahayana is characterized by its understanding of the changing nature of the Buddha and Buddhas. It justifies its scriptures by asserting that they were revealed by the heavenly rather then the historical Buddha and they are called sutras and tantras with the sutras being the more important.[23] But they are like a raft, a means to an end, rather than the end itself. The goal is to become a bodhisattva and help others and only the belief in the self or soul prevents us from doing so.

The bodhisattva can be anybody even a layperson who rejects the arhat in Theravada that is concerned with the enlightenment of the individual monk rather than the awakening of all. The bodhisattva is devoid of such selfishness. A bodhisattva became Amita or Amida the Lord of the Western Paradise or Pure Land by taking a vow in a former life as a Buddhist monk called Dharmakara. He vowed to use his merit to help people and to defer his own supreme enlightenment until others who called on him could be reborn in a land where their enlightenment would be assured.[24] He is the transcendent Buddha of infinite light and personification of mercy, wisdom, love and compassion.

There is also in the pure land, Avalokiteshvara, who dwells with Amida and shows compassion. Rituals are employed to get into contact with him and he grants grace to all. Tibetans believe he works through the Dalai Lama who is the reincarnation of the Buddha and deserves worship.[25]

The bodhisattva can also use skillful means and may even adopt, according to the Lotus sutra, deluded views (untruth) in order to bring people to liberation. For example, deception is used by a father (the Buddha) who promises his sons toys that he does not have to get them out of a burning house. Killing is also endorsed when a bandit is annihilated because he threatened the life of others. The bandit is also saved from the consequences of his intended actions.[26]

In the Mahayana the Buddha himself was elevated with superior spiritual qualities such as superhuman powers and virtues and becomes much more than a historical person, which was only one of his three bodies. The worship of him developed (bhakti) and it was held that there are other world systems and cosmic Buddhas.[27] The Chinese and Japanese believe that the Buddha can be equated with the ultimate reality underlying the whole universe. Mahayana has tremendous variety and is not a single school like Theravada. It may be that when they talk of the Pure Land it is a state of consciousness rather than a place but it became popular in China based on the sutras related to Amida. If letting go of the ego or soul was the traditional message, the Pure land monks asserted that it was letting go by the power and grace of Amida. In the light of this it is strange that some writers argue that there was not really a doctrinal difference with Theravada but simply disagreement about monastic problems.

A development of Mahayana was Vajrayana, which is found in Tibet, and this "thunderbolt vehicle" took on Tantric elements. The aim is to refine the mental, volitional and physical energies of the initiate through meditation, mantric and ritual means. The world is lustful but lust may be released in the practice of sexual yoga where it is transmuted into a power for liberation. Even sex at night with a low caste girl in a cemetry who is visualized as a deity was encouraged.

Tantrism arose in Hinduism as we noted and emerges again in late Indian Buddhism. It was based on a great number of texts that did not appear until the sixth century and were believed to have been revealed by the Buddha. The Tibetan Buddhists thought they had magical power for they contain spells, describe gods and have instructions concerning worship. Rituals involved sex but there is a debate whether to take the texts literally or symbolically. The point was the breaking down of the separation ego and concentration on interrelatedness.[28]

There was also the purposive attempt, which we have mentioned, to challenge the five precepts of Buddhism. Killing may be allowed to prevent someone doing something that would send them to hell, stealing to prevent another stealing, adultery to provide better rebirths for the recently deceased and so on. But again the texts used contain multiple levels of meaning and cannot be taken at face value.

MEDITATION

In meditation, there are various postures with attention paid to breathing, mindfulness or awareness (sati) leading to insight into the nature of things and realization of nirvana. There are things that hinder meditation such as lust, hatred, laziness, worry, doubts, but other conditions help: perseverance, relaxation of body and mind, concentration and tranquility. Concentration can be gained by using various objects such as a blue disc, breathing deeply, reflecting on kindness and compassion and casting aside sensual desires. The sense of self is broken down as we realize the impermanence of all things. An altered state of consciousness is achieved when mental activity is stilled and samadhi (intense concentration) is reached. It is a loss of all sense of separateness between thinker and thought.

Mandalas are symbolic depiction of the universe and its occupants and are used in meditation. In Mahayana, meditation is undertaken with the aim of achieving friendliness and benevolence toward all especially the suffering, and sharing of joy with those who are happy. It is moving away from the inward to the outward with the ultimate purpose of the elimination of all consciousness and the receiving of supreme enlightenment that is nirvana. But in all this a major feature is the mind and one wonders why it is not given a central place in the skandhas.

KARMA OR KAMMA AND REBIRTH

The general principle of causality is behind karma: if we act in a certain way then we experience a certain effect. It applies to the universe that could not have come into existence without a principal cause; so the Dalai Lama seems to be sympathetic to the Christian view of a creator.[29] The Buddha transformed the Brahmanic notion of karma based on the Brahmanic view by giving it an ethical and psychological orientation that focused on intention. The control of the mind rather than ritual actions leads to moral and spiritual progress.

The last thoughts before death are important for if we die craving for existence we will be reborn, which is not desirable. A good action is skillful and a good act or gift can help the dead. Feeding the monks is seen as transferring the merit to the deceased or other ancestors. The action done, not the doer, is important, and automatically affects the process of rebirth. During our life time the physical is dying, as the Buddha said: "When the aggregates arise, decay and die O bhikkhu, every moment you are born..." we are dying while we live! Our lives are a series from birth to death, a movement, continually changing and it continues as long as there is a "thirst" to be and to become.

Some see consciousness as the connecting link in rebirth but it is not an unchanging thing that passes from one life to the next but "the last act of consciousness in the old life and the first in the new life are consecutive moments in an uninterrupted sequence- this is the theoretical basis for being able to remember 'our' previous lives in the same way that we recall our childhood."[30]

DEATH

Rituals, chanting, flower decorations, and so on are used so that the dying person may concentrate on the good he or she has done and these practices continue in Tibet where it is believed that there is an "in-between state."[31]

At death cremation takes place and mourners wear white and use flags to decorate the household after the funeral. The bereaved offer meals to the monks to transfer the merit to the dead person through the water pouring ceremony. This is intended to ensure a better life in the next birth but karma determines their fate. The rituals in Buddhism follow an old tradition and reflect the belief that we are not separate selves uninfluenced by other people or our past generations. In Sri Lanka there is a turning to the gods for help.

The *Tibetan Book of the Dead* describes the intermediate state of days between one life and the next, but Theravada denied such a state and maintained that the last act of consciousness in one life conditions the first act of consciousness in the next. But the book speaks of the spirit or life force that is trying to communicate with relatives and there is a white light that is one's consciousness and if it can be recognized enlightenment is granted. However, the soul is ruled out.

There is a continual flow or progress of change so the present is followed by the next stage and the direction of the change is controlled by laws. We are an organization of energy so what it does at this moment will influence the next and later stages and it continues beyond death. Hence instead of a soul there is the process itself. But if we are composed of energies and materials, how did they come together? It is like flame; when it goes out, it is lit by another. The connection between one life and another cannot be physical or have a molecular connection so consciousness occurs again. Some say it is like a leech that before it lets go of its previous position has already got a grasp of the other. But the consciousness must have memory if recognition is possible in the next life.[32] Rebirth is preferred rather than reincarnation for the empirical self or soul is a fiction.

Speculation about the after life is to be avoided since we have no experience of it. Otherwise we can be compared to a man who has been shot by an arrow and refuses to take treatment before he knows who shot it and where it came from. What is needed is to pull out the arrow of sorrow. Yet it is difficult to avoid mentioning the soul: Thus E. Conze writes: "those

attacked by external enemies may, or may not, suffer injury to
their souls; but those who are weighted down by the senses suffer in body and soul alike..."[33]

Christmas Humphreys was an eminent lawyer and judge who
introduced Buddhism in Britain and was involved in the practice of Zen Buddhism. He points out the variety of Buddhism in
Tibet, China, Japan and Europe. He thinks that while denying
a spark of divinity or immortal soul they admit that there are
two selves, a higher and lower. It is the high self that emerges
because the lower dies and it continues from body to body for it
is Lord over the lower. The soul, he points out, was mentioned
by Apostle Paul and can be called for convenience this higher
self. In the following he embraces rebirth and questions who
dies and the condition in the after life:

> When I am dead, who dies, who dies,
> And where am I
> A dewdrop in a shining sea
> An inmate in the sky?
> Or do I rest awhile and thence
> Return for new experience?
>
> There's nothing changeless, heaven or hell
> Nor Life's oblivion;
> Only a heart at rest and then
> A further walking on.
> We live and as we live we learn;
> We die and then again return
>
> Yet who returns, what comes again
> To fretful earth?
> I know not. Only this I know;
> There is a road that comes to birth
> In everyman, and at the end
> Shall brother know all life his friend.[34]

There are many areas where we can be reborn according to our
karma. The worst is hell but it is not a permanent place; bad
karma can be worked off; it is like purgatory. It takes a long
time to deal with our sins and it is simply impossible to escape.
Then there are the animal realms, the realm of departed spirits,

the area of divine beings who lust for power, and the human realm where rebirth is possible.

The Buddhist does believe in gods who have superhuman qualities but they are subject to death. The hells and heaven can be explained psychologically or metaphorically as happens with other religions. It is stated by some that the Buddha did not reject the concept of God; he was simply silent about it hence his approach was neither agnostic nor atheistic.[35]

Another way of looking at rebirth is the patterns by which the skandhas are related to each other and these can be reproduced from moment to moment because the skandhas are causally connected. These patterns provide the continuity during the life of a person and at death the causal connections do not end for the patterns form new ones not identical to the old but connected with them. Rebirth has been viewed as the chance to advance in perfection, but in Buddhism you can go down as well as up, like the game of snakes and ladders.[36]

PHILOSOPHY

Dharma is not only the foundation of all things it is also an impersonal cosmic law or the Absolute. The Buddha's teaching is also dharma and is learned by spiritual practice, listening, reflection and joining the sangha.

Abhidharma is the higher dharma, the earliest attempt to prove the teaching of the Buddha and is based on one of the three main divisions of the early Buddhist canon of scripture, the pitaka. Later we have the development of sutras or collections that were to be used by the Mahayana and the philosophical schools.[37]

We recall that we are composed of matter and have feeling, perception, intention, habitual tendencies and consciousness. These in abhidharma are reduced or broken down into dharmas that go beyond the conventional belief in persons and acceptance of an ego or soul.

Constant change is a principle of Buddhism; the dharmas come and go; there is impermanence, temporariness; but together they make up our experience. Helen Waterhouse uses the helpful illustration of a painting by Seurat in which the canvas is covered in tiny dots of color making the picture look coherent at a distance but close up, a pattern of separate dots. Thus our experience of life is not smooth and continuous but consists of dharmas that arise together and then cease.[38]

These smallest components of existence form the basis for everything else. We might say that they are like atoms as understood in current scientific thinking. They come and go like bubbles on water but are basic building blocks and persons are merely labels for a changing collection of impersonal events that are empty, that is, lacking in inherent existence. This is true of the ego or soul. Emptiness is not a substance out of which things are made but points to the fact that nothing has ultimate or necessary being, including nirvana or the Buddhas. All is a magical illusion.[39] Our language and concepts based on cause and effect cannot grasp the ultimate truth of anything.

There are two levels of truth as we noted in Sankara. On the conventional level we talk of people and bodhisattvas and Buddhas, but on the ultimate level they do not have eternal, separate, nonrelative existence. But there is debate about this. Some groups argued that dharmas are substantial realities existing in their own right and operating momentarily for a time. If such an enduring time occurs then there is a permanent moment and unchangeability. What then of impermanence central to Buddhism? The answer of the Abhidharma was that even the analysis of the shortest conceivable moment of time shows a process rather than inert substances.[40]

The dharmas can also be compared to the quarks of modern physics, they do not exist separately but in groups that change continually. Later Buddhism was influenced by this teaching but its abstract view of emptiness was given warmth and compassion by the bodhisattva. Emptiness (sunya), which is related to the not-self (anatta), is not a negative nothingness or a vague ultimate otherwise Buddhism could be accused of pessimism or nihilism but a way to express dependent origination.[41]

Ultimate reality is ineffable; it is emptiness or void (sunya). Some philosophers thought that there were two worlds and the Buddha was the bridge between them, an incarnation of emptiness or the Absolute. Nirvana was the attempt to reach such transcendent existence. But imagine a situation where everything changes and there is no substantiality in anything, and apply the same to the teaching of the Buddha and the four noble truths. They become simply devices for liberation, thus Nagarjuna said that there is no distinction between the world and nirvana and that means there is no difference between nirvana and samsara that is transmigration or rebirth.[42]

Ultimate truth is the empty nature of phenomena, it is the absence of intrinsic reality, it is the final truth and key to liberation from suffering. All that we experience—birth, death, pain, and pleasure—take place here in the relative world and are real only as conventional or relative truths. Hence the Dalai Lama says that when the Buddha recognizes the self but at times denies it, he is adjusting his teaching to the level of truth that his audience can receive.[43] But there was a Madhyamika school that did argue that no-self (anatta) contradicts reason and is not the complete and final truth.

Yogacara, another philosophy, stressed the mind and believed that what we perceive is a mental construction. The so-called solid world is only an appearance and it applies to the soul. There is only a flow of mental experiences that is mistakenly interpreted as selves or external objects. What there is consists of a store consciousness that is like the unconscious level of the mind and it carries over into the next life. The store consciousness has impressions that are caused by the actions we have done hence the connection to karma. Consciousness or vinnana has the seeds of memories that reproduce themselves over time and account for the continuity of personality through death. Our seeing the world is governed by the unconscious mind that images what the world is like.

But the focus on the mind was criticized since it led to being too occupied with illusion rather than the relatively real. The philosophy employed yoga, which has become common in the West. It is consciousness which makes the link between rebirths and nirvana but the Madhyamikas accused the Yogacarins of making mind a substantial entity. The philosophy is metaphysical idealism creating objects out of its own inner potentialities. Berkeley is the nearest European equivalent.[44]

In both schools there was the attempt to deify the Buddha and the belief that ultimate reality is beyond definitions. It shows, as Rupert Gettin says, the problems Buddhist thought had in arriving at a proper statement of the middle way between the two extremes of eternalism and annihilationism.[45] But Yogacarins have a solution to the dualism between self and not-self. They argue that such dualism is resolved by the experience of nirvana for once this state is realized one experiences pure awareness without any object or concept such as the self.

Zen is a more positive view when compared to the philosophies, which we have mentioned. It depends on verbal transmission and passes directly from mind to mind for there is no reliance on scriptures but a concentration on experience. Ignorance must be eliminated and prayer, ritual, books and texts cannot lead to enlightenment. A teacher is necessary and rationality defeated by koans or riddles. Meditation (zazen) is practised and enlightenment comes suddenly.

Zen has different groups and they relate to the culture of the country. Koans are recorded questions or sayings that are beyond the realm of reasoning; for example, what is the sound of one hand clapping? One answer is that there is no such thing as the sound of one hand clapping because clap is a word to describe the sound of two hands when brought together. Zen is critical of the analytic, dualistic, conceptual view of Western philosophy.[46]

Another idea is the Buddha nature, our true nature that does not die. Introspection and detachments can enable us to discover this nature. It could be compared to the image of God and shows, as the Dalai Lama said, that all human beings share the same divine nature.[47]

We are basically good and need to cultivate this side of our nature which according to the Mahayana is in the womb or embryo. It is the true self according to the Mahaparinirvana Sutra[48] and means that we possess potential Buddhahood.

Enlightenment is the uncovering of what has always been there but obscured by defilements. We need to recognize what we already possess, and in meditation, according to Zen, we realize it; yet it is a long journey before we become Buddhas.

A central idea is that of sudden enlightenment that occurs when we stop talking and reasoning and is the result of many years of meditation. It is called "satori," the Japanese word for enlightenment. Zen tries to get back beyond the stress on moral ideals to the original experience of the Buddha for without it we cannot understand what the teaching is about. Only when the monk has experienced "satori" can he understand the Zen master. Until then he is sent away with a scolding and sometimes a blow on the head!

NIRVANA

The experience of Nirvana removes the delusion of the self and ends desires. It cannot be defined and if we try we would become attached to the definition! It is the letting go of false beliefs and can only be experienced.[49] Yet the Buddha did attempt to describe:

> There is, disciples, a realm devoid of earth and water, fire and air. It is not endless space, nor infinite thought, nor nothingness neither ideas nor non-ideas. Not this world is it. I call it neither a coming nor a departing nor a standing still nor death nor birth. It is without a basis, progress or a stay; it is the ending of sorrow. For that which clings to another thing there is a fall; but to that which clings not, no fall can come. Where no fall comes, there is rest, there is no keen desire. Where keen desire is not, nothing comes or goes...there is no death, nor birth...there is neither this world nor that, nor in between. It is the ending of sorrow. There is, disciples, an Unbecome, Unborn, Unmade, Unformed. If there were not this...there would be no way out for that which is become, born, made and formed...but there is release.[50]

The description is not easy to understand because our concepts are inadequate to describe nirvana just like the Tao: "the Tao that can be expressed is not the eternal Tao."[51]

But we can say that when we let go of craving we are reaching toward nirvana for it is craving that drives samsara or transmigration. It means the end of hatred, greed, ignorance and being able to see things as they really are. We cannot think of it as nonexistence since the Buddha experienced enlightenment under the tree and continued to live. It is nirvana with remainder or substrate and when we die it is nirvana without remainder or substrate that is the ultimate goal. When we detach ourselves from craving and sense experience there is freedom as in the Yogic trance. It is the parallel to being dead and it is like the flame of a candle going out. But where does it go? Buddhism says that such a question is meaningless and we should remember that the Buddha remained basically agnostic about such matters.

But the Buddha did speak of an island or other shore, and is there not a kind of immortality in the succession of rebirths? He refused to answer ultimate questions and if it is said that he did not know the answers it contradicts the view that he was omniscient. Nirvana and emptiness are associated for nirvana is experienced by emptying ourselves completely of thoughts and by blowing out of the fires of greed, hate and delusion. Since it is going beyond reason it is inexpressible and involves the abandoning of personal identity. It is the illusion of self that is the root of our desires and binds us to rebirth.[52]

There are negative as well as positive views of nirvana. A positive view is this:

> For those who stand in the middle of the water,
> In the formidable stream that has set in,
> For those who are overcome by decay and death,
> I will tell you of an island, O Kappa.

This matchless island:

> Possessing nothing and grasping after nothing,
> I call Nibbana, the destruction of decay and death.[53]

The Buddha is special but will he exist after death? Existence means to be born at a particular place and time and implies that we are part of this impermanent world. Hence we cannot say he exists, for if we do then he will be reborn. But to say that he does not exist would mean annihilation so we need to say that he has an existence that goes beyond rebirth.

Nirvana is the unconditioned, that is, other states are subject to causes. However, it is not since nirvana occurs when conditioned things like ignorance end and the chain of causality is broken. Nirvana is a state of happiness and joy that will be experienced in full when the wheel of rebirth comes to an end.

THE HEAVENS

There are many heavens where the gods live and Mahayana Buddhism recognizes them as being helpful to us, but they are mortal and cannot escape rebirth and they will decay. The gods who cannot escape sensory desires dwell in the lower heavens but others that can live in the higher. There are also four formless heavens that have infinite space, infinite consciousness, nothingness and neither perception nor nonperceptions. These correspond to meditational levels. The question is: Do these realms exist or are they to be understood metaphorically or related to psychological or meditational states. Traditionally they appear to have been taken literally but Buddhism says that it is in the workings of our minds that all these layers of understanding and experience are found.

According to Theravada there are four holy places that should be visited with reverence and awe. The first is where the Buddha was born and the second where he was enlightened. Benares, Deer Park, was the site of his first sermon and is the third place. The fourth is where he died. The Buddha promised that those with a believing heart on such pilgrimage to the holy places shall be reborn after death, when the body shall dissolve, in the happy realms of heaven. There are also hells that are for those who lie, use bad language, covet another's possessions, are stingy and backbiters. On entering the hells one is struck with iron rods, endures the fires and experiences other forms of punishment. But it would seem that they are not permanent and appear to be more like purgatory.

We have been dealing with the historical Buddha but each world age occurs in a cycle and each has its Buddha. Dipankara was the Buddha of the previous age and Maitreya will be the one of the future. Similarities between Mahayana and Christianity have been suggested: loving kindness and compassion particularly seen in the bodhisattvas who sacrifice their lives for all and have a savior role, and the second coming of Maitreya, the loving one.[54]

The last saying of the Buddha was:

> How transient are all component things;
> Growth is their nature and decay.
> They are produced; they are dissolved again;
> To bring them all into subjection that is bliss
> Decay is inherent in all component things;
> Work out your salvation with diligence[55]

CONCLUSION

In general there is a denial of the soul or self but within the religion there have been protests about it and a variety of views. The Buddha nature in all would imply a spirit or divine activity in us and might be seen as a soul. The quotation at the beginning of our reflection on Buddhism shows that the person was being denied but we will use the concept in the final chapter as a way forward in our thinking about the soul.

Buddhism is depending on the changing nature of things that rules out anything substantial but this has been challenged. Think of three sensations that we might have, namely A, B, C. We experience passing through this process ABC, which means something in us can survey what is going on as A passes to B and then to C. Something is recognized as the same through the transition from one to another and finally we have had the experience of ABC. It demands a soul that is not a mere succession of states but something permanent; otherwise it will be just a collection of perceptions without the knowledge that they were occurring.[56] In the philosophy it is conceded at times that the no-self doctrine is not a final truth. It is also worth remembering that there was a pattern seen in the elements of our makeup and it will figure in our future discussions.

The Buddha was elevated in Mahayana and worship of the gods introduced probably because of the need of some kind of grace or help from them. The savior element is seen in the bodhisattvas. Followers can draw on the merit of the Buddha and the bodhisattvas that parallels thinking in Catholicism. The discussion of consciousness was also significant providing some sort of continuity between one life and another and the idea of store consciousness might be seen as our more familiar teaching about the unconscious.

One of the attractions of Buddhism in India was its rejection of caste divisions and it even became a state religion under Emperor Ashoka. But such a rejection of a social system failed to break the concept of caste that dominated the Hindu society and, ultimately, Buddhism failed to make progress.[57]

CHAPTER 7

THE SIKH PATH

My soul, you alien in this world, why do you fall victim to it?

It is said that Guru Nanak (1469–1539) the leader of Sikhism experienced the presence of God during a period of three days. He was a government official in the Punjab state and after his enlightenment was able to preach and perform miracles until his final settlement in Kartarpur. His followers were known as Sikhs or disciples.[1]

We know little about Nanak from a historical point of view. His life is contained in the janam sakhis, which are collections of stories relating to historical events, legends, and mythology. Hew McLeod applied a historical and critical approach and concluded that little can be known about him. Some Sikh scholars agree but others disagree and use the stories as a basis for doctrine and ethics. The difficulty in knowing the facts is not peculiar to Sikhism since it applies to other religions.

What is clear is that Nanak had an enquiring mind and a wisdom that attracted attention. Many stories circulate about him. For example, one day he joined a group of pilgrims standing in a river offering water to assuage the thirst of their deceased ancestors. Turning to the west, Nanak began to throw water. Asked what he was doing he said that he was watering his fields in Kartarpur. They laughed at the ridiculous belief that water could reach fields so far away. Nanak replied that it was just as stupid to think that water could reach souls no longer on earth and who had no physical wants or needs. On another occasion he was at Mecca and went to the Ka'bah where wearied with the journey he lay down at the entrance and fell asleep. The keeper found him in the morning, sleeping with his feet toward the Ka'bah. He was awakened rudely and upbraided for daring to sleep with his feet pointing toward the House of God. Nanak apologized, said that he was a weary traveler, and asked the keeper to do him the favor of taking his feet and turning them in the direction where God did not dwell. To a startled keeper he explained that the entire universe is nothing but God's dwelling.[2]

Nanak is regarded as human but he is savior, prophet, true enlightener, and as perfect as a being can be. In a sense he partakes of divinity since he received the divine revelation. God was manifest in him, and he is without error and sinless. In the Hindu sense he is divine having his guruship from God but perhaps the best estimation of him is a charismatic prophet who had spiritual gifts and brought a revelation. As such he is the human model to follow for he portrays what God is like.

KEY WORDS

Nanak used expressions in relation to God such as word (sabad) and name (nam), divine preceptor (guru), divine order or will (hukam), truth (sach) and grace (nadar). Nadar shows that God must reveal Himself if He is to be known and sabad means a form of divine self-expression: "the word is my Guru." The action of God takes place through the sabad, which implies both a model of God as agent and has a similarity with the Word (logos) in Christianity. Understanding these terms and using them will bring us into harmony (hukam) with the divine order or will.

Nanak's religion was for the householder and not for the ascetic or the monk. He advocated a casteless society unlike Hinduism and founded the guru ka langar, a community kitchen for all to eat together. Worship must be in the Name: "when sin soils the soul, the Name alone shall make it whole." It means repeating the Name not in a mechanical way but meditating on the nature of God that would conquer the ego or haumai. The ego, unlike Buddhism, is recognized but must be dealt with if we are going to conquer the deadly sins of lust, anger, greed, attachment and pride. The mind and its control are important for once it is quite peaceful, it can attain a state of divine bliss or superconscious quietness and a vision of God. Thus the Nam or Name of God is something special.

Names are our identity but in religions, they stand for character and nature. For example, Mary was instructed to call the baby Jesus for he would save his people from their sins. In Sikhism the Name (nam simaran) of God reveals His being, character and nature and time must be spent in meditation upon it. The Sikh hopes that by so doing he will be filled with God just as in the secular sense our interest in work or home or hobbies may fill our whole lives. The Name designates an indwelling power and the parallel in Christianity is hallowing the Name of God in the Lord's Prayer.

SCRIPTURE

Before Nanak died he was able to appoint his successor and he and those who followed him were called Gurus or holy men. They were very important in leadership, administration and governing the Faith. The title Guru appears in the hymns of Nanak as identical with God but he did not claim it. It was given to him by his followers. The Sikhs apply it to God, the scriptures, human masters and the community. At the death of the final Guru a curious thing happened, a book became the Guru: the Guru Granth Sahib or Adi Granth. It consists largely of hymns by Guru Nanak, other Gurus, some Muslim and Indian writings, and is revered as the voice of God and consulted constantly for guidance. The Sikhs have been accused of being book worshippers since the Guru is put to bed every night and in the morning throned on a dais above the congregation. Is this not idolatry? They say that the accusation is false for in every religion material objects can symbolize a spiritual power, for example, bread and wine in Christianity.

The Sikhs believe that it is necessary to wash before handling the scripture and when it is opened the first paragraph gives guidance for the day. It is also central in the naming of children, marriage, and the initiation to the Khalsa brotherhood. Then there is the Dasam Granth that has the hymns of Guru Gobind Singh but it does not have the same authority since it contains legends and events dating to a later period. The collection was compiled during the eighteenth century and includes legends from Hinduism. In practice it is used little.[3]

GOD

The Sikh has a high view of God who is ineffable but pervades the world in a personal way. It resembles the Semitic religions. God reveals Himself to the person in the depths of the soul and by a response to His Word (Sabad) receives the experience of His grace. The incarnation of the Hindu gods such as Vishnu in ten or more avataras and the authority of the Vedas are rejected.

God is one and does not have a second. He is indescribable in His essence: "If I know Him should I not tell His story but He cannot be described in words."[4] Nevertheless the universal must be expressed in the particular if we are going to say anything at all about Him; thus He is immanent as well as transcendent: "the Unseen One dwells in the soul."[5]

It is by the will of God that all things come into being, particularly the soul:

> Through His will souls come to be,
> Through His will excellence is obtained.
> Through His will some are high born, others low;
> Through His preordained will some receive pain, others pleasure.[6]

WORSHIP AND FESTIVALS

The earliest Sikh meeting places (dharamshalas) were not places of veneration but accommodation for pilgrims and are now known as gurdwaras. They are open at all times for meditation but corporate worship is essential. It must have a bearing and effect on daily work that should be performed with diligence. Faith and good work go together. The Guru Granth Sahib is central in the devotion but there are no priests. Any member can read the scripture and conduct the service but usually it is done by the committee of the gurdwara who organize it.

Sometimes there is a granthi who acts as a religious teacher and custodian of the building. Nanak rejected the use of images in worship (diwan).

The men remove their shoes and the women cover their heads and approach the scripture that has been placed on a raised platform with a canopy over the top. A fly-whisk made of Yak's hair, a sign of royalty, is waved continuously over it and as each worshipper passes the book, he bows and places an offering in front of it. Prayers are said, passages of scripture repeated and devotional songs (kirtan) sung. The service is very lively, using a variety of musical instruments and the hymns are read first and then explained before singing. A sermon is preached and at the end of the service there is the distribution of food (karah prasad) in the langar. It is a mixture of ground wheat, sugar and butter in equal parts. The seated congregation receive karah in their right hand, which is the Punjabi name for a gift or present. The purpose is to show that they are one united family of equals with caste distinctions rejected.

Women enjoy equality and participation in worship. Amar Das, the third Guru, recognized the quality of their work and appointed four women manjidars to be responsible for preaching and the collection of tithes in the areas that they governed. Mata Guijri, the wife of the ninth Guru, Tegh Bahadur, assumed leadership of the community after her husband was murdered and her daughter-in-law, Mata Sundri, succeeded her. Celibacy is not prized, although some groups do exist, and there are no taboos regarding women's impurity. Marriage is encouraged for Sikhism is a householder's religion with monasticism considered as an escape from one's duties in the world. As in all religions the mother is highly honored.

For the Sikhs the holy place is the Golden Temple at Amritsar, which is linked with previous Gurus, Hindu gods, and houses the Guru Granth Sahib. Pictures of Gurus who have died are not in the same place as the scripture but hung in other rooms. There is also at Amritsar the Akal Takht (the eternal throne), once the residence of the historical Gurus and now the most important of the five seats of authority. It means the unity of spiritual and temporal power. The impressive Golden Temple is a model for all gurdwaras.

The Sikhs have various rituals introduced by Guru Amar Das that were augmented to preserve the cohesion of the community. There are those that accompany the birth of a child, entering the Sikh brotherhood (the Khalsa) and marriage. All must take place in the presence of the Guru Granth Sahib. Prayer (ardas) is to be offered twice a day, in the morning and in the evening. It contains invocation, remembrance of those who gave their lives for the Faith, the blessing of God on the Khalsa and all humanity, protection against evil and any special miracle that has occurred. It concludes with praise to God. Such a prayer is also offered during public devotion. In the conclusion of the diwan there is the prayer: "O my soul, live with God forever, and the soul is the gift of God." The soul is paratma, which means that it is part of the Cosmic Soul. We are made in the image of God so the soul/spirit is bound up with the divine and never dies.[7]

There is also the celebration of many Hindu festivals and the birthdays of Nanak and Guru Gobind Singh. They are joyous occasions accompanied by fairs, animal races, wrestling contests and other sporting events. Diwali, the Hindu festival, is remembered as it coincided with the return from prison to Amritsar of the sixth Guru, Hargobind. The birthdays of other Gurus are celebrated, especially those who were martyred.[8]

Nanak was opposed to rituals that he saw as the external trappings of religion, but the protest was probably intended to mean that purity of heart and intention are more important than any ritual. Without it pilgrimage, for example, is useless. It is in line with the Hebrew prophets condemning ritual divorced from justice and mercy.

CREATION

There is one God, the creator, eternal, omnipresent, pervading the universe and it is by His grace that we worship Him. He is the Truth and we cannot know Him by thought alone, fasting or other devices. Man has been infused with life by Him and is predestined to do what He wants. He is self-existent, creating the world by an act of His will, sustainer and present as light in every heart.[9]

Creation may be viewed as emanation from God and due to His will. The process may be evolutionary or due to an accident but the consequence is the intention of God.

HUMAN NATURE

We are ignorant of our true nature and destiny, which is governed by karma. Haumai is self-reliance and the belief that the world is important that prevents us from freeing ourselves from rebirth.[10] We need to turn to God and be obedient to His will so that His grace (nadar) might operate.

Maya is the temporal world and it is a delusion not an illusion as some Hindu philosophers believed. We cannot live without the materialistic things that it confers upon us but maya can give us the wrong perspective and keep us away from God. It deceives us and leads to lust, greed, attachment, wrath and pride. These are the five evils whereas the duties of the Sikh are nam japan, kirt karna, vand chakna (remembering God), earning an honest living, giving gifts to charity and helping others. Mankind is blind and self-centered (haumai) and such egoism causes violence, sorrow, doubt and the inability to see God. The problem is the ego for it causes us to disobey God and leads us away from Him.[11]

Manmukh is loyalty to self but not to God unlike gurmukh that obeys the voice of God and is free from haumai. The soul governs our activity and can be affected by good or evil. It decides our spiritual life but it depends on God being present or absent. The soul is the seat of temptation being allured by the attractions of world. It is called at times jiania, a Punjabi term, and is subject to delusion but it is foreign to the present life and belongs to another sphere:

My soul, you alien in this world, why do you fall victim to it?

When the True Lord dwells in your soul, why should you be snared in death's net?

The fish is separated from the water with tearful eyes when the fisherman has cast his net,

The world of maya is a sweet attraction, in the end the delusion is exposed . . . Make devotion, apply consciousness to God and rid yourself of mental apprehension.

Nanak speaks the truth, consider it my soul, you foreigner soul.[12]

Calling the soul "foreign" is significant; it does not belong to this world.

Sikhism accepts the reality of the world, it is not the Hindu maya (illusory), but is impermanent. The soul is attacked by weaknesses, lust, wrath, avarice, love of the world and pride. Maya makes us blind and deludes us into accepting the values of this world. God has placed the soul, divine spark, or conscience in us and it (the term jiva is sometimes used) is immortal being of the essence of God with His Name inscribed upon it.[13]

LIBERATION

The soul that is filled with goodness is the seat of God and enters into union with Him. The ego disappears so that our thoughts, speech and everything else is an expression of God. The union, sahaj, means that the Light so fills the soul that man becomes an extension of it. It is an illusion that we are separate from God; we have always been united with Him, so there is no need for an absorption into Him ultimately.[14] But it requires concentration and the training of the soul for it is prone to forgetfulness.

How can honour be achieved in His court if the Lord does not dwell in the soul? . . . My Soul! Day and night repeat the virtues of the Lord."[15] But where there is self-interest, haumai, the soul cannot be in man. Only when the Satguru (God) is met does the Name and the Word dwell in the soul:

When the self is overcome, then doubt and fear are also overcome and the sorrow of death and rebirth removed.[16]

The soul must make an effort to reach the grace of God but yoga and asceticism are rejected for fasting and penance do not soften the soul. Holding to the Name is the way to reach the stage of gurmukh that is God-mindedness. If sahaj can be obtained, transmigration of the soul ends. It does not mean absorption into the Absolute or supreme Being but rather love for Him and internal devotion.[17] There is no need to renounce marriage and become an ascetic for one can live a life of piety in ordinary circumstances and resist the temptation of worldly things. In brief the separation of man and God is to be overcome not through rituals, pilgrimages, or celebration of festivals but by responding to His grace and obeying His will. Again and again the way of escape for the soul from spiritual death is by remembering the Name (Nam japan): "Past actions determine our garment, His grace gives us the door of salvation."[18]

Repetition of the Nam japan is like taking a boat by which the soul crosses the ocean of existence on a voyage that transforms the personality (nam simaram). Concerning our likeness to God there is identity-in-difference as we noted in the teaching of Ramanuja the Hindu philosopher. Such a unity (sahaj) removes the sorrow of birth and rebirth and means that the soul recognizes both God and itself. Like most religions it is not the achieving of academic knowledge of God but becoming tuned to His initiative. It involves various stages culminating in being filled with the love of God and being able to say: "He is me and I am He."[19] It is a state of complete gurmukh where the law of karma ceases to operate.

Sikhism has a number of prescriptions that express the basic formula: "My Soul repeat the Name of God and seek refuge"[20] and the prescriptions summarize the danger to the soul: "Forgetting the Beloved even for an instant means great sickness in the soul."[21] Love is a prime element in salvation:

> My Soul how can you be saved without love? ...
> My soul let your love of the Lord be like that of the fish for
>   water ...
> Without water, even for an instant, it cannot live ...[22]

> My soul repeat the Name of God and seek His refuge ...
> The ocean of life is crossed by a boat, namely the repetition of
>   God's name as a rule of life ...
> The waves of avarice and greed are overcome by the pre-eminence
>   of God's Name in the soul ...[23]

Haumai, self-centeredness, is the major problem in attaining
liberation but the grace of God is there to assist us. There is the
need to deny oneself and rely on God who reveals Himself in
the depths of the soul.

BEHAVIOR

The ethical way is essential to Hindu and Muslim so Nanak
prays for the Muslims pleading that mercy will be their mosque,
Faith their prayer carpet, justice and law their Qur'an, modesty
their circumcision and civility their fast. The same must apply
to his followers but in the development of the religion this way
of peace was soon to be transformed since the Sikhs had to
defend themselves against their enemies.

The tenth Guru, Gobind Singh (died 1788), changed them
into a fighting force by creating in 1699 a new and unique
brotherhood, the Khalsa. Its founding was dramatic. In 1699 a
large group of Sikhs had gathered at Keshgarh when suddenly
Guru Singh appeared with an unsheathed sword in his hand and
announced that his sword thirsted for blood. Would a true Sikh
volunteer to offer his head? He made the request three times
before Daya Ram offered himself and was led to a tent nearby. A
few minutes later, the Guru reappeared before the assembly his
sword dripping with blood and demanded another volunteer.
At that point many decided it was time to leave! But a second
Sikh, Dharam Das, came forward. He too was led to the same
tent from which again the Guru returned with his bloodstained
sword. Three other volunteers were called and experienced
apparently the same fate. There was a dead silence until finally
the Guru emerged from the tent leading the five Sikhs who had
volunteered to offer themselves to his sword. They were dressed
in saffron colored robes and turbans of the same color and each
wore a sword on a belt. The assembly greatly depleted stared
in amazement and disbelief but the Guru announced that they
were the Five Beloved and would form the nucleus of the Faith
that he christened Khalsa, the Pure or God's own. He then
proceeded to administer amrit (nectar) to them.[24]

After such an initiation ceremony the numbers of the Khalsa
increased with men and women joining through baptism and

swearing to obey a new code of discipline. An obligation was
requested of them: to wear the "Five Keys" comprising the kes
(uncut hair), the kangha (comb), kirpan (dagger or short sword),
kara (bangle), and kachh (breeches) that must not reach below
the knees. Tobacco smoking or eating meat slaughtered in the
Muslim way (halal) and sexual intercourse with Muslim women
were forbidden. The membership added a name to their present
ones: Singh being for men and Kaur for women.

No doubt the martial Jats contributed to making the Sikhs
militant for they were good at war and numerically strong in
the community. But there has been a reaction to all of this by
the Sahajdhari Sikhs who follow the devotional patterns taught
by Guru Nanak and his successors. Their numbers are difficult
to determine but they do remind us of the love and devotion
and patience of Nanak, something that every religion should
pursue. The Sikh code of conduct confirms their position when
it states that there should be altruistic voluntary service, prayer
in the morning and evening, reading and reciting of scripture,
meditation, remembrance of the martyrs and so on.

The practice of the Faith includes many things but we can
mention only the following: there should be a denial of caste,
magic, untouchability, fasting on a new or full moon or other
days and wearing of jewelry. Educating children in the Faith
is very important and the need to encourage them when they
reach adulthood to earn an honest living. There is to be no sex
outside marriage and the woman does not need to wear a veil
but the male must wear the turban. Meditation, honest work,
generosity are to be praised and manual labor in particular is
stressed. Most Sikhs are vegetarians and meat is not served in
the langar. The sexes are equal, which is proven by the fact that
women do not wear veils, do participate in the services and can
be members of the Khalsa.

When someone does not keep the Faith he or she must come
before the congregation, acknowledging their sin and asking for
forgiveness. Penalties include cleaning the langar or the shoes
of the congregation outside the gurdwara and reciting prayers,
reading the scripture and a monetary donation to a religious
or social institution. The Akal Takht deals with very serious
matters.[25]

REINCARNATION

To escape reincarnation souls need to be united with God.
Karma occurs because of the will of God hence caused by Him
with both good and bad effects. Past actions determine us. How
then can there be a balance between what God determines and
free will? One suggestion is that while God wills the salvation
of men He permits the law of karma to operate thereby preserving the relative autonomy of man, so we are free to move within
the sovereignty of God.[26] It is significant that Islam, Sikhism,
Christianity have the same problem with predestination and
free will.

DEATH

The Sikh is taught to be aware of the unexpectedness of death.
Nanak uses the favorite analogy of the fish:

> The fish did not recognise the net in the salty and unfathomable
> sea;
> It was very clever and beautiful, why and whence its confidence?
> Because of its action it was caught, death does not pass it by.
> Brother know that likewise death hovers over your head
> As with the fish, so with man, the net falls unexpectedly.
> The whole world is in bondage to death, without the Guru death
> is unchallengable,
> Those who are immersed in Truth are saved, leave doubt and
> vices behind
> May I be a sacrifice to the truthful who repose in the court of
> Truth.[27]

When Nanak died, the Muslim wanted to bury him but the
Hindu contended for cremation. He had left instructions
to cover his body with a cloth and place flowers by it with
Hindus on one side and Muslims the other. Those whose flowers remain fresh could do with the corpse what they wished.
Nanak was not worried about the body for it was the state
of the soul that mattered. If it had not attained liberation it
would suffer loss.

The belief is that at death the soul will live in the presence
of God and not be reincarnated if the person has disciplined

his life and dwelt on the Name of God. There will be a recording angel who catalogues all deeds from the cycle of birth and
death and it is good acts that govern the judgment. At death
consciousness and the ego die but the soul does not. It is the
precious jewel within our breasts and if we have cared and cultivated it we will merge with the Deathless One at the end. The
soul thirsts for God throughout life and in the hereafter.

Death is not feared by the Sikh. When he dies the body is
bathed and dressed in clean clothes and there is the singing of
hymns on the way to the cremation beginning with

> The dawn of a new day
> Is the herald of a sunset,
> Earth is not thy permanent home
> Life is like a shadow on the wall
> All thy friends have departed.
> Thou too must go.

And ending with:

> Says Nanak, he alone can cross the sea of being
> Who sings the songs of God.[28]

During the time of mourning the Guru Granth Sahib is read
and the distribution of karah prasad. Death is not a mourn-
ful experience, it is a time of singing: "The Guru said when I
am gone sing only those hymns which will lead the devout to
blissful deliverance. God dispenses His love to every soul and
such love contrasts with the fleeting experience of earthly love.
The world is unreal, a deceitful image, but the Name of God is
exalted forever."[29]

Usually the body is covered by a white shroud and it is cremated or committed to the river and karah prasad and fried
cakes given to the mourners. There is a reading of the complete
scripture in the days that follow but rituals and ceremonies are
considered spurious. Attendance at the sangat is required and
showing submission to God by cleaning the shoes of those who
are there. The Sikh believes that singing the praises of God,
obeying His commands by not eating fish or drinking liquor
and caring for parents will bring to an end the transmigration

of the soul. But if the soul has misbehaved Nanak spoke of it "burning" because of worldly desire that results in separation from God. After death it is troubled and wanders in anguish bitterly regretting its sins.

Tegh Bahadur (1621–1675) had 115 hymns in the Adi Granth and writes of the conditions that the soul will have to fulfill in order to mingle with the Lord:

> He who in adversity grieves not
> He who is without fear
> He who falls not in the snare of sensuality
> Who has no greed for gold knowing it is like dust.
>
> He who does not slander people when their backs are turned
> Nor flatters them to their faces.
> He who has neither gluttony in his heart
> Nor vanity nor attachment with worldly things.
> He whom nothing moves,
> Neither good fortune nor ill,
> Who cares not for the world's applause,
> Nor it censure.
> Who ignores every wishful fantasy
> And accepts what comes his way as it comes.
> He whom lust cannot lure
> Nor anger command,
>
> In such a one lives God Himself.
> On such a man does the Guru's Grace descend,
> For he knows the righteous path.
> O Nanak, his soul mingles with the Lord
> As water mingles with water.[30]

HEAVEN AND JUDGMENT

Heaven is the bliss of being in the presence of God, it is not a place of comfort and pleasure. Judgment as we have said will be based on actions as the soul appears before God, Yama is the God of the dead and he has authority over them who have a kind of half existence between rebirths. It is not a pleasant existence and from there man is projected back into another birth, high or low, according to his karma. Yama judges the souls and if they have sinned and not placed their Faith in the Name of

alien to the world. It is like conscience that must
divine spark that needs cherishing.
proaches death without fear because he believes
. The goal is not heaven but ultimate union with
es not mean being absorbed into God but a com-
Him. On the other hand if His commandments
obeyed there is separation. The self is the enemy
ealt with by the grace of God, the doing of good
ending to worship. While there is a stress on this
he Sikh must prepare himself for it by good deeds
anity that stresses that the grace of God advances
ner whatever his/her condition.[36]
w sought to understand the soul in the context
eligions and it is time to see what philosophy has

God they will be sent to one of the twenty-one hells for purification prior to rebirth.[31]

MYSTICISM

Nanak had a mystical experience and his followers also testify to it. An example was Khushwant Singh who had an experience of one God who pervaded the universe and advanced toward him by His grace. Afterward he gave away all he had and despite the charge of madness started to preach and travel extensively.

Nanak's life of good works earned the approval of both Muslims and Hindus who were present when he died in 1539. As a monotheist he did not believe in the incarnation of God or gods or the worship given to idols. God, he believed, is Truth so we cannot speak an untruth, cheat, fornicate, or steal. It is impossible to define God but He could be called Father, Lover, Master, Giver, the True Creator or the True Name (Sat Nam). He understood the Nam or Name of God as invoking adoration.[32]

DIVISIONS

Like all religions there have been divisions in the Faith. Fortunately Nanak named Angad as his successor before his death in 1539 so there was no initial power struggle such as in Islam. Angad was a pious man whose poetry is included in the scripture and he was followed by Amar Das. He condemned suttee, advocated monogamy and widow remarriage. Ram Das followed and developed a settlement later to be called Amritsar that with its magnificent Temple soon became famous. The next Guru Arjan Dev incurred the wrath of the emperor Jahangir and was tortured to death becoming the first Sikh martyr. It led under Ha Gobind to the replacing of pacifism with active armed resistance and the construction of the Akal Takhr, the seat of Sikh authority. He was imprisoned but eventually released. Har Rai succeeded him and he was followed by Har Krishen who was only five years of age. It caused conflict with other members of the family who had ambitions to be Guru but Krishen behaved wisely as he matured and was deeply spiritual. Another martyr was his successor, Teg Bahadur, who was executed by the Muslim emperor in 1675.

The final Guru was Guru Gobind Singh, a formidable man, who composed the Dasam Granth and accepted the use of the sword in self-defense. He founded the Khalsa and engaged in battle with the Mughals and insisted that when he died the Guru would now and always be the Granth Sahib. The authority would rest on it and the Panth or community. But divisions began to show since the original pacifism had been succeeded by a warlike spirit. It was difficult to reconcile this trend with a peaceful founder who spoke about the delusion of worldly values and the need for a quiet and patient meditation upon the Name of God. The pacifism was embraced by a group called the Sahajdhari mentioned earlier. They continued as if the changes had not taken place and the Namdhari also protested since they were not happy with the replacement of the living Guru by the scripture. A third group is the Nirankari who insisted on behavior rather than ritual and thus followed in the footsteps of Nanak. The opposition to the place given to the Adi Granth continued with the Radhasomi movement that did not install it in their gurdwara. They opposed caste and attracted many untouchables. The movement was also responsible for establishing a line of Gurus.

The Nirankari met with opposition in recent times with Sant Jarnail Singh Bhindranwale embarking on a campaign of violence against them. There was much unrest that included the assassination of the Indian Prime Minister Indira Gandhi by her Sikh bodyguard and the death of three thousand Sikhs. The Sikhs want a homeland of their own, Khalistan, a separate state with no interference from Muslims or Hindus. They deplored the creation of a Muslim Punjab and thousands left the area. It meant not only loss of property but also difficulties in accessing the sacred sites of their Faith. Their home became the new state of Punjab (1947) but it remained one of the states of India.[33]

Today it is estimated that there are around eighteen million Sikhs many of whom are farmers but also soldiers, artisans, carpenters, metal workers and mechanics in industry and the fine arts. There are many Sikhs in the professions.

C

Critics say that Sikhism i It is true that these religi also inspired by Kabir and that had a devotional sch was shown by his writing composed. They attained any of his predecessors.[34] its Gurus and the Khalsa, phenomenon.

Nanak respected other l humanity should be like Hi a temple and a mosque, nor a Muslim. Though differen all men are in reality the sam would like to see the Punja independence from Pakistan perous as compared with otl is that militant members are about.

One striking thing is that ing rituals and rules as did th tion was direct, a personal ex is usually associated with the happened, however, in the Fa or a system. Perhaps it was bou rience God they want to share munity develops it needs rules seen in all religions.

Concerning their doctrine of religions. He is transcendent a grace to us but we must advanc God is indescribable, the univer particular.

The soul is given by God an forever. Since it is part of Him i tual is attracted to worldly things ject to delusion. God dwells in t

Cosmic soul s be obeyed or

The Sikh a in immortalit God, which d munion with have not beer and must be deeds, and a grace of God unlike Chris toward the s

We have of six world to say.

CHAPTER 8

THE PHILOSOPHER AND THE SOUL

In this chapter we enquire about the link between mind and brain and what place is given to the soul in philosophy. There are various views in the history of philosophy and we discuss briefly some of them.

EARLY THOUGHT ABOUT THE SOUL

The ancients dreamed that their spirits or souls moved around freely without their bodies; hence it was believed that the soul lived on when the body was dead. Food and drink were left near the abandoned bodies in case the soul wanted to refresh itself and gradually the idea of transmigration developed: the belief that at death the soul left the body and inhabited another. The Indian religions, as we have seen, postulated the law of karma: deeds done in the former life determined the status in the new. Good deeds could result in an upgrading to a higher caste whereas doing evil meant denigration.

The concept of the mind or soul as a substance is very old with the Egyptians believing that the physical body would turn into a spiritual one at death. Homer accepted the Greek belief in an immortal soul and in the sixth century Pythagoras argued for the transmigration of the soul that inhabited a tomb-like body.

The Indians and the Greeks believed in the preexistence of souls. True knowledge is recollection of what was known in the preexistent state, it is not gained by sense observation that deceives. The Hebrews did not separate body and soul as the Greeks did and there is only slight evidence of any kind of belief in immortality, as we have seen, until the Book of Daniel written sometime in the second century before Christ. The concept is found in the Second Book of Maccabees but it is the whole person not simply the soul that is raised by God to eternal life. These views had some influence on the fully developed doctrine of the resurrection of the body that emerged in Christianity.

We have mentioned Plato (429–347 BCE) and Aristotle (384–322 BCE) already and refer to them here because they are essential to our theme. The greatness of the former is asserted by Whitehead when he said that the whole of European philosophy consisted of a "series of footnotes to Plato."[1] We recollect that Plato emphasized the universal or general. Justice exists, for example, and is a reality over and above any of the particulars: the river is above the flowing water and justice is above particular acts of it.

When I know the form of anything, the idea of it, I know the essence and must have some prior knowledge to enable me to say this particular thing is a cat, dog or horse. The form is the essential feature making a thing what it is. If I want to make something I have an idea of what it is like and impress it upon matter just as a sculptor takes a slab of marble and creates a statue. Forms do not belong to the world of the senses since they are unchanging. Plato believed in a creator, the Demiurge or World Architect who brought the world of ideas and matter together. He speaks of gods but sometimes seems to believe in one supreme God or Form of the Good, the master of the universe and source of souls.[2]

The soul must be trained in mathematics initially but to apprehend the Form of the Good eventually a mystical vision is required. The progress of the soul requires an advance in the knowledge of the forms that are the innate tendency of anything to realize its good. This end or teleos becomes a controversial issue in the theory of evolution as will see.

We know the forms by reason but knowledge of the world is provisional since it is always changing. The soul was in the eternal realm before entering our world so we remember and the recollection is the proof of immortality. Sadly we lose knowledge of the eternal world because of our life here. Plato was a dualist and held that the soul is tripartite: reason, spirit and emotion. Just as a charioteer controls the horses the soul must control the body.

Mind (nous) is the rational part of the soul. In the myth of Er he discusses the fate of souls after death and the choices offered to them before reincarnation. The forms are guiding principles and bring nourishment to the soul resulting in its longing for completeness. Philosophy must elevate the soul from the fleeting objects of this world into the area of knowledge when it will meet with the forms.[3]

Aristotle brought the forms down to earth and said that we must rely on our senses for knowledge. Form was equivalent to function and we knew it by what it did and the way it did it. It can be embodied in matter and the soul is the form. He seemed to think of the soul as a life principle rather than an entity and it made things grow, reproduce, move and perceive. It enables the body to function and dies with the body. Perhaps he did believe that nous or mind survived death but it is impersonal rather than personal.[4] His forms are not transcendent so he may not have been a dualist like Plato.

Aristotle made clear that we cannot separate form and matter for the latter always tries to realize the former, that is, the acorn strives to become a tree. Plato saw the sculptor as independent of the marble but Aristotle thought he was dependent on the marble for the form or idea is in it.[5] Purpose is evident everywhere in the world and there is no such thing as chance.

Mind or soul then is in us as the form of matter and instead of division there is an intimate relation between the two. You cannot have the one without the other. Form is a potential that becomes actual and there is a pull in things to realize an end so again we have teleos.[6]

DUALISM

Rene Descartes (1596–1650)

One day Descartes decided to spend time doubting everything and at the end knew there was one certain thing left: he had spent the day doubting! He said, "I think therefore I am" (cogito ergo sum). Treating it as a self-evident truth he was able to move to understanding both mind and body.

In a world that behaved in a machine-like manner being determined by cause and effect he was a thinking thing. Body and mind are two substances and quite distinct from one another. A substance is something that is unique and depends on nothing else for its existence. For example, a triangle is unique having three sides, other properties are incidental.

We have bodies but the essential thing is the mind that thinks. Descartes was a mathematician and reasoned that only clear and distinct ideas were to be trusted. He could see clearly that 2 + 2 = 4; hence knowledge lay in the area of mathematics. Clear ideas were the way to truth. I have a body but it does not mean that I am a body.

I am an immaterial and immortal soul that is mental without any physical extension. But Descartes never really explained the interaction of body and mind, that is, how changes in the brain can induce changes in the mind and vice versa and to say that the soul is located in the pineal gland, at the base of the brain, is hard to justify.

He thought our knowledge of the world was indirect and thus man feels pain in the limb that has been amputated. We have the experience in our minds. But Descartes detached himself from people to think and did not take into account how we are affected by the social. He treats the inner experience of the individual and forgets the external.[7]

Today, some have no meaningful role for mind, believing in epiphenomenalism that states that the mind simply accompanies the brain. Or that conscious experiences are identical to brain states, a different way of seeing the same thing, the former internal the latter external.

Innate ideas were challenged by John Locke (1632–1704) who said that the mind was like a blank sheet of paper, tabula rasa, and it was experience that impressed itself upon the mind. The humorist nowadays rephrases Descartes: "I do not think therefore I am not"![8] But the mental appears to cause something. It is not merely an accompaniment to the physical for it interprets and makes meaningful what I see. Descartes had opened up the way for a separation between nature as he saw it and the mind or soul. Science could then study nature in a mechanical way and put forward laws without paying any attention to purposes and goals characteristic of the mental faculty.

Dualism can also contend for the freedom of the will since my mind can act independently of my body. Descartes argued that animals were determined but the human was special because of the working of the mind. We will look at animals and their training in the next chapter.

Empiricism

David Hume (1711–1776)

David Hume is a contrast to Descartes since he placed stress on experience. We know "perceptions," that is, experience of heat and cold, light and shade, love and hatred, pain and pleasure and so on. Since all we have are these impressions from the senses only those things that are perceived exist. Hence the mind or soul is a jumble of perceptions with no unifying center. I only feel that there is a bond, but it cannot be observed. The Buddhist while agreeing goes further than Hume contending that once the delusion of a personal center is removed we are no longer subjected to desires and suffering that flows from wanting things. Eliminate desire, and the way to nirvana is open.

But Hume like Descartes tried to work out a theory of personal identity without taking into account other people and their minds. It cannot be done. He refused to see that knowledge comes from more sources than sense observation, for example, memory is important in establishing my identity. I remember someone or something and relive the experience, and while I have changed I know that I am not another being. Again, I have thoughts and no operation on my brain will disclose what these thoughts are.

Hume was very puzzled about self, on the one hand arguing that we cannot have direct knowledge of it and on the other assuming that we do experience it. He wrote, "Upon a more strict review of the section concerning personal identity; I find myself involved in a labyrinth that I must confess I neither know how to correct my former opinions nor how to render them consistent."[9] His problem is how we remain the same person throughout life. He writes: "But when I reflect on my self now and that of twenty years ago or more I know that they are not two but one and the same self."[10]

Immanuel Kant (1724–1804)

Kant was not satisfied with Hume's conclusions but admitted that his work had awakened him from his dogmatic slumbers. He agrees with Hume that knowledge arises from experience but believed that the mind supplies the form by which we know that experience. The mind is active on sensations not simply receiving them, as Locke had said, for it is not a tabula rasa on which experience writes. But both Locke and Kant have a relational view of personal identity rather than a substance.

We cannot, through reasoning, prove that there is a self or soul but we may act as if there was one since there is value in it. Kant believed in a moral law with the soul as its basis and it requires a good will that shows itself in our acting from a sense of duty, not acting because it will benefit us. Yet the good man will fail to achieve his ideal and needs more time than this short life provides, hence immortality.[11] Kant spoke of a thing in itself, ding-an-sich, which we do not experience directly and is transcendent. It was the noumenal world in contrast to the phenomenal or empirical that we experience through the senses. The argument has been used today to prove that we cannot know the soul in itself but only as it functions.

MODERN DUALISM

Dualism of body and soul continues to persist as we see in the dialogue between John Eccles, a Christian, and Karl Popper, an agnostic. Popper stresses that the development of language was important and the individual or organism does affect evolution by selecting a new environment. The consciousness of self from lower levels to higher emerges and man is able mentally to create a new world of myth, scientific theories, poetry and religion.

This is World 3, in contrast to World 2, which is the subjective or psychological and World l of physical objects.[12]

Popper rejects reductionism, which is the attempt to explain everything in terms of the lower and leaves out downward causation. Emergent evolution is shown by new things and events that have unexpected properties and objective propensities. A novelty of arrangement can lead to physical and chemical properties displaying something different. Quantum mechanics has jettisoned strict determinism and introduced objective probability statements into the theory of elementary particles and atoms. Rigid causality has been replaced by the probabilistic.[13]

He does not think that matter has an inner aspect that we could call the soul but he does believe in a self and argues that David Hume did, for he says that the impression of ourselves is always intimately present with us and speaks of character from which our actions flow. Memory is important for self-awareness and we interpret what we see. We are engaged in mental activity and problem solving posed by observation.[14]

Peter Strawson agrees that the self is the pilot, not a bundle of experiences or stream of consciousness as in Hume and William James. The baby has an inborn attitude toward persons and smiles at us so person is prior to self or mind. We can lose parts of our body but still retain the self. The case of Helen Keller who was blind and deaf refutes empiricism that relies on sensory input.[15]

Students who listened to Popper told him that he was advocating the theory of Gilbert Ryle (1900–1976) but he said that the distinction was that he believed in the ghost in the machine. Eccles pointed out that the nonmaterial ghost is an aid to understanding the self. It is a crude way of thinking but we cannot ignore it entirely. The self interacts with the brain, selecting, organizing, initiating, and integrating it. There is an openness of the brain even when we describe it in the reductionist way.

The Cartesian model of interaction has broken down being inapplicable to modern physics but there is interaction, such as the self trying to remember a name interacts with the brain. It is interaction between W l and W 2. The self waits for the brain to answer its requests and we examine the response. It is on a higher level and is active, judging what the brain turns up and playing on it as a pianist plays on the piano. Both Eccles and Popper see the position in this way.[16]

Dreams can have a revealing function. Otto Loewi in a dream had a vision of how to do an experiment on the chemical transmission from the vagus nerve to the frog heart but forgot it. Fortunately the dream was repeated and upon wakening he made a full plan of the experiment and carried it out in his laboratory. It was successful and for the discovery he was awarded the Nobel Prize in 1936. Popper points out that it shows the activity of the self-conscious mind in immediately impressing the dream on the conscious memory.[17]

Eccles believes in another existence but Popper is not sure and does not like an unending period of time. Eccles thinks that mind with its creative imagination is superior to the brain and sees the self or soul surviving the death of the body. He reacts against a materialistic science that dismisses the spiritual nature of man. The self is unique and the emergence of the mind from the brain does not make it a mere spin off, he thinks there is a supernatural origin of the self and soul. Popper says that evolution does not give us a full explanation of how the mind arises from the brain. We know little and science cannot help us with the ultimate mysteries.[18]

OTHER DUALISTS

The value of this discussion is that it attempts to find some solution to the problem of interaction. Richard Swinburne is also concerned about it and associates the soul with mental sensations such as pain, thrills, beliefs, feelings, thoughts and purposes. These interior experiences are private and are known only by each individual. Events in the brain can cause mental problems like pain but what happens in the one is distinct from the other. The brain itself feels no pain.

It seems that at a certain stage of evolution the animal brain became very complicated and the soul developed, which means that we rise above the animals that seek only survival. But the sciences find difficulty in measuring the soul's thoughts and feelings. He goes for soft dualism and contends that sensations are not physical events. They are distinct internal events and only individuals have access to them and control them.[19]

But science shows the effect of body on mind and maintains a psychosomatic unity. A soul that was immune from genetic, biochemical and environmental factors would not be related to the experience of the person who is a multileveled unity. It is a holistic view contending that the self or soul is not a static substance but a dynamic activity at various levels of organization.[20]

IDENTITY

We identify someone by physical appearance and peculiarities, character, voice, finger prints, DNA and physical movements. But there is also memory and when it fails we forget our past and who we are.

I can imagine myself to be someone else, indeed an actor like the late Peter Sellers became the character he was playing to such an extent that his friends did not recognize him. Most actors, however, while entering into the character they play do not lose their self-awareness. Sellers never understood who he was! His mother went to see him on one occasion when he was acting and collapsed in a flood of tears in the taxi that was taking her home. She kept saying, "He is not my son . . ." The taxi driver said, "But I saw you talking to him." "That was not he," she cried, "it was some duke or other?" Well if his mother could not penetrate his disguise who could!

On a more academic level there was the case of Schopenhauer the philosopher who was found wandering in a park late at night. He was challenged by a security guard with the question: "Who are you"? Schopenhauer looked at him and replied sadly, "Who am I. I wished to God I knew"! Was it a case of spending too much time with the questions raised by philosophy or just a loss of memory?

Memory is very important for it enables us to realize that we are the same person now and in previous experiences but the self cannot be known or described like external objects in terms of special attributes; this is possible only in awareness. We need to go beyond physicochemical processes to a higher level of understanding; yet if mind has evolved from matter it cannot be that different from it. Perhaps we might talk of mental and physical predicates or alternative languages.

What then of my identity? There is a humorous story about a Greek debtor who said to the lender that he was not the same man to whom he had loaned the money (due to the self always changing) so he owed him nothing. The lender hit him and replied in response to his complaint that he was not the same person who struck him a moment before![21]

People change over time but is there not something that remains the same? How is my identity preserved throughout life and in the hereafter? Personal identity requires more than having the same body? Our cells change constantly during life yet we do not have changed bodies; identity of body does not depend on identity of cells. Perhaps the memory criterion is best providing psychological continuity. If I can remember what I did in this life then I am the same person in the next and it would be necessary for any kind of judgment. But memory is remembering something in time and implies continuity of existence here and now whereas life beyond death will transcend our time. Eternal life is not everlasting life implying quantity but quality.

Then there is the first person perspective: I use the personal pronoun when referring to myself and it is not simply a label as the Buddhist says. I think of myself as myself, which makes me a person, and it does not depend on the matter I am made of. In saying this some are really talking about an inner life but then go on to assert that it does not require an immaterial substance like a soul. Yet oddly they go on to admit that belief in immortal souls can be held. Becoming persons is due to the development of a first person perspective that is not explained by biology.[22]

In sum personal identity is held for a number of reasons: experiences of the same person by reason of association with a persisting mental substance or with the same body, or a special relation between the two or on the basis of memory.

CONCLUSION

The question of the origin of the soul is still disputed, some say given by God but others think it emerged as part of our evolutionary development.

We have noted arguments for and against dualism and that, despite criticism, it still persists. But it has not explained properly how mind and matter can interact with each other. Consequently there has been a movement away from trying to understand what substance or essence is to thinking of soul in terms of its function. And there is now an emphasis on the development of the soul or personality in the social context.

We saw that the form of Aristotle meant function, what something did, and some have applied this to the soul. Soul for him is the life principle. We focus on its activity not the essence, which is difficult to penetrate. But can we define someone by his profession? Surely more is required. Form for Plato was what someone is not simply what he did. Form did not change.

We will continue to pursue these and other questions in our next chapter.

CHAPTER 9

CAN WE AVOID THE DUALISM OF BODY AND SOUL?

In seeking to answer this question we want to consider consciousness and the concept of person. The philosophy of behaviorism will also be taken into account but it will be seen to lead to materialism. Finally, we will ask if there is any way of verifying life after death.

CONSCIOUSNESS

The contents of conscious experience include colors, shapes movements, tone qualities, and thought so some equate having consciousness with qualia. They are the qualities of the world as we experience it: our subjectivity. If you examine my brain when I am seeing, hearing, smelling, it will not tell you anything about my experience or why I disagree with others about how these senses affect me and them. Some scientists think that brain mechanisms produce consciousness and that machines will have it eventually.

Consciousness is my awareness of being alive and having a self but the self is difficult to grasp as David Hume said: "For my part, when I entered most intimately into what I call myself, I always stumble on some particular perception or other. I can never catch myself at any time without a perception."[1] The brain is very important here but study of it with its feedback mechanism cannot tell us what is going on inside us so the problem of consciousness remains.

The mind has a depth that Freud explored. He postulated three levels. The first is the consciousness of emotions and memories, the second is the preconscious in which memories are placed but not accessible except under special conditions such as questions. The third is the subconscious or unconscious in which memories are locked and can only be released by hypnosis. Dreams are important but they have to be interpreted. Freud is considering things that are not material but so does physics: fields of force, inertia, numbers and so on. He believed that the conscious and unconscious mind controls behavior. Before Freud little attention was given to the irrationality of the self or how much behavior was due to unconscious causes. Like an iceberg the mind lies beneath and controls consciousness on the surface.

Jung put stress on the collective unconscious or archetypes, which is the result of our experience as a species. He believed in self-realization or what was later called self-actualization, Social psychology showed that we are products of social interaction and opposed Descartes who thought that knowing one's mind preceded knowing that of others.

Thomas Nagel in What is it like to be a bat argues that physicalist theories of mind do not explain how subjective experience can be identical with physical events. The subject is not given full credit in reductionism, which fails to take into account conscious experience. The physical operation of the organism cannot inform us what is going on in our private experience or explain the point of view that we have about it.

As we will see in the next chapter, it has been the impact of neuroscience that has stimulated the study of consciousness. The brain can now be scrutinised in a way unthinkable by Freud and Jung. As a result some contend that the physical is different from the mental and there is an interaction. Hence dualism is still with us but others reject it and insist that there is only the physical and the mind can be explained in that way. Daniel C. Dennett favors materialism and tries to explain mind away by rejecting an inner self that controls our behavior. We need to reduce everything to its smallest, material, mechanical parts, and that includes the self that turns out to be an illusion. Opposed to him are Roger Penrose and David Chalmers who argue that you cannot reduce consciousness in this way. Hence, as one reviewer says of Dennett's book, announcement of the final demise of mind-body dualism is somewhat exaggerated.[2]

Behaviorism

It is an easier option than dualism. I know what is going on in your mind by the way you behave and it operates on the basis of a series of reflexes to stimuli. The unobserved mind is known by the observed. Mental phenomena such as sensations, feeling, emotions, thought and dreams are just pieces of behavior. The Guru of behaviorism was B. F. Skinner who contended that behavior is explainable in terms of genetic predispositions and what he called reinforcements, the technical term for rewards and punishments. If we know what these latter factors have been it will enable us to predict what will be done next. Mental terms such as thoughts, intentions, emotions and so on have meaning only when they are associated with behavior.

But can I really know your thoughts in this way? Suppose I am standing in a crowded room and watching you lift a glass to your lips. What are you doing? Having a drink for refreshment or drinking poison? I cannot tell directly by observation and need to talk to you to discover how you are feeling and if you are intending to do something that might be drastic. If it were possible for me to examine your brain I would still not be able to detect your thoughts. Or take the case of the man who does not use the indicators of his car but puts out his right hand. What is he intending? Is he going to turn right? Or stretching out his hand to feel if it is raining? Or pointing to a house over there where a relative lives? All our guessing about his action is wrong because he suddenly cries: "Look I can drive with one hand"! Intentions cannot be observed and I need to accept what you tell me.[3] There is a difference between subjective feelings and bodily actions and I can be wrong when I try to read off the former from the latter. I say I have a pain and you notice me whining about it but you cannot see the pain. It is the other minds problem, that is, knowing what is going on in the mind of others.

Scientists observing the behavior of Einstein and his views thought he was crazy. He engaged in thought experiments and came up with ideas that puzzled and baffled his contemporaries. He said that they believed the only difference between him and the inmates of an asylum was that he was outside and they inside! He was indifferent to clothing and often was seen dressed like a tramp. At Princeton, a professor's wife when she opened the door said: "Sorry, I cannot give you anything today" and closed the door. It was left to the professor who was greatly embarrassed to run after Einstein and apologize for the mistake.

The dualist is confident that he knows why he is doing things and how he feels because he looks into his mind but the behaviorist will have nothing to do with such introspection. Basically he thinks that the mind is a set of dispositions to behave in a certain way, but there is more to mind than that. Often we have to settle issues by logic and the meaning of language, as in the trick question; Has it ever happened that a man has married his widow's sister? The answer rests on the meaning of the word used, namely widow. A man has to be dead to leave a widow.

Gilbert Ryle in "The Concept of Mind" called the mind the "ghost in the machine." Thinking and knowing are not invisible operations of the mind but as visible as jumping and skipping. How did he arrive at such a conclusion? Let us think of a lump of sugar. There is a lot we can see about it: shape, color, and structure, and we can estimate its volume and weight. But it has other properties that are invisible and can be made visible. If the sugar is placed in water it dissolves because it has a tendency or disposition to be soluble. We can think of the mind in a similar manner; knowing and thinking are its dispositions. How do we make them visible? We test by asking questions and evaluating the answers. Knowing is not the operation of a ghost in the machine but the exercise of an ability or capacity. But Ryle does not tell us what the source of the dispositions is and often there is a lot more going on in the mind than revealed by its capacities.

He does think that mind and body are not equivalent things. It is a category mistake. Mind describes bodies and the way they operate. Watch someone's behavior and decide what they are thinking for there is no inner self when we speak of mind. Mental activity is the exercise of behavioral dispositions and skills. But behavioral skills may not reveal what is going on inwardly since they may mask the real thinking. The attempt to explain behavior without taking into account internal factors fails: it is like a chemist trying to explain the behavior of a molecule without reference to its internal structure.

Mental calculation is done in my head but there is nothing being experienced of what is out there. It is different when I see a tree out there and think about it. In both a modification of my consciousness takes place but in one, the mental, the experience terminates within my own mind but with the external tree there is an experience of something beyond me, there is something objective. In the mental there is only an internal modification of my consciousness.

Interaction of mind and brain means a correlation, one influencing the other. Stimulation of the temporal lobe of the brain can cause delight or disgust so changes in the brain affect consciousness and when I think or will a correlative brain state is produced. In psychological laboratories it was discovered that mind can influence the nervous system responsible for heart beat, blood pressure, body temperature, which is comparable to the exercises and practices in Zen and yoga.

Is the mind preprogrammed? Chomsky said that the use of language was innate and not learned so moving to the Cartesian notion of an innate rationality distinct from the conditioned responses postulated by behaviorists. The behaviorist thought that the study of mind and soul was impossible since they cannot be seen or analyzed directly but it was demonstrated that we could have controlled experiments showing how the mind worked and the roles of thinking and remembering.

The mind is not simply passive recording and analyzing information but influences perceiving, remembering and thinking. We are special in the use of imagination. It has concepts that classify information and differentiate between objects and schemas. They are broader than concepts and contain ideas, plans, memories and possibilities for future actions. A schema would include basic knowledge of what we do when driving or getting into a train and so on.

Behaviorism is false because it cannot deal with sensations that are distinct from such behavior. If I have a color image or feel pain it is not behaving in a certain way and sensations are distinct from brain events though they may cause them. There is interaction between mind and brain. The ignition of a fuse is distinct from the explosion so firing of neurons is distinct from the visual sensations or pains they cause. Purposing is active in contrast with desires, sensations and beliefs and we believe that our puposing will affect the brain. Mental features help us to develop since they convey an evolutionary advantage. Otherwise to suppose that they are a mere by-product of brain states would mean no evolutionary advantage but experience shows that this is not a starter. Thoughts, desires and beliefs direct actions and are essential factors.

MATERIALISM

Materialism asserts that the mind and body are identical and disagrees with the behaviorist that mental states are dispositions to behave in a certain way. They are identical with bodily states and thoughts arise from the pattern of the neuron network. The dualist is also wrong when she says that the raising of her arm is an act of will and causes something to happen in her brain that in turn causes her arm to rise. The will cannot cause any change in brain energy.

But if I am identical with my body and it is determined like some machine, where is my freedom of choice? It was this that worried Descartes and he argued that while the body was determined the mind was not. Of course the materialist does not believe in anything that he cannot see but there are many forces in our world as we mentioned that the scientist cannot see such as currents, fields and subatomic particles. He knows that they are there by their effects and the theist can argue that God exists because of His effects on us. How can I be a moral creature if I am mechanically determined? There is no point in talking about an "ought" if I cannot do it. How can I do my duty or strive for any kind of goodness? We do not blame the animals when they misbehave for they do not have a sense of "ought."

Functionalism is a philosophy that seeks to resolve some of the difficulties of materialism by using the computer analogy. Thoughts are like software and the brain processes them. Software does not have a spatial location and we can think of thoughts existing on a different level and having an impact on the brain. Without the software the hardware will not function and the same applies to mind and body. The mental is an activity not a state or structure thus behaviorism has given way to functionalism that identifies mental states by the causal roles they play in behavior. But it like materialism can reduce thoughts to the firing of brain neurons so we are back with the physical.

John Searle is not happy about the materialist use of the computer analogy. He contends that the computer is similar to a non-Chinese speaking man locked in a room that receives, rearranges and then posts a whole series of Chinese characters according to a set of rules. Like the computer he does not understand what he is doing and even if a computer could become conscious it would throw little light on what consciousness is. In any case how could it experience pain or the passions that we have?[4]

There are those who hold that artificial intelligence is a genuine possibility but is it another example of projecting what we can do onto other things? We do it continually with dogs and cats. A robot simply moves about as a result of its electrical wiring and its program and we cannot see human intention there. AI (Artificial Intelligence)projects this intentionality so mind is to brain as program is to the hardware but mental states are a product of brain operation whereas the program is a product of the person who made the computer.

Consciousness is elusive and when we try to grasp it, it slips away like a bar of soap. No wonder for the brain has one hundred billion neurons and the problem is how to get from these firing to consciousness? The mind has been compared to a pattern in the brain. I am doing one thing but stop and decide to do another. This decision causes another pattern to form in the brain and physics cannot tell me why it should be. Rational consciousness and decision making is the crown of evolution and it is absent in the computer since there is no growth.

It would appear that mind and body are different concepts existing on a different level. I can describe a book by its style, expression, printing, word constructions or by its content showing how the characters behave and why. These complement one another as do neural and mental activity. What we have is complex activity in the brain and out of it emerges consciousness. There is a correspondence. The justification for such emergence would be emotion, character, aesthetic response, yearnings for God, in short what makes us into persons. And these cannot be reduced to the material aspect. They identify us and could persist after death.[5]

If we accept the mind as a pattern in the brain we also see it as the center of our subjective personal life. In contrast to the physical causes of the brain's operation the inner life has intentions and motives that require the probing of the why, rather than the how question and are unexplainable by mechanical forces.

PERSONS

We need at this point to take a closer look at what "person" means. Knowing how the brain works is helpful but it does not explain the feeling that I am me. Philosophy makes an attempt, taking into account consciousness, self and person. Peter Strawson puts forward a double aspect view of a person who has both states of consciousness and bodily characteristics. The concept of person unites these because one thing is viewed from two different aspects, hence we cannot reduce the person to mind, as the idealists try to do, or body and brain only as the materialist insists.

Philosophers distinguish between the biological development of a human being and the morally significant concept of person. Being a person is a moral concept, which means a concern for others and is developed in the moral community of parents, teachers, friends, and employers.

As a person we are aware of being the subject or unity of both the mental and physical. A distinction is made between the conceptual and the empirical. The neurosurgeon looking at the brain is following the empirical approach but the conceptual refers to ideas or concepts that involve the meaning and use of language. Concepts are abstract but we cannot do without them: citizenship, names of the days of the week, nationality, justice and so on.

Person falls into this category since we need a term that indicates unity or wholeness. When we explain personal relationships we do not use the terminology of electrons, protons, atoms and molecules but talk about emotions, intellect and volition. The two aspects do not belong to the same class or category. We think of the first as things and the second as states of the person.

It connects with holism and opposes the view that we can understand the person in terms of his parts. Gilbert Ryle writes of the man who seeks to understand the Oxford colleges in terms of the parts and has to realize that the university and colleges cannot be placed in the same category. The parts cannot be confused with the whole and the real cannot be reduced to the observable. The University is not another institution apart from the colleges but they differ in the way they are organized and coordinated. They cannot be placed in the same category.

The University is not apart from the colleges and the mind is not separate from the body; they affect and interact with one another. In being persons we have reached the highest levels of our being and in this connection we operate downward controlling the activities of the lower parts. It was the high level activity of mind that ensured survival against animals that were stronger and faster than we were.

In brief, the dual aspect theory recognizes that it is the person who transcends his body and mind. And it is the person who can ascribe to himself/herself feelings and volition. It is how he/she feels. For example, a person says that she is tired and we may challenge this by saying that she is bored but it is difficult to challenge for it is the experience of an individual and its meaning cannot be determined objectively.

NEAR DEATH EXPERIENCE

In recent times considerable data on the subject has been amassed, including accounts of near death experiences, psychical research and claimed memories of former lives. It would seem that near death experiences are particularly relevant and many cases have been documented. Clearly agnostic and atheistic accounts carry more weight than those of believers in God for the latter could be dreaming about what they already believed.

With regard to these experiences we mention the atheist and philosopher, the late A. J. Ayer (1910–1989). After a heart attack he was rushed to hospital and was clearly dying. But he recovered and afterward reported that in such a state he saw a red light that showed that someone was in charge overall of the universe. He observed two ministers who controlled space but it appeared to be out of joint. He wanted to extinguish the light but could not and he was unable to attract the attention of the ministers.

His friends judged the experience to be a hallucination but Ayer who lived for a year after it reflected on mind/body issues and said that in a future life there may be a prolongation of our experiences without the presence of body. He thought that the view was inconsistent with the concept of personal identity adopted by both Hume and William James, which was that one's identity consisted not in the possession of an enduring soul but in the sequence of one's experiences guaranteed by memory.

But the main problem is to discover the relation or relations that have to hold between experiences for them to belong to one and the same self. Ayer said that he had not been able to account for personal identity without falling back on the identity through time of one or more bodies that the person might successively occupy.

He goes on surprisingly to refer to Christianity where personal identity through time requires the possession of a resurrected body. He pointed out that two Cambridge philosophers, J M. E. McTaggart and C. D. Broad who, though atheists, believed in survival after death. The former based his view on metaphysics and the latter on psychical research. Since Ayer experienced not God but rather survival he concludes that it may be possible to have the one apart from the other. He wrote that his previous conviction that there is no life after death had been slightly weakened but he had not ceased to be an atheist.[6]

Scientists are now taking these phenomena seriously since there have been many cases similar to that of Ayer. We will continue to discuss it in the next chapter.

Reincarnation

A number of Jews did believe in the doctrine and the belief persists today as shown in the Kabbalah. It is prominent in New Age religions where the belief has its advantages as well as disadvantages.

Buddhism prefers thinking of rebirth rather than reincarnation because it denies the soul. The new life as in Hinduism will depend on the goodness or badness of the former but in Buddhism intentions as well as deeds are stressed and the last thoughts before death are important. It is claimed that the Dalai Lama, the head of Tibetan Buddhism and the leader of the Yellow Hat monks, is the reincarnation of the Bodhisattva Chenresi. The Sikhs believe that to escape reincarnation we need the grace of God and good deeds.

The Modern Position Regarding the Self

Much attention is now paid to the influence of the social on us. We notice others early in life and try to imitate them so the social self is born and the identity of the individual self is found within the social and cultural. But modern philosophers still try to maintain personal identity though analytic philosophy attacked it. Existentialism as represented by Sarte held that there is no private self, it is public, an object in the world and it is only in the experience of the other that I become conscious of my self. Existence preceded essence and we are not determined by anything for we are free. We mentioned his example of the waiter: no one is determined to be a waiter yet he might so identify himself with the role that he thinks that is what he is. But there can come the time when he decides to refuse to play the role. He realizes that he is more than that. Hence it is difficult to accept that we think of ourselves only in terms of our social identity.[7]

Dualism contends that the mental and physical are different but monism insists that they are of the same kind of material. A via media is to argue that there is only one kind of material but different mental and physical realities cannot be described adequately solely in terms of the other. We saw in Greek thought the understanding of two different kinds of things, namely soul and matter but in Hebrew it is argued that there is only one kind of material, that is, matter or energy. In that case modern thought has seen the mind as an evolved property of the body. Darwin stressed our similarity to the animals and it led to the view that we have no souls just brains that produce minds to help us survive. The middle way is the dual aspect theory, which means that there are two distinct ways of thinking of me. I am a brain but something more for I have an inside life and can be called a subject not an object. Minds taste but brain circuits fire. Minds arise from the workings of brains in terms of qualities (qualia) and meanings.[8]

CAN A FUTURE LIFE BE VERIFIED?

A. J. Ayer had a lot to say about verification but the response was that the principle itself could not be verified: historical statements or general laws of science could not be verified. In response Ayer argued for a weak form saying that all that was needed for something to be meaningful was some sense experience. But God's attributes are nonempirical, therefore, not intelligible. But there is no sense experience for the verification principle itself. Ayer later admitted that the principle allowed all statements to be classed as meaningful and it was intended to understand if statements were meaningful, not true or false.[9]

John Hick put forward eschatological verification. Two men are walking down the same road, one believes that the road leads to the Celestial City, the other that the road leads nowhere. Both check signs along the road and interpret in different ways, verification is possible since there either is or is not a city. But we can know the truth only at the end, which religions have always contended is the case.[10]

Anthony Flew believed that believers kept qualifying their claims to avoid falsification, which produced death by a

thousand qualifications. If religious statements had no empirical consequences they asserted nothing. But the believer can
point to many differences in his life as a result of religious
experience. Hare contended that religious language may be
noncognitive but still meaningful and important for the beliefs
are "blicks," unfalsifiable convictions, that have consequences
for conduct.

CONCLUSION

The question of the origin of the soul is still disputed, some say
given by God but others think it emerged as part of our evolutionary development.

We have noted arguments for and against dualism and
that it despite criticism still persists. But it has not explained
properly how mind and matter can interact with each other.
Consequently there has been a movement away from trying
to understand what substance or essence is to thinking of
soul in terms of its function. And there is now an emphasis
on the development of the soul or personality in the social
context.

We saw that the form of Aristotle meant function, what
something did, and some have applied this to the soul. Soul for
him is the life principle. We focus on its activity not the essence,
which is difficult to penetrate. This issue will reappear in the
next chapter.

Perhaps the way forward is a dual aspect monism, that is,
mind and matter are complementary aspects of "one world
stuff."[11] Waves and particles are complementary, but when we
think of light, they are not contradictory, so it is argued that
mind and matter complement one another without contradic-
tion. Correlation of mind/soul and brain is put forward by
some thinkers.

Subjectivity, our feelings, thoughts, willing has to be taken
into account and are characteristic of persons and this means
the inward factor. The soul and the mind are the inner factors
and psychology finds it difficult to deal with it since we are so
unpredictable. But recognition of inner and outer aspects of the
person makes for a unity.

The soul is the whole person and it is expected that this will be raised in any resurrection. Memory is important for any future assessment of the person.

We now turn to science to see if it has anything to say about the soul.

CHAPTER 10

DID DARWIN KILL THE SOUL?

*We must however acknowledge . . . that man with all his noble
qualities, with sympathy which feels for the most debased,
with benevolence which extends not only to other men but
to the humblest living creature, with his god-like intellect
which has penetrated in the movements and constitution of
the solar system—with all these exalted powers—man still
bears in his bodily frame the indelible stamp of his lowly
origin.*

Descent of Man (1871)

This is Darwin's balanced view of man and we want in this chapter to see if he went as far as denying the soul and if so how it would affect our understanding of the human.

Science in his day was fighting for its authority but now it has become the high priest of our generation with its mathematics, physics and biology, so perhaps it can weigh the soul. Dr. Duncan MacDougall used a balance to weigh the departing soul believing that it must possess the attributes of a material substance. He placed the body of a dying man on platform scales and in the last seconds noted a change of weight as if something had left the body. Other experiments with dying people and dogs showed a weight loss in the human but not to the annoyance of dog lovers in them! He did not publish his work for many years until forced by ridicule and press misunderstanding.[1]

The criticism was justified for the soul is a spiritual not a physical entity and in any case current science states that weight itself is a problem. But MacDougall was not alone in his attempts for Leonardo da Vinci looked for the physical location of the soul and Descartes placed it in the pineal gland.

CHARLES DARWIN (1809–1882)

It was Darwin who set the cat among the pigeons. He was born in 1809 and had the opportunity of first hand research when he sailed on the Beagle in 1831. His account of the voyage, from 1831 to 1836, was based on keen observation, attention to detail, and candid assessment of the people he met. *The Journal* also reveals his attitude to Christianity and the missionaries. Asked by some people near Santiago why he had entered their church he said that he was a sort of Christian and in New Zealand he commended the missionaries for their work in changing the attitude and lifestyle of the natives. Many of the men that he met in various parts of his travels were barbaric being in the lowest and most savage state and he sees the distinction between savage and civilized man like a wild and tame animal.

Darwin says that the introduction of Christianity meant improvement thoughout the South Seas. In particular he was impressed with the Tahitians who under the guidance of the missionaries had abolished alcohol from their country and were the kindest and most hospitable people he had met. He admits that someone who is shipwrecked on an unknown coast would do well to pray, "that the lesson of the missionary may have extended thus far." But he also commented on the goodness of the many people he had met who were ready to offer him the most disinterested assistance.[2]

A sort of mystical feeling takes possession of him as he gazes at the mountains, and the great silence and solitude they offer, and writes of the sublimity of the primeval forests that are "temples filled with the varied productions of the God of Nature. No one can stand in these solitudes unmoved and not feel that there is more in man than the mere breath of his body." Was he thinking of the soul when he used the word "breath"? Again he stated: "There is grandeur in this view of life, with its several powers, having been originally breathed by the Creator into a few forms or into one; and that, whilst this planet has gone cycling on according to the fixed law of gravity, from so simple a beginning endless forms most beautiful and most wonderful have been, and are being evolved."[3]

The words "by the Creator" were in the second and subsequent editions of the *Origin of the Species* (1859) but later he regretted using the term saying that he had "truckled to public opinion" and that he really meant "appeared" by some wholly unknown process. Yet he did nothing to change his compromise in the three editions of the *Origin* that appeared after 1863, that is in 1866, 1869, and 1872.[4]

In the *Origin* he concluded that everything had developed slowly and that natural selection was the driving force of evolution. He opposed the idea of God constructing everything directly, but in 1879 he denied being an atheist, preferring to be known as an agnostic. Disbelief in Christianity, as he said, came slowly but was at last complete.

Variation and Species

Darwin devoted the first two chapters of the *Origin* to variation under domestication and under nature. Variation in plants and animals do occur, but how? He approaches the subject cautiously recognizing that the laws of heredity are quite unknown with regard to animals and whether they have descended from one or several species. He inclines to the latter view but confesses that the matter is vague. The important thing is that selection leads to modification and change and acts on variations.[5]

In chapter 2 he tries to define a species that he thinks contains the unknown element of a distinct act of creation and with variation there is community of descent. But among naturalists there was a difference of opinion and he thinks that a well-marked variety may be called an incipient or initial species. He believes that the term species is given to a set of individuals closely resembling each other and does not essentially differ from the term variety that is given to less distinct forms. But if the variety is great there is the raising of the form to a species.[6]

One definition of a species is that it is a group of actual or potentially interbreeding populations that are reproductively isolated from other such groups. Darwin's finches are an example but another would be the squirrels in the Grand Canyon. They live on opposite sides of the Canyon, having divided as the great chasm developed. Following their own evolution they are now quite different and unable to interbreed. Different environments cause populations to diverge, but species can become more alike so we can conclude that there is also convergent evolution.

NATURAL SELECTION

Favorable variations will enable an organism to survive in the struggle for life and these advantages will be inherited by the offspring. He uses the expression struggle for life in a metaphorical way, including dependence of one individual on another and success in having progeny. Such a struggle is necessary, otherwise as T. R. Malthus in his *Essay on Population* (1798) pointed out if there were no checks on populations the world would not hold them. The struggle that we see going on is due to the hazards of nature that selects those best fitted to survive.

The struggle is most severe between species of the same genus when they come into competition. Such a struggle between allied species means that intermediate forms or missing links between species are quickly eliminated because they lack the advantage of the two closely allied species. He also contends that the nonexistence of intermediate forms is due to the imperfection of the geological record.[7] Optimistically he believes that links will be found. Natural selection is much more powerful than what the human can do for it preserves favorable variations and rejects the injurious. Why is this? The reason is that nature has the stamp of a far higher workmanship than man. Who did this stamping? Would we not say, the Creator? He does not commit himself.[8]

He deals with sexual selection, reproduction, and does not reject Lamarckian acquired characteristics. Isolation with its checks on immigration and competition will help in the production of new species especially if it is a great open area with a large number of the same species. But natural selection is slow, requiring millions of years. He denies that nature ever takes "leaps."

Divergence of character is important since the more diversified the descendants from any one species become in structure, constitutions and habits, the more likely it is their numbers will increase. Those that diversify the most are less likely to be eliminated. Species are not fixed but become gradually modified, no change will lead to extinction. Unfavorable conditions can cause it and those that survive do so by having some advantage. Yet he does admit that species of the same genus have a common parent and retained their form for long periods.[9]

The change in species remains a difficulty as B. S. Beckett points out: "It is easy enough to argue that one species may have evolved from another by a number of small changes but it is another matter altogether trying to prove that this is so. Such proof may never be available,"[10] hence we continue to speak of a theory or theories of evolution and natural selection. It is necessary also to remember that artificial selection has not yet produced an entirely new species.

Darwin investigates the laws of variation and denies that they occur by chance. It really means that we are ignorant of the cause of a variation but it is probably due to the reproductive system and changes in the conditions of life. He notes that our ignorance of the laws of variation is profound.[11]

When we see a remarkable development of any part of an organism that gives it an advantage in the struggle of life, it is liable to variation but why should this be? There is no explanation in believing that species have been independently created, he says, but if we accept that groups of species have descended from other species and have been modifed through natural selection we can make progress.[12]

At this point he tries to deal with difficulties in his theory. One that disturbed him greatly was the production of the eye. How could such a complex instrument have been produced by gradual modifications preserved by natural selection? Here he is confronted by natural theology and in particular William Paley who asserted that one could prove design in nature from the example of the eye alone. Darwin meets the objection by showing that in the early stages of its evolution rudimentary forms of the eye could have conferred an advantage in the struggle for existence. Yet he has doubts for he says in his transmutations notebooks, "we may never be able to trace the steps by which the organisation of the eye passed from simpler stage to more perfect preserving its relations—the wonderful power of adaptation given to organisation—this really perhaps is greatest difficulty to the whole theory."[13]

The eye is very complex. How could such a structure have been evolved by chance? It consists of many interrelated parts most of which are useless without the others. For any one of these parts to have survival value they must have appeared at the same time as other related parts. Useful mutations that are rare must have occurred simultaneously and some critics consider that it is inconceivable.[14]

He admits that anyone who concentrates on the difficulties of his theory will reject it. These are the problems of accounting for complex organs and instincts, the alleged fixity of species grounded on the sterility of hybrids, and the gaps in the fossil record of the modification of species.[15] He devotes three chapters to them and subsequent work has confirmed the success of his response.

Natural selection, he said, did not act for the good of another species and structures have not been created for the display of beauty. The difficulty here is that we see many things that are beautiful and he is not convincing with his example of the ants and how the aphides, small sap-sucking insects that voluntarily yield their sweet excretion to them. He can only say that probably the aphides do it for their own convenience. It is not by logical deduction but imagination that leads him to say that instincts are guided by the principle: let the strongest live and the weakest die.[16]

Darwin though accused of it did not say in the *Origin* that humanity was descended from the apes. Indeed he hardly mentions them. There was a common ancestor so it is more accurate to speak of cousins. But it was more sensational to say that he did see our descent from the monkeys and the implication gave popular newspapers a field day. It was only with *The Descent of*

Man (1871) and *The Expressions of the Emotions in Man and Animals* (1872) that Darwin investigated the possibility.

He believed that instead of the independent creation of species the Creator had impressed laws on matter so that the production and extinction of the past and present inhabitants of the world should be due to secondary causes like those determining the birth and death of the individual. Since we have said that God normally uses the natural instead of direct intervention there seems to be little difficulty with it.

He had problems, however, with inward changes since he did not know about genes and struggled to understand how character was modified. The struggle is for food and mates, involving the individual rather than the group. Darwin argued that in sexual selection the strong get the females who are beautiful and desirable. He believed that we were a superior species and mounted the doubtful argument that the struggle for existence brought out the good in us. The wonderful universe did convince him that it could not be the result of brute force so he was inclined to look at everything as resulting from designed laws with the details, whether good or bad, left to the working out of what we may call chance.

He said that Asa Gray's (1819–1875) teleology pleased him greatly and as a youth he accepted the whole of Christianity literally including the earlier chapters of Genesis. But his commitment eventually was to deism rather than theism accepting an Unmoved Mover (Aristotle) who works through unbroken laws rather than an intervening divinity. God planned everything beforehand and watched it all unfurl as He intended. Evolution would confirm rather than refute God.

After the *Origin* there was an uneasy compromise between those who thought the higher faculties of mind, soul and morality had been specially created by God and those who believed that they had developed naturally. Darwin continued to stress natural laws and did not see any necessity for divine intervention in evolution. He was not happy about the situation and decided to write *The Descent of Man* and *Selection in Relation to Sex* (1871) and *The Expressions of the Emotions in Man and Animals* (1872).

The *Descent* had to struggle with the belief that ape ancestry was incompatible with an immortal soul. It stressed sexual selection as well as natural. He admits the limitations of the natural or the survival of the fittest for he had not considered properly in the *Origin* structures that are neither beneficial nor injurious.[17] He admits too that the difference in mental power between the highest ape and lowest savage is immense though they have many emotions in common.

There is no evidence that man had an innate belief in God because races exist who have no such ideas, but he acknowledges that a belief in the Creator and ruler of the universe has been held by some of the highest intellects who ever existed. It is also admitted that less civilised races believed in unseen or spiritual agencies because the soul of man in imagination and dreams conceived it.[18]

One of the great differences between the human and the animal is the moral sense or conscience. We have an "ought," a sense of duty, which holds up "the naked law in the soul" and demands sacrifice for others and devotion. Even if the animals had rudimentary forms of it they would not acquire the same moral sense as ours. But there is a kind of sympathy among animals that reflects some moral sense for they care for one another.[19]

The dog (Darwin was very fond of his) is obedient and sympathetic to the needs of the master and could be credited with having a conscience. Altruism shows itelf in sacrifices for kin but rarely for strangers unless they were comrades. We cannot credit animals with morality since unlike man they are unable to compare past and future action and the approving or disapproving of them. Conscience is not innate but acquired like the moral sense from the social. While he does not deal with the soul he assumes that we have one by various references: "the soul-shaking feeling of remorse" and the Hindu "stirred to the bottom of his soul" and so on.[20] There is an immense difference between the mind of the lowest man and that of the highest animal but it is one of degree not kind. The golden rule "As you would that men should do to you, do you to them likewise" lies at the foundation of morality. In brief he is arguing that both mental and moral faculties have evolved and tribes that have the moral qualities strengthen their communities and enable them to overcome others.[21]

Darwin spends a lot of time on sexual selection comparing it with natural selection and showing the different attitudes of male and female to sex. He concludes that man has developed from an ape-like creature that had a highly organized form and possessed language, a large brain, and was moral. He admits that the belief in an all seeing Deity had a potent influence on the advance of morality[22] and asserts that man has an immortal soul but says it is difficult to determine when the belief arose.[23]

The Expressions were written in the context of the "gorilla wars" sparked off by the *Descent*. Thomas Huxley (1825–1895) and Richard Owen (1804–1892) debated the uniqueness or otherwise of the human. Darwin challenged the belief that our higher faculties such as mind and morality distinguished us from the animals. Science he argued had laws and they could not be compromised, they were the tools to explain what was going on in nature. God could have designed such laws and would not need to interfere with them. He wrote: "Of course it is open to everyone to believe that man appeared by a separate miracle though I do not see the necessity or probability."[24] Thus he maintained both in the *Descent* and *Expressions* that the human had qualities that the animals did not possess, the difference was one of degree not kind.

He saw religion developing from animism (spirits in nature), polytheism (many gods), and then to monotheism (one God).[25] In the *Descent* sexual selection based on a sense of beauty played a part in developing the higher faculties and natural selection favored cooperation and community over individualism. He investigated our expressions and showed that they also appeared in animals. The exception is that the human blushes but the animal does not![26] It is possible to draw from the expression that it reflects awareness of right and wrong implying conscience. We attempt to cover the face to hide from others blushing. With regard to the soul Darwin made no attempt to explain it since he thought it was one of the hardest problems and better left for others to deal with![27]

ALFRED WALLACE

As is well known Darwin was compelled to publish because Alfred Wallace (1823–1913) had come up with the same theory. But though agreeing with Darwin he had unorthodox beliefs concerning spiritualism and socialism. Wallace thought that humans because they had special minds had a new and distinct order of being. He followed Richard Owen in believing that man's brain was unique and the seat of a rational and responsible soul that was not evolved. He appealed to T. H. Huxley who replied that science investigated natural subjects and the spiritual was not one of them. Wallace, however, went on to study spiritualism that he saw as manifesting the spiritual and contended that being scientific meant considering all phenomena even those that were considered impossible.

Darwin was impressed with the encyclopaedic knowledge of Wallace and admitted that he was terrified and distrusted himself. They did not disagree about natural selection but how much it could explain. Wallace was posing questions about the mind that Darwin feared would lead to the murder of their child that is evolution. It is interesting to note that the point made by Wallace is still debated: Does the mind evolve by natural selection?[28]

Wallace held that primitive people not only possessed mental capacities far in excess of their survival requirements but had physical features that were useless except in a civilized state. These had all evolved prospectively long before they were needed, which showed intelligent foresight and natural selection being blind could not have been the cause hence he invoked a supernatural power to guide evolution.[29] They had language, which is a distinctive human characteristic and differs vastly from animal signs and natural selection could not account for artistic, ethical, or musical capacities.

Wallace was pessimistic about the moral progress of humanity and Huxley agreed that ethical standards could not be derived from the struggle in evolution. Our concern for the weak repudiates the gladiatorial theory of existence. Science had no objections to a theology that insisted that God had set the process going but it led to deism, something, as we have said, to which Darwin inclined. Revd. Charles Kingsley then put forward an idea that has been embraced by scientists and theologians in our day namely that God could have created animal forms capable of self-development rather than divine intervention to create distinct species. Darwin was so pleased with the idea that he included it in the preface to the second edition of the *Origin*.[30]

What was difficult for Darwin to counter was Wallace's belief in the natural equality of savage and civilized people. Wallace joined the Society for Psychical Research which did not prevent him being proposed for a Fellowship of the Royal Society in 1893. For Wallace the appearance of man was a fundamental change making a difference not only in degree but in kind from what went before: "My view...is that there is a difference in kind, intellectually and morally, between man and other animals; and that while his body was undoubtedly developed by the continuous modification of some ancestral animal form, some different agency, analogous to that which first produced organic life, and then originated consciousness, came into play in order to develop the higher intellectual and spiritual nature of man."[31] He did not believe that mankind had come into being through some random event. There was a Mind guiding the process.

Some writers today follow Wallace contending that what has evolved is qualitatively different from its origination in matter. Humans have an inner life of sensation, thought, purpose, desire and beliefs, the mental aspect, which is caused partly by the brain. But the mental can cause the brain to act and there is an interaction. While natural selection could enable us to understand a lot it was unable to explain human consciousness or how man felt in his soul.

The contrast between the two men is quite startling showing that there can be different opinions concerning the same subject. Perhaps the weakness of Darwin is shown in the comment that his wife made about him. She was a Christian and was perturbed that he was not considering Christianity carefully because his mind was directed by science. She wrote: "It seems to me also that the line of your pursuits may have led you to view chiefly the difficulties on one side and that you have not had time to consider and study the chain of difficulties on the other…May not the habit in scientific pursuits of believing nothing till all is proved influence your mind too much in other things which cannot be proved in the same way and which if true are likely to be above our comprehension?"[32]

Darwin did admit that he gradually lost interest in music and poetry since he did not attend to them. He does deal with use and disuse in the *Origin* but he may be an example of "what you do not use you lose" and it could be applied to the neglect of the practice of Christianity.

Darwin's theory emerged in a century of religious doubt with the publication of *Essays and Reviews* (1860) which repudiated traditional doctrines and challenged literal interpretation of Genesis. It also denied a Designer God. Together with the Free Thinkers and secularisation, the atmosphere was conducive to scepticism. But it is unlikely that Darwin would have extended his theory to accepting Social Darwinism or agreed that the class war propounded by Marx (he refused Marx's request to have *Das Kapital* dedicated to him) and Engels had a relation to his biological theory. War they said was a biological necessity and only the fittest could survive. Two world wars and its continuance in our time in various parts of the world have dampened enthusiasm for the theory in other than biological contexts. And it opposed Darwin's view that sympathy and co-operation had survival value for communities.[33] We are called upon not only to be human but humane.

CONCLUSION

Darwin did not kill the soul but probably would have contended that it had evolved. Others continued to believe that it was given directly by God at some stage in the development of the human. He seemed to think that the soul has the faculties of conscience and moral sense.

At one time Darwin appeared to accept that God was behind all things and if this is so then the theist can accept natural evolution. A contrast is that Darwin stressed natural selection but some of the religions we have considered believe in divine selection commonly called predestination. Natural selection works on an organism that has some advantage but divine selection aids those with no advantage. Huxley the great supporter of Darwin was not happy about natural selection with its implications of favoring the strong and neglecting the weak.

In the next chapters we will consider those who follow Darwin today and arrive at a more materialistic outlook.

CHAPTER 11

AFTER DARWIN

In this chapter and the next we consider how Darwin's work could lead to reductionism and materialism.

With regard to the development of new species it is held that it results from "reproductive isolation" and geographic separation of different populations over many years. Mutations and genetic divergence help the adaptation to the environment and result in speciation. These are random events, difficult to predict and not always helpful but evolution depends upon them.

Their opponents or theists deny the random nature of the process arguing that it shows evidence of design for it is difficult to maintain that every link in the chain of evolution is the result of mutation and natural selection. A single instance where evolution was shown to be driven by some other means would undermine the whole edifice. But it is impossible to identify since there is such a long period of time. Karl Popper goes as far as to say that the Darwinian theory is a metaphysical program rather than, in a strict sense, a scientific one.[1]

DESIGN

The teleologist believes that an organism exists because it was made for the conditions in which it is found but the Darwinian thinks that an organism exists because, out of many of its kind, it is the only one that has been able to persist in the conditions.

It was the belief of Huxley who stressed function not form, but slow development has its problems since so much can go wrong. These slow steps need integration if complexity is to be reached and it points to some kind of organization.

Today the theist argues that evolution is the way in which God achieves His design but Peter Atkins and Richard Dawkins contend that a Designer is not needed since random changes can lead to order and complex systems can be self-arranging. In response, some point to patterns in nature that are everywhere and God is the whole of the pattern.

Michael Ruse argues that too much has been made of natural selection as an alternative to design and attention should be paid to function. It is what a thing does that is important, not what it is or its nature. But there are values because ends are desired. When speaking of design we use a metaphor which means that you take an idea from one field and apply it to another: to regard the heart as a pump is to think of it in a new way. We take note of ends when we consider features possessed by organisms that help in the struggle to survive.

With Darwin something is of value because it helps survival and reproduction but these are the reasons why they exist. It is a cyclical situation where the first leads to the second and then back to the first.[2]

Evolution depends on chance mutations, copying errors in the genetic code, which are enhanced by chemical and radioactive means. But it is difficult to believe that we are here because of errors! What causes mutants? In general they result in an improvement but require an initial organization. In computer simulations it is the operator who selects the shapes and rules that will give the desired results. Natural selection is very important but we have seen that Darwin while insisting on it admitted that it was not the exclusive means of modification and put forward sexual selection.

Adaptation figures in Darwin's scenario for it is those who can adapt to different circumstances who survive. According to Darwin it did not mean purpose but a response to the environment. The chance variations enabled life to survive in a hostile context so that birds evolved wings that gave them a decisive advantage. He contended that birds did not evolve wings in order to fly, which could be seen as purposive, but by enabling them to fly, the wings were a major contribution to survival.

As he grew older he had doubts about seeing the universe as the result of blind chance and compromised saying that design could apply to the whole process rather than the details. God was the framer of evolutionary laws but he was still worried about making Him responsible for a nature "red in tooth and claw."

Michael Ruse says that the design metaphor reflects values and he accepts them in a relative sense. Since organisms have a distinctive complexity, the design argument is appropriate. There is a forward looking understanding to final goals hence there is more to evolution than unaided selection and blind chance. There must be the creation of souls. He supports a theology of nature as an aid to revelation and faith, and doubts that random mutations can produce adaptations and organized complexity.

The Catholic Church is interested in the debate because of its natural theology. Pope John Paul II was friendly toward science and with the exception of the soul he allowed evolutionary thinking. The Church believes that the soul is incorporated by God forty days after birth, but others think that when the brain reaches a complexity the subsistent form of the soul emerges.

Jacques Monod argued that contingency and chance are alternatives to God and purpose and he uses the illustration of the Monte Carlo casino. But Mary Midgley replies that casinos are not chancy but purposive with human devices producing an arrangement that is never normally found in nature: a calculated disorder that baffles prediction.[3]

The reductionist is not impressed believing that we are the result of a string of accidents beginning with a fortuitous conjunction of molecules in a primeval oceanic soup. These accidents were guided by natural selection of favorable combinations and was due to chance. But an organism functions according to a pattern imposed on the parts: the organs are subservient to the organism; the tissues serve the organs, the cells the tissues, and proteins serve the cells. There are lower and higher levels and we cannot explain the whole in terms of the parts, rather it seems to transcend the parts. The parts of a watch are assembled in a coherent pattern to alert us to the time; thus the watch as a whole is the explanation of its parts rather than the other way round.

But even if nature works in a random way through physicochemical interactions, they have evolved into the pattern of order that God designed. It was He who supplied the starting point for the random interactions in the first place. We might say that we have chance and necessity for all follows the pattern that God has mapped out. Everything in the world is related to something else so that the earth and planets obeying the laws of physics give rise to gravitational forces that sustain the atmosphere without which there would be no life on earth and so on. Evolution is God's way of working.

If we ask why there is a universe, what the ultimate causation is, science cannot answer. Did it happen by chance, necessity, high probability, universality or design? There is no way science can answer these questions. The theological belief is design on the basis of the balances and fine tuning but natural selection with its wasteful effects sees no design. But how can random events have maintained biological adaptation over millions of years in the face of changing conditions? How can chance alone be responsible for the emergence of new and successful structures such as a nervous system, brain and eye? The more intricate and complex a system is the more vulnerable it is to degradation by random changes.

Paul Davies having enumerated these objections points out that "a minor error in copying the blueprint of a bicycle would probably make little difference in the performance of the assembled machine. But even a tiny error in the blueprint of an aircraft or spacecraft might well lead to disaster."[4] How can random gene shuffling be responsible for all our marvelous faculties? Should it not lead to disorder rather than order? Science with its analysis and measurement cannot prove there is no purpose in nature as Jacques Monod conceded.[5]

Davies believes that the order of the universe points to God and when the laws of physics are studied they point to a Designer. The laws of quantum physics, thermodynamics and gravitation interleave each other in a manner that bestows a beautiful harmony and self-consistency. He says that the scientist is concerned with the why questions as well as the how. Why the laws, why can we understand them, why the world is as it is, why did the world come to exist and so on. He says "there is something going on behind it all. The impression of design is overwhelming" but his God is timeless, not personal.[6]

Darwin did not reject an overall plan. He wrote about the extreme difficulty or "rather the impossibility of conceiving this immense and wonderful universe including man with his capacity of looking far backwards and far into futurity, as the result of blind chance or necessity. When thus reflecting I feel compelled to look for a First Cause having an intelligent mind in some degree analogous to that of man; and I deserve to be called a theist. This conclusion was strong in my mind about the time, as far as I remember, when I wrote the Origin of Species."[7]

Yet despite this statement, as time went by, he concentrated on the defects of nature with evolution seen as a blind process and refused to give priority to the beauty of the world, which could have led him to a Designer.

CAUSES

One way of reconciling science and religion is to talk of two different types of causality: Conan Doyle getting tired of Holmes decides to kill him and he does it by Moriarty. Doyle is the primary cause and Moriarty the secondary. God made us and the evolutionary process that brought us into being are theories related to each other in much the same way.

Some scholars use the illustration of a novelist who does not preplan his novel in detail but starts with a setting, characters and theme, and lets the plot work itself out in the writing as he goes along. The theme remains under his control making an overall framework. In the same way God restrains His omnipotence and omniscience to allow the world process to unfold itself but still guides toward its conclusion. The setting had to be right for evolution hence the basic laws of the universe are finely tuned to produce life and govern the action. It does not look like chance.

Evolution and creation complement one another for God operates through natural processes and gives meaning to them.

LIMITATIONS OF SCIENCE

Darwin never gave the impression that science would explain everything but many free thinkers of his time did. W. K. Clifford, professor of mathematics at London University, denied the separate existence of a mind or soul for which immortality might be claimed and contended that morality was due not to any divinely imparted conscience but to the social instincts bred in mankind. Professor J. Tyndall declared to the British Association for the Advancement of Science in 1874 that science would wrestle from theology those domains that once were considered its province namely the mind or soul, the creation of the earth and the origin of life.

These claims appear odd today as science admits its limitations. Science deals with the impersonal and with experiments. Problems are resolved by cause and effect, not by meaning or purpose. There are measurements not values, and concentration is on part of reality not the whole. But how can we judge music, for example, by neural response to vibrations in the air and not deal with our personal experience of it? In short, religion uses a personal explanation whereas science an impersonal one. They complement one another.

Induction is used making a move to the universal from the particular. But the statement "all swans are white" can be invalidated if eventually I find a black one. We must according to Karl Popper proceed by falsification; we can never prove that all swans are white; one can disprove it the first time we see a black. Hence there are no ultimate statements in science for they can at some time be refuted. Einstein offered tests for his theories but Karl Marx did not, nor did Freud. There should be the repeatability of experiments to falsify but we cannot do it with evolution and cosmology.

Popper insists that what we have in science are conjectures but it is doubtful whether falsification alone can distinguish science from nonscience. There is a creativity about genius that puts forward new ideas and they are not the consequence of falsifying previous theories.[8] It was Thomas Kuhn who fastened on this creativity that does not simply grow out of the old. There are paradigm shifts such as the Copernican revolution and the theory of relativity and a departure from normal research under the old order. But Kuhn overdoes it since new paradigms are accepted more willingly than he thought and did Newton not say that he built his ideas on the old?

Einstein admitted that science can only ascertain what is, not what should be, and outside its domain, value judgments of all kinds remain necessary. The scientist continues to have faith in the rational order of the universe and that laws persist in all parts at all times. Does this not point to a Designer especially since theories are simple and elegant and beautiful equations may take precedence over experiment?

GENES

Genes contain information for the design of the organism. Some are turned on and some off as the organism develops in interaction with the environment and the effect is probabilistic rather than deterministic.[9] Genes form the code by which cells and bodies are built and determine our physical characteristics, that is, brown hair, blue eyes and so on. Genetic change occurs because genes do not always make exact copies of themselves, a bit of information is missed out of the genetic code or switched around and mutations occur. They can be good or bad and spread through the population with good mutations resulting in more offspring.

Gregor Mendel worked out that inherited characteristics are transmitted through the generations as distinct and permanent units, some dominant and some recessive. These we call genes. Mendel was experimenting with peas about the same time as Darwin published the Origin and showed that color and texture were transmitted to the next generation in rearranged combinations. Genes control reproduction and are transmitted intact and are not blended.

The study of cellular chromosomes opened up the way to understand the internal chemistry of the genes. The word gene has many definitions but a simple one is a unit composed of DNA forming part of the chromosome by which inherited characteristics are transmitted from the parent to the offspring. Evolution came to be seen as change in the frequency of the genes in populations but it was not until the twentieth century that the genetic code was understood with the identification of the DNA. Genes and mutations were shown to be the reason for variations that diminished the role of natural selection.

DNA

Genetics advanced with its discovery, the chemical constitution of genes, revealing the process by which like begets like. It was shown that nucleic acids includes DNA (Deoxyribonucleic Acid) and RNA (Ribonucleic Acid). They are long chain-like molecules constructed from repeating units, and the bases are of four different kinds. Francis Crick and J. D. Watson in 1953 discovered that the sequence of the four bases form a code of genetic information. It is RNA that regulates the proteins.[10]

The DNA is made of two spirals of atoms, intertwined as a double helix. Its structure showed that genes were sections of the DNA molecule and explained how certain characteristics are transmitted. The DNA during fertilization in the eggs unzips down its double helix length and allows the mixing of genes from male and female and the inheritance of characteristics across generations.

Thus the way was opened up for the creation of a new branch of science: molecular biology. The DNA is self-replicating genetic material and is the carrier of the hereditary information. It is an encoded message. The double helix is like a twisted ladder and with the four kinds of molecule there can be different combinations along, each double helix spelling out the genetic code. The set of information gives instructions to the cells in the body enabling them to develop in certain ways. The genes in the DNA have strands grouped together into large units known as chromosomes and they are arranged in pairs. It is the chromosomes that determine what gender we are: with X for female and Y for male.

The DNA is the basis of genetics, cloning, GM technology, forensic genetics, finger printing, Designer babies and paternity-testing. But critics point out that information from the DNA might fail in providing the right messages for building bodies, mutations might not be right for natural selection to work on, and the environment might not support the life forms. It could happen by chance but more likely if there is a Mind behind it all. The DNA is required for natural selection to operate but where did it come from? It shows signs of both design and purpose. Some say that the DNA comes into existence spontaneously but this is difficult to maintain.

Anthony Flew thinks that what the DNA material has shown is the unbelievable complexity of the arrangements that are needed to produce life. Intelligence must have been involved in getting these diverse elements to work together in a subtle way. It could not have happened by chance.

All life forms have coding and information and the cells are processing replicating systems. How are we to explain the origin of this information and the way the machinery came to exist? A gene is a set of coded instructions that has a meaning but how can such meaningful information emerge from blind molecules?

We cannot be reduced to genes even when we map and sequence them for it gives us the genotype not the phenotype. It does not give us the map of human life. When we speak of genes being selfish or the mutations as mistakes in copying or the battle in nature for survival, we are using metaphors. It reflects the reductionist point of view but the theist sees genes as organic parts of the building up of complex carriers for consciousness. Mutations are vehicles of emergence and of the striving for life in the realization of new values. The reductionist cannot account for the beginning of culture and moral obligation unless as by-products of the process. But how can moral obligations survive in a world where "dog eats dog"?

The Human Genome Project confirms that genes differ from person to person and has advanced our knowledge of the process but it will take many years to know the functions of all genes and even when we do it is debatable that we will understand everything about what it means to be human. What we know is that children inherit not a blending of characteristics of parents but a unique recombination of the genetic determinants transmitted to them by their parents. Changes or mutations in the DNA can affect our bodies and it is on these variations that natural selection works.

SALTATIONS OR JUMPS

Thomas Huxley had already put forward the idea of "jumps in the process of evolution," which was to figure in subsequent discussion. William Bateston (1861–1926) agreed with him regarding these saltations and Stephen J. Gould in our time developed punctuated equilibria. He postulated that new species are created by evolutionary changes that occur in rapid bursts over periods as short as a few thousand years, separated by periods of stability in which there is little further change.[11] The theory states that the reason intermediate stages have not been found is that they do not exist. Species change very little for millions of years and then abruptly give rise to a large jump with no intermediate steps.

Barbara McClintock (1902–1992) stressed the idea of "jumping genes" based on her study of mutant genes in maize. She insisted that the function of some genes is to control other genes and that some are able to move on the chromosome. Following her work it was proved that pieces of bacterial DNA do indeed "jump" on the chromosomes. Jumps could produce adaptations and they could be seen as the products of God.

The slow and gradual that Darwin insisted upon does not fit easily with the uneveness of the fossil record. Stability is interrupted by rapid change. There is the admission of jumps in his letter to Hooker dated April 12, 1859: "I would advise you to be cautious about stating so broadly (I thought that you perhaps knew of distinct cases unknown to me) about species not varying for many generations and then suddenly varying. To a certain extent I quite believe it that a plant will not vary until after some generations (perhaps a dozen or so) and then will begin to vary possibly suddenly, more likely gradually . . ."[12]

ANIMALS

Is there a distinct difference between human beings and the animals as Wallace believed? The Victorians not only agreed with him but were also horrified by the thought that we were related to them!

Now we know that the apes are our cousins and have genes in common with us. We differ from the higher apes by about 2 per cent but if much of the DNA is junk, the difference is very important. A minor alteration or error in a single gene can cause serious disability or death. It is the interaction between genes that gives us the various qualities.

With humans there is a progressive increase in brain size leading to intelligence, inventiveness, and upright gait conferring speed and mobility. There is a consciousness that has the power of abstract thought, awareness of self and of a future, communication in making and using tools, ethics, social and family relationships. Homo sapiens developed three hundred thousand years ago with language, artistic ability and spirituality.

We do not descend directly from chimps or orangutans as we mentioned, but share a common ancestry. Much effort has been expended in finding "this missing link" between humans and the animals. Mary Leakey searched for hominids in East Africa and in 1959 found a skull that was a possible ancestor of man—a species of Australopithecus.[13] Marie Dubois had already in 1891 discovered fragments of homo erectus or Java man who walked upright and Otto Zdansky found examples of homo erectus near Peking in 1926. Despite disputes about these findings it is now accepted that the human family originated in Africa from ape-like ancestors. "Lucy," a female hominid, was discovered in Ethiopia in 1974.

Chimps can operate simple tools such as sticks, pass on their skills, and show the emotions of compassion, altruism, rage and brutality. Darwin showed it in *The Expressions of the Emotions in Man and Animals* (1890). They kiss, embrace, pat one another, tickle, laugh, swagger and beg. But when we learned to stand upright we had hands free to do other things and our brain was much bigger. Chimps cannot tie shoe laces for their thumbs are not mobile. We buried dead bodies and there was a belief in spirits and language was a great asset enabling us to teach simple skills more quickly and communicate ideas.

Chimps have photographic memories and do better than humans in some memory games. In a test to locate the position of numbers on a screen, six chimps were pitted against a group of university students. The chimps had been trained to recognize the numbers from one to nine and place them in sequence. The numbers were flashed on a screen and then covered in white squares. The chimps were faster at pointing out what numbers had been and where. A chimp called Vashoe used signs and knew their connection with objects. Others in the group, Sarah and Lana, were more advanced with Sarah understanding signs and Lana could communicate by pressing keys on the computer. Further experiments showed that chimps are like five-year-old children in being able to understand words and stories.[14]

But only the human has the brain that is capable of understanding how we came to be here and could rebel against the process. Without it we would not have survived. Darwin admitted that we were unique in asking questions about the world, develop concept formation, have complicated social relations and exhibit a sophistication that animals do not possess. Our symbolic language can transmit advanced information and we have abstract thought, creativity, morality and religion. Why do we engage in religion and the animals do not? Do we have something innate such as an inner spiritual light, conscience or moral sense or soul?

Darwin in his notebooks describes the faculties of the soul that includes the moral sense and conscience. He thinks that these develop early in life and evolve, not being planted in us by God. The moral sense is the greatest good and society would not make progress without it. He thinks that morality evolved because it had survival value.[15]

In the *Descent of Man* Darwin developed an argument for the view that conscious intelligent behavior "for the good of the community" was a natural product of evolution.[16] As we mentioned in the last chapter, he refers to man as "god-like because of his noble qualities with sympathy which feels for the most debased and with benevolence that extends not only to other men but the humblest living creature. His god-like intellect has penetrated into the movements and constitution of the solar system. Man has exalted powers even though he still bears in his bodily frame the indelible stamp of his lowly origin."[17]

There is also the question raised by Wallace. Why did the human have a brain that had a far greater capacity than what was needed for survival and showed itself in artistic and creative powers? Wallace postulated latent power or soul in the human that could have been given to him by a higher intelligence, which distinguished him from the animals.

At times Darwin struggled with the problem of religious feeling and described its characteristics: dependence on a superior, reverence, gratitude, hope for the future and said that no one could experience it until advanced in his or her intellectual and moral faculties. As always he wants to find similarity with the animals and sees it in the attitude of his dog who has a deep love for him coupled with submission and fear.[18]

CONCLUSION

We have noted that there is a variety of views about evolution and that problems about the theory are still being raised. But there has been a move from concentration on the essence of something to the consideration of its function. This will be considered in our last chapter.

Contrast with the animals shows that we have something innate that is spiritual and strives to realize values. Is the distinction between us and them one of degree or kind? Darwin held the former and Wallace the latter. However, it can be maintained that the degree is so great that it could amount to a distinction in kind.

In the next chapter we continue to consider how evolution can lead to materialism with the effect of denying the soul.

CHAPTER 12

THE DARWINIANS

The theory of evolution is about as much open to doubt as the theory that the earth goes round the sun...

Richard Dawkins

In this chapter we focus on Richard Dawkins, who is a prominent opponent of religion before going on to note continued problems with the theory of evolution. We also discuss among other things what science says about life after death.

Richard Dawkins coins the word "meme" for a cultural unit of replication that propagates itself from body to body by sperm or eggs leaping from brain to brain. Memes are like songs and recipes passed between individuals and across generations. The word is derived from the Greek mimeme meaning likeness and like a gene it can mutate through accidental miscommunication or learning errors but need not have any direct genetic basis. It is not an adequate measure of cultural evolution that depends not only on imitation but also reason and synthesis.

It is now contended that cultural evolution is more important than evolutionary in shaping human behavior. Margaret Mead (1901–1978) was a pioneer in showing this and reasoned that such behavior was alterable in favorable circumstances.[1] Culture becomes the way to transmit the past and conscious choice alters the future. Moral norms come from culture that includes religion and was not necessary for the survival of the species. But if morality was not necessary how did it emerge in the culture of a people? You cannot get an "ought" from an "is." It is we who change our environment to reflect our values, choose what we will do, what we will believe, and science, art and religion are the result.

A PROMINENT REDUCTIONIST

Natural selection will promote genes that are selfish favoring their own survival at the expense of alternative competing ones. Why then do organisms at times risk their own lives? In response, Richard Dawkins, the most prominent reductionist in the UK, speaks of altruism related to kinship. It happens because of gene sharing. Someone jumps into a river to save his son but would hesitate to do this, especially if it was dangerous, for a person who was not related to him. If the rescuer knows that he is related, then by saving him he is perpetuating his own genes. He may think that even if he dies in the attempt it is worthwhile.

It is doubtful, however, that most of us think of genes; we make sacrifices because of love and compassion and it extends beyond our kith and kin. A father can put his life in jeopardy for an adopted son and there are many cases of people risking their lives for those they do not know. The parable of the Good Samaritan is about a man who risked his life for the injured traveler on that dangerous road to Jericho. He could have been attacked by the robbers still close at hand (Lk 10.30–37).

Huxley argued for social groups rather than individuals as the units of evolution but Dawkins maintains that the gene is the unit of survival. Natural selection requires that variation be transmitted to the following generation but at what level does it take place: at the level of genes, individual organisms, kin or groups? The group suggestion supports altruism: similar genes of relatives will be protected by the sacrifice of their kin.

Religion teaches that we are selfish and can agree with Dawkins' belief in selfish genes. Indeed he records that clergymen wrote to him saying that he had established the doctrine of original sin! But genes are physical and the doctrine is referring to the spiritual death that separates us from God. Still we can rebel against genes not only by our own choices and strength of character but dependence on the power of God. It is anthropomorphic to speak of selfish genes for it is the organisms that are selfish.

Religion is a virus according to Dawkins, a meme or a unit of cultural inheritance acted upon by natural selection. It spreads but is not critically questioned. It is agreed that we learn about religion from parents, church, school, friends and it can be viewed as indoctrination but it is not necessarily so. If it was we would expect more religious people! If we can rise above our genes, why not also our culture?

Often reformers in religion reacted against the values of their society. We adapt to our environment but make protests about it and we can change nature for the good or the bad. Religion has contributed to the solidarity of the tribe and the preserving of the social order but not simply following its values for it has brought about change. The gene then could be the unit of selection but it is the phenotype that is the physical manifestation of the organism. The genes have the instructions but the phenotype is the product.

Dawkins contends that we are simply survival machines. Unlike most biologists he has launched an evangelical crusade against religion in his books and TV appearances. Yet since natural selection confers an advantage not wastage he admits that religion must have functioned in this way; otherwise it would not have survived. He thinks that religious ideas have been maintained because they were compatible with other memes but this was hardly likely since there have been many persecuted religious movements. Strangely, when he speaks of design in religion, he selects Scientology and Mormonism as intelligently designed!

His attack on religion is in his book *The God Delusion*. Just in case we had any doubt about it, the publishers state that the book is nonfictional! For him natural selection does it all, there is no need for supernatural agents and chance is the slow power of accumulation. To postulate a Designer only raises the point who designed Him but he does admit that there may be something in nature that eludes the scientist.

Morality predated religion, and is a by-product of something else. It does not have its roots in religion. Morals based on the Bible are weird. How are we to know what to take symbolically or literally in the story of Noah? How can we think that earthquakes are punishments of God instead of shifts in techtonic plates? He omits to say that generally religious people would accept the latter and not the former.

He selects problematic stories from the Hebrew scripture that reflect badly on persons like Lot and Abraham, pointing out that we pick and choose the scripture that suits our point of view. He does it himself with a deliberate omission of the great ethics of the Hebrew prophets who stressed justice and the mercy of God. But his point is that we must have some moral criteria for rejecting some scripture and accepting other parts. It raises again the question discussed by Darwin of the moral sense and where we got it. It is a development he thinks arising from a more civilised environment. But the argument does not hold since modern civilisation often shows man's inhumanity to man.

He allows some progression in the understanding of God, citing Jesus as an example. He was a great ethical innovator and the Sermon on the Mount shows that he was ahead of his time. But he does not ask how the sermon looks in the light of natural selection! Religion divides and causes all kinds of harm though some good principles can be found in holy books. He tries to justify atheists, which is difficult when he is dealing with Stalin and Hitler, and then attacks the Nobel Peace Prize winner, Mother Teresa of Calcutta, for opposing abortion.

He estimates that knowledge of the Bible is poor but how can this be if pupils are indoctrinated at school as he says? The influence of the Bible is still with him for he is able to quote many of its verses, which have entered into our common speech. He thinks that ignorance of it would impoverish the appreciation of English literature and should not be dropped from the curriculum. He does not believe in prayer but in the power of science to open the mind and satisfy the psyche that is the soul. Having dismissed the mysteries of religion he accepts the mysteries of quantum mechanics.

Dawkins is aware that science needs to take notice of morality for evolution wedded to genetics has posed problems for ethics by germline engineering, therapy and cloning. These call for ethical and religious judgments since they concern not only where we came from but who we are and what we might become. But he and others think that morality can be reduced to biology, which provides us with a set of moral behavior patterns useful for survival. But this is proceeding on the basis that you think you know what a thing is by its source or its development. It is the genetic fallacy.[2]

Returning to Kenya where he was born he discusses evolution with a bishop and enters a new museum that holds a lot of fossils. He does so with an air of awe resembling the feeling of a religious person entering church. When he lifts the first edition of the Origin of the Species he does it with a reverence that the believer has for the Bible but does not mention that in subsequent editions Darwin included a creator.

Dawkins still seems to be worried about how he views altruism since he has a feeling that there is more to it. How can he explain the feeling he has when he sees a stranger weeping? What drives him to comfort such a person? He sees that he is rising above his origins and that he must tame the natural selection that insists on competition and struggle, but how since he refuses the grace of God?[3]

GAPS IN THE THEORY OF EVOLUTION

It has been impossible to discover how life originated because we cannot replicate the conditions that existed 3.8–3.5 billion years ago. Nor did Darwin know about self-organization that we now realize plays a part together with natural selection. Again, we do not know what the last ancestor of humans and chimpanzees looked like, where and how it lived, and what processes sent us down our separate evolutionary path.[4] When Dawkins was asked why there was lack of definite fossil evidence he replied that we have been looking for it in the wrong place!

Another factor is that doubt has been thrown on Darwin's tree of life that he uses extensively in the Origin to explain the evolutionary relationships between different species. The tree with its branching structure shows how one species can evolve into many and was as important to him as natural selection. Each branch represents a single species and branching points are where one species becomes two.[5]

The criticism is that we have no evidence that it corresponds to reality. Proof of the tree rested on showing that the more closely related two species were the more alike their DNA, RNA and protein sequences ought to be. Darwin had assumed that descent was exclusively vertical with organisms passing traits down to their offspring. But it was discovered that species swapped genetic material with other species or hybridized with them so the neat branching pattern degenerated into interrelatedness with species being closely related in some respects but not others. Hence we have HGT, the horizontal gene transfer, which could be a major player.

Amid all the controversy it emerges that the tree is no longer an adequate description of how evolution in general works. One reaction is that the theory of evolution is not wrong but more complex than we thought but another one is that the tree concept is now buried.

DID RELIGION PLAY A PART IN EVOLUTION?

Michael Brooks points out that scientists nowadays have suggested that religion is an evolutionary adaptation that makes us more likely to survive and pass on our genes. It enabled our ancestors to form tightly knit groups that through cooperation competed successfully with other groups. Others doubt this and trace its origin to our brains being wired for it. The debate will not be settled easily though some think we can have both explanations.[6]

We do have a predisposition to believe, which is confirmed by the survey that 84 per cent of the people in the world believe in a supernatural force of some kind and in the existence of the soul. Even agnostics and atheists are prone to supernatural thinking, attributing purpose to significant moments in their lives as if someone was intervening to make it happen.[7] Such belief often arises when disasters strike.

MIND AND BRAIN

There must have been a point in evolutionary development when self-consciousness emerged. It would require a brain that consists of electrical currents and chemical changes unlike the mind or soul that has thoughts and feelings. It seems likely that primitive animals possessed feelings and learned to avoid predators, which would cause them pain and death. Thought developed as to the distinction between them and others hence self-awareness. Animals generally are genetically deter mined by their genes but with the human they are more of an influence.

Some emphasise that mind evolved from the brain and our behavior is programed by genes. The brain is a kind of digital computer and hence mechanical. Against this it is argued that we are not like computers being composed of flesh and blood and understand what we are doing. Computers simulate our behavior but simulation is not thinking and we have conscious-ness, reason, free will, and there is the unpredictability of brain events.

It is likely that mind and consciousness being emergent qualities of the brain are a new configuration. Consciousness is not just a brain spin-off with no causal function for we con-struct theories, compose music and use imagination. The mind initiates changes in the tissue of the brain. Mental effort pro-duces new neural states, and meditation in the various religions appears to show a change of brain structure and function that makes possible a new form of consciousness of the self or innate Buddha nature. There is a focus on breathing to get away from the usual thinking so mind is interacting with the brain and not passive.

Consciousness remains a mystery but on the basis of quan-tum mechanics, Roger Penrose thinks that it arises from tube-like structures in the brain cells so consciousness is due to subatomic processes. Drugs can affect these microtubules and cause problems for us but the theory does not deal with how subjective experiences and thought processes arise.

However, the reductionist contends that the brain is an organization of molecules brought about by evolution and our decisions based on free will are really adjusting the atoms in the molecules inside the cells. The soul is a delusion but objectors ask about love, beauty, good and evil, free will, reason, and morality. Can love and meaning be reduced to the level of atoms?

It is impossible to say that the working of the brain is fully explained in terms of synaptic firings of electrochemical processes for it would mean loss of these qualities. They are complementary just as the mechanical operation of a traffic sign complements the meaning. In the physical operations of the universe nature is an advertising sign for the creator. J. B. S. Haldane said, "If my mental processes are determined wholly by the motions of atoms in my brain, I have no reason to suppose that my beliefs are true...and hence I have no reason for supposing my brain to be composed of atoms."[8]

The brain is complex with a hundred billion nerve cells but unlike the mind it has a location in the human body. A surgeon stimulates the brain that causes the conscious experience but he has no means of knowing that this activity is producing a beautiful vision of something in the consciousness of the patient. The physical enables the rise of the nonphysical thoughts, values and purposes, which we possess. But it is unlikely that the basic physical particles that only have such properties as extension, mass, velocity and position can account for the quite different properties of color, smell and touch.

Functionalism seeks to throw light on the problem. In one form the mind simply accompanies bodily events and has no causal effect but in the other there is a causal role for consciousness. The latter is more appropriate for if consciousness has no executive power why has it evolved? A better analogy of brain and consciousness would be this: two dancers always move together but sometimes one takes the lead and sometimes the other. There is correlation without identity.

Another suggestion as we mentioned is that the mind is the pattern in the brain. There are holistic properties in it and what matters is the pattern of neural activity, not the detailed functioning of individual neurons. At this collective level new qualities of self-organization appear that cannot be derived from the laws governing the neural function.[9] Different laws may operate at the higher level of the brain that do not conflict with the lower laws but are additional to them.

The dualist insists that the mind influences the brain and it responds and science cannot disprove the claim. It is as well for if the brain predetermines everything where is the free will to make decisions? What we do know is that we continually make decisions that affect our lives and it is very difficult to convince people that they are predetermined.

HIGHER AND LOWER LEVELS

There is a movement from the simple to the more complex due to emergence and downward causation. A new phenomenon appears that could not be predicted in the study of the parts and requires its own language and terminology to explain it. The higher level laws relating concepts are irreducible to those of the lower levels. Meaning and purpose emerge that describe the function of a machine due to the organization of the parts into a whole. A book is not reduced to the mechanical parts of the computer or the meaning derived from them. In the human is seen the emergence of consciousness which relies on the organization of cells in the brain but cannot be equated with them.

DNA molecules obey the laws of chemistry and physics but do not explain higher level concepts like information transfer or natural selection. Information is meaningless except with reference to the function of the whole cell. There is the emergence of new properties when parts are combined hence the stress on holism. It might be that future work will be able to explain the higher or more complex in terms of the lower and simple but the hope resembles religion, which says that the future will explain its mysteries.

We noted the use of the chariot illustration in Buddhism but only when parts of a chariot are assembled do we know what the use or function is going to be. Similarly, looking at different parts of the brain will not tell us about brain function. Rules, laws, procedures are not part of the structures of things, for example, the laws of chess are not contained in its structure but they, like the laws of the universe, are due to inferences.[10]

It is the whole not the parts of the brain that gives us consciousness. The brain receives and processes information but we are more than information processors having feeling and willing. The religious concept of the soul was more than the intellect for it has the meaning of "living being" in the Genesis account: it is nephesh coming from and belonging to God. Perhaps there is something in the view of Aristotle and Aquinas that the soul was the form or pattern of the body. It is that which actuates a body and has the characteristics of personal identity. Some scientists think that the soul may be the dynamic pattern that provides continuity between this life and the next.

We cannot observe memory, imagination and reflection. When I think of some object I have sensations, perceive certain things and have feelings toward it. The mental is causing the physical, a form of top-down causation. Biological accounts of the brain require the investigation of beliefs, desires and feelings as well as neurons, synapses and serotonin, but the physical sciences cannot handle subjectivism and it is left to psychology and sociology. They have difficulty because the material they are dealing with is unpredictable.

Mind may be the result of evolution but it can stand outside the process and make judgments. It is related to the physical but distinct from it and requires a different type of explanation. Currently a house and flats are being built at our seafront and I often watch the construction as it develops. There are the builders using bricks that are the raw material at the lower level, then there is the architect with his plan, and on the final level there is the town planner whose permission is essential before building begins. It is a top-down scenario. I cannot explain the process by the lower but must take into account the whole especially the higher level.

To change the illustration, the parts of a plane do not have the capacity to fly, it is the way they are organized and their shape, a holistic property. There are patterns of organization within the composition of an entity. All living organisms have goals of survival and reproduction and can modify these goals. Even the simplest organism can sense its environment and alter its behavior so there is self-direction based on information received from the surroundings.[11]

There is also the power of the mind so that Hindus can endure embedded meat hooks in their backs and parade in front of others. Tibetan monks sit meditating overnight in temperatures well below freezing and in addition being repeatedly covered by cold wet blankets though with no ill effects.[12]

The mind appears as a global attribute of the brain and not a local product of any of its parts. It has awareness, insight and creativity and programs the mechanical brain. The study of the brain does not tell us what it is like to be a person but we are persons and more than the material elements of our bodies, something that the religions except Buddhism hold firmly on the basis of soul or mind. William James was a functionalist and treated the mind like other organic faculties, but C. Lloyd Morgan argued that the evolution of organized complexity produced a qualitatively distinct level of being.

Lovelock put forward the holistic idea of Gaia, which means that the earth is a single organism and the properties of the planet could not be predicted from the sum of its parts. The parameters of the environments are finely tuned for us to be here: both the rise of the sea and oxygen content of the earth's atmosphere seem to be controlled; otherwise life would cease. The idea leads some to see the world as God's body, a Mind interacting and controlling the world as we do the body. But the idea resembles paganism with the mother earth whereas God is a Spirit and the heaven of heavens cannot contain Him (1 Kings 8.27). It is a transcendence that is held in tandem with His immanence.[13]

THE SOUL

Is the origin of the soul at birth, conception, the result of evolution or enters sometime after birth? The Catholic Church believes, as we mentioned, that the soul is created by God and does not develop naturally from genetic material. And the theist holds that the soul is the center of consciousness and reason that cannot be reached by scientific analysis.

Keith Ward takes into account the evolution of the soul and uses mind and soul interchangeably. Soul is dependent on the brain but in perceiving and understanding goes beyond it and is an organizing principle of life that interprets and gives a sense of continuity. It is like a compact disc storing information but the disc is a material thing and it must be read by someone. The reader is the soul that works with the brain but directs and coordinates. We are embodied souls with personality and the hope of resurrection is for a new body that will express the true nature of the soul.[14]

Eschatology

There is little agreement over how life started and how it will end. It may have begun in a warm little pool (Darwin imagined this) or out of sight of the sun, in deep rocky fissures as Dawkins surmises.

How will it end? Our universe is running out of hydrogen fuel that is needed to make new stars. Without them there will be no light, heat, energy or life so eventually it will become a cold dark place. The sun is getting warmer at the moment and in a few hundred million years it will be so hot that we will be unable to endure its rays. It is reckoned that by eight hundred million years everything will be dead, with the earth becoming a desert. Hence the need to escape to a more youthful planet, but perhaps recycling will take place with the ashes of the sun and the earth providing the material.[15]

Some scientists such as Freeman Dyson think that we will be eventually exported to other planets and that consciousness could be reproduced in forms detached from flesh and blood. Frank Tipler also speculates saying that the mind is a software program within the hardware of the brain and could be transferred to other hardware. He thinks that immortality will be achieved at what he calls the Omega Point.

Our way of processing information is a close equivalent to the idea of the soul and such information could be the basis of a future life. According to this view the soul is like a complex computer program. But we are more than information processors, and can replicas be the same as we are? Some forms of the scheme oppose biblical eschatology, which means the recreation of humanity.[16]

John Polkinghorne believes that Christian hope is intelligible in a world of science and disagrees with Peacocke who thinks that Christian eschatology is empty speculation. Science argues that the world will collapse or decay but he believes in continuity and discontinuity between this world and the next. The God of love is our hope, which means that realized eschatology is not enough; we need the future oriented element.[17]

John Hick points out that there are various opinions regarding survival: the materialist and humanist rejection, the Western belief in the personality beyond death perhaps as disembodied mind or reconstituted psychophysical being in a heavenly state. Or the Eastern belief in the continual rebirth of the soul until its realization of identity with the eternal spirit. Hick states that different words are used to describe the nonphysical: mind, soul, self or I, person, spirit, ego, consciousness, psyche, the subconscious, the unconscious, the id, the superego, jiva, atman.

The Latin Fathers believed in traducianism, the soul that Adam had was passed down by continual division; thus he sees a parallel with the gene pool flowing down the generations via our parents. But creationism means that each soul is newly created and attached to the fetus between conception and birth. Hick does not think it holds up because of the genetic process, which implies that our characteristics are derived from nature and nurture not something added that forms the core of personality. He thinks we might identify the soul with our moral and religious attitudes that would fit the linga sharira of vedantic teaching and we can add our freedom in making choices.

But he holds that so long as one person freely differs from another in his moral and spiritual attitudes, it will be impossible to disprove the claim that the difference is due to basic dispositions that were either implanted by God at conception or formed in previous lives. Soul is a value word meaning a relation with the creator and hope of eternal life. If we follow the Darwinians it can be maintained that the soul was produced in the same way as the body but the whole process of evolution has God behind it, meaning that both body and soul are a divine creation.[18]

Others insist that any discussion on eschatology needs to take into account what Einstein thought of space and time. They stretch and shrink and time is related to gravity that makes it go more slowly. For the physicist time is not one event after another but something that is there and space is not a finite space but related to time, which means it is not possible to explain eternity in terms of time or heaven in terms of space. At death we leave the world of space and time and in this context how can we explain the world to come in terms of ours?[19]

CONCLUSION

A mystery that still eludes us is consciousness. Is there a possibility that it could continue after the death of the body? Certain things point to survival after death. The mind, for example, may be a pattern in the brain and could continue to exist after we die, and we will, in the next chapter, pursue what near death experiences can tell us and whether or not they point to the possibility of a life after death.

We now consider what we have learned from the study of religions and the views of philosophy and science on the soul.

CHAPTER 13

THE WAY FORWARD

In this chapter we reflect on what philosophy, science, and the religions tell us about the soul and see if we can go forward in our thinking about it.

CAN THE SOUL BE DEFINED?

The soul, psyche, was regarded in Greek thought as the principle of life, a substance, and souls could exist apart from bodies. A substance (ousia) is the essence of something, according to Locke and Kant, and remains the same through change.[1]

Descartes accepted this but had difficulty in explaining the interaction of body and mind/soul. They are inseparable and influence one another. The brain has an impact on moral behavior, personality, recognition of others, and any injury to it can change us. There is a correlation of mind and brain without identification.

Descartes and other dualists saw the soul as breathed into us by God (Gn. 2.7) but if animals have souls then we are not special on that account. Soul means the principle of life. But why is it that man is singled out by receiving the breath of the creator? Some scholars go as far as to say sharing in the attributes of God, but this could lead to a pride that scriptures condemn.

Nowadays one substance or entity is accepted with two aspects, a physical examined by neuroscience and a mental investigated by psychology. Some dualists think that from the physical there emerges a completely new entity of mind or soul. It means, unlike Descartes, that the precedence is given to the physical.

CAN THE SOUL BE DEFINED IN A FUNCTIONAL WAY?

We are known not by what we are but by what we do. The stress is on activity. We cited various aspects of this but from the religious point of view it means a unique role of exercising dominion over and fulfilling stewardship of the creation.

The mind or soul is a functional part of the brain. It is a process like the program run on a computer.[2] The use of process reminds us of Buddhism which insists that we are a changing bundle of characteristics. The software organizes the program and it could be transferred to some other system. Likewise the soul could be transferred to another body in the after life.[3] But someone is needed to operate the machine and the most likely candidate is the soul regarded as a person. It is possible to say that someone displays intellectual abilities without mentioning any nonphysical entity but the question persists: what kind of person has these abilities or capacities? Has she got some essence that shows itself in this way?

CAN THE SOUL BE DEFINED WITHOUT REDUCTIONISM?

A praiseworthy attempt has been made in recent times by a group of thinkers who while accepting reductionism want to go beyond it. Their basic belief is that soul is a functional capacity of the body rather than something spiritual within it. Various positions regarding body and soul are stated. Dualism equates the soul with person, holistic dualism with the whole of the person, but the nonreductive view stressing the functioning of the person gives rise to higher capacities such as morality, spirituality and religious experience. Reductionism is limited since it concentrates on the physical aspect of the person and tries to explain all that we are by science.

Morality is more than a necessity for survival and genes do not determine our nature. There are two aspects of the human, mental and physical, which do not rule out free will. Our higher human capacities distinguish us from the animals and are due to emergence of the higher from the lower. It is admitted that dualism cannot be proved false but spirit and soul do not denote entities within us. They represent the whole person. Soul means the core unity of a person and depends on God for continued existence.[4]

We have spirit bodies, which is preferable to dualism: body or soul or trichotomism of body/soul/spirit or the mental substance of idealism. The spiritual acting on the higher level of the human supervenes on the material. Roger Sperry agrees believing that consciousness is an emergent property of brain activity not reducible to the neural events of which it is mainly composed: there is no conscious awareness in nerve cells or in the molecules or atoms in the brain.[5]

Nonreductive physicalism means that we are able to be addressed by God and heed His calling which distinguishes us from the animals. We can think rationally and carry out experiments into the nature of the universe. The soul was regarded traditionally as the site of religious and moral experience but it is now replaced by God acting through our bodily capacities.

Nancey Murphy contends that interaction with the environment and higher level evaluative processes alter neural structures; hence we are not determined by them and we can resist biological needs, obey reason and choose to act. Downward causation can reshape the neural system hence we are more or less free spirit bodies.[6]

But what of personal identity if there is no soul? How can I be the same person with all the changes involved in getting older and how can I be identified after the resurrection with a very different body? Identity through time was preserved by the dualists with their account of the soul as an entity in its own right. But Murphy concentrates on the body and eventually proposes the same body after death but one that does not require spatio-temporal continuity or the same material constituents.[7]

Memory shall be required as well as awareness. If a resurrected body had my memories, I would know that I am myself but we would also need the same moral character that is the kind of person we want to be. Hence the development of virtue ethics and moral perceptions that are downward evaluative processes, which reshape lower level factors.[8] She believes that a body not tied to a spatiotemporally continuous material object would be of different "stuff" like the resurrection body of Christ.

The soul was introduced to explain our capacities for reason, morality, spirituality and free will but leaving the soul aside or discarding it does not mean losing our higher capacities. She believes that it is personality that survives death.

Two key factors are mentioned: supervenience and the action of God. Murphy argues that mental states are supervenient on brain states. Supervenient means inseparable from the other properties of something. Two objects may be identical except that one is red and blue, one is beautiful and the other not, so beauty and color are supervenient properties. But she admits that there is no proper definition of supervenience and the matter is controversial.

What it means is that when I say someone is good it supervenes on his particular characteristics and would constitute his goodness so mental characteristics would supervene on physical ones. There are two descriptions of something: light switched on is a signal that I am at home but by prearrangement it could be changed to a different message. The message of being at home is supervenient, the light on is subvenient.

It will depend on circumstances which play a crucial role in making a difference between supervenience and identical relation. There is one state of affairs with two descriptions and these can be variable. The circumstances dictate whether there is goodness. St. Francis the monk and R. M. Hare the philosopher could be equally good but the latter did not live like the former because of circumstances.

She then stresses emergence. Higher levels of reality cannot be seen as causal reduction to the biological level. There are emergent levels as we proceed from the neurological to the mental, to the interpersonal, to the political, economic and legal, to the moral and the spiritual.

Warren S. Brown attempts to apply this to the evolutionist versus creationist accounts of human origins and thinks that under certain circumstances the concept of creation supervenes on the explanation of evolution. That life was created would supervene on the claim that life evolved under the circumstance of the evolutionary process. It supervenes on but does not replace evolutionary theory.[9]

Murphy concedes that dualism cannot be proved to be false but neuroscience has confirmed Darwin's views and capacities once attributed to the soul are regarded as functions of the brain though it cannot explain our feelings, emotions and choices. The soul emerges as a property of a person, it is a natural development. Morality, spirituality, religious experience and being related to God point to spirit bodies. The problem of personal identity is solved by arguing that we are persons. To be a person is to have a body and subjectivity and continuity of memory that depends on the brain. Of course, the brain dies so we are dependent on God to resurrect us and give us a new body. She does recognize an embodied self but neglects to mention that the self and the soul were often equated.

Science, she admits, can never prove that there is no soul whose capacities are correlated with brain functions. But those who try to prove the existence of the soul rely on intuition and introspection that are unreliable. This too is controversial since intuition has often led to scientific discovery. How much, for example, did Einstein use his intuition? Her argument too would require greater attention to the mysticism that we have mentioned, which has such an experience of the soul in relation to God. If there is no soul, how is my identity preserved in the after life? She repeats that God can create a new transformed body and provide it with my memories and include the other elements mentioned above.

For her proposal to work, there is a need for divine action at the higher level of the body. But we have the thorny problem of the laws of the universe; can we get past the violation of them? Here she relies on quantum mechanics where the

laws are statistical and could give God more freedom to act.
Despite criticism of this idea I think she has a good point in
making such a choice. But what about the point of contact
between God and us that was traditionally viewed as the soul?
It was seen in Christianity and the other religions that we have
reviewed.

She and her colleagues replace it with the imago Dei. But
what does it mean? There are different views as we noted in
past chapters. Their belief is that it means a personal relationship with God and the neighbor. Sin destroys both divine and
human relationship.[10] But if the doctrine of the Fall is taken
into account, the image is already marred by sin and only by the
grace of God can it be restored. In the light of current developments in science Murphy endorses the need for an entire series
of conferences to study divine action.

I think the discussion, since we live in a global context,
would profit by attending to more religions than Christianity
and Judaism. The soul is a very important concept in Hinduism,
Islam, Sikhism and cannot be set aside or neglected. Even
with Christianity she and her colleagues admit that there are
many conflicting interpretations of the biblical view of the
soul.

But the work attempts to move beyond the reductionism that
understands the organism as a whole playing no role in organizing, directing or influencing its behavior. She is right when
she notes that top-down causation and emergence oppose it recognizing that organisms can have properties that do not exist
within its molecular elements.

CAN WE KNOW THE NATURE OF THE SOUL?

Murphy is influenced by functionalism and we recall that the
form of Aristotle means function and it appeals today because
it is difficult to know the nature of something. Hence concentrate, as Russell Stannard stresses, on what the soul does. The
soul he points out is employed in different ways for mind or
consciousness but he uses mind when referring to mental experiences that are correlated to what is going on in the brain and
spirit for personal relationship to God.

Murphy too speaks of spirit bodies yet spirit can be used ambiguously as when we talk about Einstein being a spiritual man because he had a sense of awe at the immensity of the universe. But he did not believe in a personal God hence there was no personal relation with Him.

Stannard does not want to talk about things as they are in themselves either body/soul or body/mind/spirit but explanatory frameworks. The physical is used when we are dealing with the body in its relation to the world and the mental when making decisions and so on. The spiritual arises when we talk of ourselves as human spirits in relation to God and His purpose for our lives.

He cannot define what the soul is in itself or what God is in Himself just as physicists cannot say what physical entities are in themselves. There is, for example, electric charge but what is it? All we can say is that sometimes the presence of one object alters the motion of another and accounts for it. Objects carry something extra that we call electric charge and these charges exercise forces on each other. The same applies to space, time and mass; they simply tell us about changes of behavior and relationships. It is these that we deal with, not things in themselves. In other words, time is being wasted trying to define whether mental experiences are the same as brain processes, when we have defined neither.

God's essence is not known; we can only know the ways He chooses to reveal Himself, that is, the way he relates through His energies. Our spirit in itself is unknowable and we are unable to understand whether the mind and the spirit are the same thing. It is impossible to know the nature of things but whether they are the same things or not we switch from one framework to another continually. In other words do not look for the meaning of anything but its use. Soul is functional and that is all we know.[11]

In the above context attention is being paid to Kant's view of the unknowability of the thing in itself and the noumenal world. There are also shades of Ryle in considering how a thing behaves. But though the proposal is attractive there has been much attention given to the nature of God in the religions that has resulted in doctrines that are not easily set aside.

Others, of course, will welcome the proposal since it is admitted that we do not have knowledge about God in Himself. The religions we have examined apart from Buddhism portray the majesty and glory of God but how can we know Him if His revelation does not tell us something about what He is in Himself? How can we rely on it? In the Gospel of John it is claimed by Jesus that he who has seen him has seen the Father and it runs through not only John but can be inferred from the other Gospels and the Epistles of Paul. In making such claims according to the record Jesus incurred the charge of blasphemy.

If we do not get true revelation we are talking about an unknown Ultimate Reality which St. Paul in his address to the Greeks said he would reveal to them. It is not realistic to set aside our description of revelation simply because it reflects human concepts and our experience of it.

IS THE SOUL AN ABSTRACT CONCEPT?

Scientists such as Paul Davies argue that the soul or mind is an abstract holistic, organizational pattern, and capable of disembodiment. The soul is nonspatial and though it cannot be seen is the seat of thought and consciousness. Abstract terms are continually in use: justice, humanity, nationality, and governing our actions.[12] But we can be asked for evidence of our nationality and need a passport for travel so the empiricist still demands that evidence be seen.

IS THE SOUL THE INFORMATION PATTERN IN THE BRAIN?

Such a pattern could be transferred to another body: reincarnation or a spiritual body suitable for the new dimension that we call heaven. A piece of music continues to exist even when we stop playing; similarly the mind or soul could continue even when transferred elsewhere.[13] The power of the mind has been demonstrated in quantum theory for our observation affects what happens. Left on its own an atom cannot make a choice and needs our observation to determine whether there is an atom-at-a place or an atom-with-speed hence our minds reach into the physical world.[14]

John Polkinghorne thinks that evolution poses problems for the traditional idea of the soul. It links us in a continuous way with our primate ancestry. But what if the creator gave a spiritual component when bodies reached a complex stage? He thinks this is contrived and puts forward the idea of the soul or mind as the complex information bearing pattern in which matter is organized. The pattern is not static but changes.

He illustrates it by calling attention to how water boils in a pot. It circulates from the bottom in a pattern of six-sided cells, rather like in a beehive. Trillions of molecules have to collaborate and move together in order to generate the pattern. It is what scientists now call complexity theory that applies to complicated situations displaying behavior according to a pattern.

We pay attention to the whole system and the information that specifies the pattern. It is the pattern that provides the continuity in "my" body and we can call it the soul, the real "me." There is a parallel here with what Aristotle said about the soul as the form of the body: the pattern is the form.

Polkinghorne holds that the soul cannot be detached from the body but God will remember it and recreate the pattern in the world to come. This is not survival of the soul but resurrection of the body.[15] Yet he says that the soul will not be lost but reembodied in a new environment. We would agree that the brain does display strategies of information processing and Polkinghorne is relying on it but we also think of ourselves as a collection of subjective qualities and one wonders if Polkinghorne is doing justice to them.[16]

In a further explanation of his position he believes that Jesus rose from the dead in bodily form and we will do likewise. Here he states that in some extraordinary way the soul may have "doors into the information bearing patterns of the body." I tried to get him to comment on the odd phrase about "the soul having doors" but his response concentrated on "information" that would need to be seen in some vastly enhanced sense to be adequate to the human soul. He states that the body has a code or formula expressing its entire nature and structure and the formula will be reembodied.[17]

At first one might think that he was contending that we would be subsumed into God but he is using an analogy when he says that we will be in the mind of God. It means a relationship and a form of being that is continuous with our present experiences as persons. It is an intimacy, not a literal union that we have noted in some of the mystics. What is held in the mind of God is our identity, our continuity, our value and he prefers this to the immortality of the soul.[18]

But it is doubtful, even if we accept that being in the Mind of God is an analogy which preserves the kind of form and being that we know now. The scripture seems to teach that in some way the dead in Christ are alive and are even watching our progress. On the other hand the Book of Revelation while recognizing disembodied souls in heaven does go on to say that they will come alive in the first resurrection. It would agree with the soul sleep taught by some of the Reformers, accepted by Polkinghorne, and coming alive would be bodily resurrection. But Ramanuja's view of communion with God and with one another in the after life does appear more definite and preserves continuance of identity beyond the grave.

In the science chapters we noted that the gift of a soul by God has problems in the evolutionary development of mankind but the theist responds by saying that God is behind everything, with evolution as His method of creation, so accepting the natural development of the soul is reasonable and not contrived. We have argued that God works through the natural.

John Hick commenting on Polkinghorne's position says that it goes beyond process theology. We all exist eternally after death in the divine memory and God uses that memory to reembody us, which he thinks is not unlike the "replica" theory we noted. But the problem here is that people die at various ages and the information, code or formula is that of the person at that age. This he says complicates the theory and is as implausible as going to heaven immediately after death since none of us are ready for it. We need to develop and change morally and spiritually hence the need for another finite life. It has the implication of purgatory or the need of a number of finite lives requiring reincarnation. At this point he refers to Buddhism and could have also mentioned Hinduism and Sikhism.

He thinks that the soul is our basic nature but it changes as we respond to life's tasks and is to be distinguished from our empirical self that expresses itself in our basic dispositional attitudes to be compassionate, generous and forgiving or to be unloving, grasping and resentful. The soul can be described independently of these.

He speculates about where reincarnations can take place and thinks of other worlds that could serve as environments for the growth of the soul. The self dies but the soul will be reembodied in another empirical self, which means the transcending of our natural self-centeredness. He calls it multiple resurrection that accepts the principle of bodily resurrection but extends it to allow for further moral and spiritual development beyond this short life. As always Hick is influenced by religions other than Christianity but he knows that reincarnation is difficult to prove and living on other planets is speculative.[19]

Russell Stannard makes a relevant point regarding Hick's problem. He says that most people think that the new life will be how we are at the time of our death: the mature older person. But do we need to consider those who end up with Alzheimers or some other debilitating disease? Will God not prefer the earlier healthy person? He refers to Jurgen Moltmann who contends for the resurrection of the whole of one's life history. God transcends time and finds our childhood, for example, as close to Him as any other stage of our life including what we are today.

Stannard's thinking on the matter dovetails in with relativistic physics. Physical reality is a four-dimensional spacetime where each of us is represented on a "world line" consisting of our whole life story with each instant of time on an equal footing. From God's perspective, it would appear to make sense that He would resurrect the totality of that life rather than just what happens to be at the end of the line. Stannard concludes that if there is anything in this then it does challenge our understanding of what a resurrected body will be like.

Concerning Polkinghorne's position he is not happy about continuing to exist in the memory of God. He is not sure about "memory" because it implies remembering something in time that happened at an earlier period. The after life should not be viewed as a continuing existence in time. Eternal life is not "everlasting life." Life beyond death will transcend time because it is a property of this physical world. It came into existence when the world was created and is limited to our existence here. Polkinghorne says that God will give us a new existence, the continuity lies with Him rather than the preservation of some thing or substance called an immortal soul or spirit. Stannard believes that beyond our physical death and the cessation of our physical brains it will still be meaningful to talk in the spiritual explanatory framework about ourselves in relation to God.[20]

We will be raised as recognizable individuals rather than being incorporated into some kind of homogenized spiritual "soup." Here we are recognized as individuals separate from other individuals by having a distinctive (physical) body; thus we can expect some kind of body by which we shall be recognized in the next life. It is not our present body, but a spiritual one.

Since the theist places such emphasis on God and what He will do in the resurrection we have to establish arguments for His existence, which I have tried to do elsewhere.[21] Theists point to the setting for evolution and bring in the anthropic principle, which means that a world with life must be a world capable of supporting it. Or on a stronger basis a world that supports life is so unlikely that its existence is no coincidence and is evidence of a power beyond nature. It is difficult to accept that the efficient laws of the universe just popped into existence without a law giver.

PERSON

It may come as a surprise that philosophers distinguish between persons and human beings. A human being belongs to a certain class of being and has characteristics that make him/her different from the animals. With the human we have reached the highest point of the evolutionary scale. We show our respect by the rule, "You shall not kill human beings" but such regard needs to be given also to the animals remembering that the Hindu believes the cow is sacred and it is necessary to have reverence for all life. When the contrast is between us and machines we remember that they can do only what we have programmed.

Peter Strawson as we saw puts forward a double aspect view of a person, who has both states of consciousness and bodily characteristics. The concept of person unites these because the one thing is viewed from two different aspects.[22] The person cannot be reduced to mind, as the idealists do, or to body and brain as the materialist insists. A balance is needed. It means not only the use of different language for the mental and physical but ascribing states of consciousness to ourselves and others. We can do it only if they have corporeal characteristics that are publically observable.

A person indicates unity or wholeness. When we explain personal relationships that we need to become a person we do not employ the terminology of electrons, protons, atoms and molecules but talk about emotions, intellect and volition. The two aspects do not belong to the same class or category. We think of the first as things and the second as states of the person.

Gilbert Ryle's example, which we mentioned, is well known concerning the parts that cannot be confused with the whole. The Oxford colleges are observable and make up the unobservable university. It is not another institution apart from the colleges but the way they are organized and coordinated, likewise the mind is not apart from the body but interacts with it. In being persons we have reached the highest levels of our being hence we operate downward controlling the activities of the lower parts of our bodies. It was the high level activity of mind that ensured survival against animals that were stronger and faster than us.

Descartes rightly refused to equate our conscious states with the physical but his position had the defects that we mentioned. Double aspect theory is preferred since it maintains a unitary self or soul that gives rise to double descriptions. There is one substance, a unity in duality. Mental states and physical characteristics are ascribed to a person: a monistic unity. As persons we have certain characteristics such as communication through language, a developing self-consciousness, moral awareness and the ability to make choices and relationships. The person transcends body and mind and can ascribe to herself feelings and volition. It is how she feels. She says that she is tired and we may challenge this by saying that she is bored, which is third person assessment, but it is difficult to challenge for it is a first person statement.

We are persons-in-relation and Descartes failed to take it into account. He paid attention to the individual and we do not neglect this but place him in his social context. Relationship with others makes us into persons and being created in the image of God means our capacity for relatedness to Him, something that the animals do not possess.

THE SOUL AND THE AFTER LIFE

We recall at this point some of the beliefs in the world religions. In Judaism there were intimations of the soul's immortality in the Psalms and the mystical writings of the Kabbalah but the real development occurred in the apocalyptic writings. This affected both Judaism and Christianity.

Today the chief Rabbi believes that we are a body conjoined with a soul, the dust of the earth joined to the breath of God, hence in each of us there is a moral spark that requires nurturing. We have seen it in other religions expressed as the imago Dei, the Buddha nature, the inner light and conscience but it requires modification due to our frail or sinful nature. The image of God confers moral responsibility, religious awareness and the ability to relate to God. It together with reason and imagination, language, and use of symbols distinguishes us from the animals.

An after life is necessary in order to right the wrongs experienced by the Jews. They were killed by their enemies because they refused to fight on the Sabbath (1 Macc. 2.20–38) hence the need for justice and the reward of immortality. The hope of a messianic age developed (Isa. 24–27) with the coming of the Son of man (Dan. 7.13–14), the vindication of the faithful and the rewarding of the just. The Maccabean literature also teaches that the living can assist the dead by prayer and sacrifice.

In Christianity the resurrection of the body is a fundamental belief but today there are some Christians who believe in the immortality of the soul. However, as we have seen, the Gospels teach that Jesus appeared in some kind of bodily form to his disciples and gave them empirical proofs that he had risen. Greek thought influenced Christianity as we have seen but though this meant a separation of body and soul it was held that they would be united in the after life. The soul is coupled with the spirit or pneuma and designates the whole person (1 Cor. 5.3–5). "The Holy Spirit bears witness with our spirit that we are children of God" (Rom. 8.16) and the spirit and soul are vehicles for salvation. Some scholars see both participating in the divine.[23]

Another question occurs frequently which relates to the origin of the soul. Was it given directly by God or did it evolve naturally? Islam generally accepts the former but some Muslims are willing to believe in the latter. It is understood by some Islamic philosophers, influenced by Aristotle, as the form of the body that stresses a unity but others contend for a dualism between body and soul. Some Muslims think of resurrection as the assembling of the old body that may form the basis of their reaction to cremation. Such a belief is hard to maintain.

In Hinduism, jiva is embodied in the present self and registers the moral, aesthetic, intellectual and spiritual dispositions that have been built up during one's life or succession of lives until finally united with Brahman. The atman is different from the empirical self that acts in a functional way. Atman is the eternal soul and Sankara with his monism made it identical with Brahman. Ramanuja opposed this and his opposition appears more in line with the Semitic traditions. A good life can earn release from the cycle of rebirth and the soul either merges with Brahman or enters into communion with Him or It. One could argue that since reincarnation means the soul taking a new body one would be necessary for the Hindu in the after life.

In Buddhism there is a denial of the soul or self but there have been internal protests about it and a variety of views. It is difficult to identify simply the self with passing states for it seems to transcend these. When I feel pain it is "me" that is suffering, I am not just my sensations or thoughts, though they are part of "me." Thoughts come and go but I remain "me," I am the person who has the thoughts and cannot be submerged in them. There is continuity for we live on as the same person from one experience to another but it is probably true that we can never properly know the self. The Buddha nature in all might be seen as a soul.

In Sikhism, God is transcendent and immanent and extends His grace to us but we need to prepare ourselves for it by doing good deeds. The soul had been given by God through the process of evolution and is destined to live with Him forever. It is central to our actions but is attracted to worldly things. But it is also alien to these things and is like conscience that must be obeyed or a divine spark, which must be cherished. If cared for it is immortal since it is of the essence of God. There is no question of it being finally absorbed into God because it will be separated from Him if His commandments have not been obeyed.

In Christianity and Judaism there is, like the other religions, difficulty in understanding the nature of heaven and hell. Some modern theologians in the Protestant tradition contend for a kind of purgatory as a necessary preparation for the perfection of heaven. Unless the concept is treated in the Catholic way of a purging of those who have faith, it could lead to universalism in opposition to the general trend of scripture.

A lot depends on whether or not the accounts of heaven and hell are taken literally or not. To interpret the Qur'an literally would refer to a Paradise of sensual pleasure where the good are served by boys and maidens. But the contribution of the Islamic philosophers shows that they preferred the symbolic to the literal. There are traces of purgatory in the Faith that exist for healing before getting admittance to paradise. And there is division about whether or not hell is eternal or temporary. Some see it as a period of time.

In Hinduism there are many hells but there are evidences to suggest that they may be temporary and they would depend on the cycles of rebirths coming to an end. The immortality of the soul is crucial and the concept of incarnation is accepted but the avatars are many and temporary and do not have the permanency of the unique incarnation claimed by Christianity.

Nirvana is a key concept when discussing the after life in Buddhism. The experience of it removes the delusion of the self and the end of desires. It is the letting go of false beliefs and can only be experienced. Though sometimes spoken of as a realm, it cannot be described, for our concepts are inadequate to do this.

We cannot think of it as nonexistence since the Buddha experienced enlightenment under the tree and continued to live. It is nirvana with remainder or substrate and when we die, it is nirvana without remainder or substrate, which is the ultimate goal. Death is like the flame of a candle going out, but where does it go? The Buddha said that such a question is meaningless and he remained agnostic. But he did speak of an island or other shore and there is a kind of immortality in the succession of rebirths. Did he mean a literal island or simply a state of mind that is content to possess nothing and grasp after nothing? He does call it nirvana or nibbana, which is the destruction of decay and death.

There are many heavens where the gods live and Buddhism recognizes them as being helpful to us but they are mortal and cannot escape rebirth and their heavens will decay. The gods who cannot escape sensory desires dwell in the lower heavens but the higher beings live in a realm above. Higher still there are four formless heavens that have infinite space, infinite consciousness, nothingness and neither perception nor nonperceptions. These correspond to meditational levels. Again the question is: Do these realms exist or are they to be understood metaphorically or psychologically or as meditational states? Traditionally they appear to have been taken literally but Buddhism says that it is in the workings of our minds that all these layers of understanding and experience are found. According to Theravada there are seven hells for those who lie, use bad language, covet another's possessions, are stingy, backbite, and so on. On entering the hells one is struck with iron rods, endures the fires and experiences other forms of punishment.

The belief in Sikhism is that at death the soul will live in the presence of God and not be reincarnated provided the person has disciplined his life and dwelt on the Name of God. There will be a recording angel who catalogues all deeds and liberation from the cycle of birth and death. It is good acts that govern the judgment. The soul does not die for it is the precious jewel within our breasts and if we have cared and cultivated it we will merge with the Deathless One at the end. But if the soul has misbehaved it continues "burning" because of worldly desire that results in separation from God. After death it is troubled and wanders in anguish bitterly regretting its sins. Heaven is the bliss of being in the presence of God; it is not a place of comfort and pleasure. Yama is the God of the dead and he has authority over them who have a kind of half-existence.

In sum it would appear that the Semitic religions have a belief in the immortality of the soul though it was a development in Judaism, doubtful at times in Christianity, and sometimes appears in Islam. In the Indian religions the soul is denied by Buddhism but is a central belief in Hinduism and Sikhism.

THE SOUL/MIND AND NEAR DEATH EXPERIENCE

A mystery that still eludes us is consciousness. Is there a possibility that it could continue after the death of the body? The foetus does not have it in the womb and it takes twenty weeks after birth for the brain to become active. In near death experiences patients are conscious apparently when the brain has ceased to function and if there is any truth in the assertion then the soul that is the center of consciousness could survive death.

We mentioned A. J. Ayer in the last chapter who was clinically dead but resuscitated. He spoke of a spiritual world. The experience has become common nowadays owing to the development of cardiac resuscitation techniques.

Dr. Sam Parnia who leads the research team at the Hammersmith Hospital, London, asserts that technology and scientific knowledge is now available to explore this ultimate question. He says that he started off as a skeptic but having weighed all the evidence he now thinks that there is something going on. There is evidence that consciousness may carry on after death and patients are being monitored who can be brought back to life if their heart suddenly stopped. They reported emotions, visions or thoughts while they were clinically dead, lost awareness of their bodies, saw a bright light and entered another world where they encountered mystical beings.

There was no evidence of brain activity or hallucination. Skeptics abound but Parnia believes that the mind or soul, the thing that is you, carries on instead of drifting into nothingness. It does not seem to matter what the religion or culture of the patients is, the experience results in spirituality and a removal of the fear of death. What is interesting is not only the possibility of life after death but also whether the mind can function without the brain.

Is the mind or consciousness produced by the brain or is the brain just an intermediary—in the way that a television set is an intermediary that turns radio waves into sound and image? The mind may be still there after the brain is clinically dead, but some doubt it and think that such experiences can be triggered by electrodes in the brain. It may be that there are pathways in the brain that control near death experiences so that when death approaches the body goes through many chemical and biological changes to keep itself alive.

The NDE could be a kind of chemical hallucination caused by the imbalance of the brain due to lack of oxygen or the experience could have been induced by the patient for comfort. But experiments on many patients in the Southampton hospital showed that oxygen levels in the near death patients were as high as or higher than those who had no NDE.

There are many mystifying cases. In a NDE a man sees his dead uncle who says: "Look for my old overcoat. I sewed a large roll of bills in my inside pocket and the money is still there." When the man recovered from his illness the overcoat is found and the money discovered in the inside pocket. Where the money was hidden was known only to the uncle and not to any other! Another factor is that during such an experience some patients were able to describe what the doctors were doing on the operating table. The doctors were puzzled by this and insisted that the nurses must have told them afterward! Another surprise occurred for a nurse who had put a patient's false teeth in a drawer on a special trolley during his cardiac arrest that induced a coma. When he awoke from his NDE he told them that the nurse knew where his dentures were. No one was more amazed than the nurse! Other studies in the United States revealed similar findings.

If the mind existed apart from the brain then there would be support for conscious life beyond death. If conscious perception can even for a moment be separated from the body the link between consciousness and the brain is questioned and leaves life beyond death an open question. Parnia says that we can now explore the question whether or not we are dead when the brain stops functioning. Other parts may still be operating namely the organs and cells. What if the brain stem had died and the neocortex that supports our capacities for consciousness and social interaction had not? It is clear that science has problems defining when we are dead.[24]

Susan Blackmore writes that out-of-body experiences are difficult to deny and she had one herself. They can be induced by trauma, shock, illness or effort and are psychological. There are experiences of peace, separation from the body, journeys, tunnels, darkness, light and passing into a beautiful world of angels. The different interpretations of the experiences do not alter the likelihood or depth of them or their result. Visions of Jesus are recorded by some, a hell-like experience is rare, and there is a life review. She is inclined to dismiss paranormal theories and favors a psychological approach but how can psychology deal with the extraordinary since there is little success in dealing with the ordinary. She says OBE is an altered state of consciousness but she is skeptical about it. With regard to survival after death she does not know but hopes there is![25]

Parnia discusses neuroscience and the nature of consciousness. Is neuroscience right that it is impossible for consciousness to continue when all brain functions are absent or does the NDE occur either before or after the cardiac arrest though it is interpreted by the patient as occurring during unconsciousness? Parnia responds by arguing that death is a continuum so that when someone has a cardiac arrest, attempts can be made to restart the heart and the lungs otherwise there would be permanent damage and death would ensue. The prestige of his work arises because he had worked on the problem with well known doctors both in the UK, America and Europe.

Research has been carried out in Holland on 344 cardiac arrest survivors from 10 hospitals over a two-year period and 41 reported a NDE that resulted in a spiritual transformation. It was also found that since all cardiac arrest survivors underwent the same biological changes and were given the same drugs, NDEs were unlikely to occur as a consequence of these factors. There was peace, pain-free feeling and a separation from the body.

This raises again the question of the link between mind and brain. There are billions of neurons in the brain and they generate electricity through a network of cells and the connections are called synapses. It may be that consciousness arises at the level of the synapses. The brain is a neural network but how can it produce thoughts? How do we realize the self from the inputs of millions of brain cells? How do chemical or electrical events that are not conscious become conscious? What happens to free will if we are determined by such mechanical events? The materialist says that the brain observed and the observer are one and the same; however, this is puzzling: how can a physical event of my watching my brain be the same as me who is doing the watching?

Sir John Eccles, as we mentioned, is a neuroscientist believing in the distinction between mind, consciousness and the brain. He argues that the unity of conscious experience is provided by the mind and not by the neural machinery of the brain. The mind plays an active role in selecting and integrating brain cell activity and molding it into a whole and it is wrong to think that the brain does everything. We are not passive spectators who meekly watch what is going on in the brain otherwise we could not make decisions or have control of our lives. The brain is just an instrument providing communication from and to the external world and we need to read the coded patterns of the information that it provides and make selections. It is interesting to realize that the amoeba or earthworm has no brain but has senses to feed, rest and escape from predators.

Parnia contends that neuroscience cannot provide us with a theory of the relation between mind and brain; there is no explanation of the electrochemical events producing the feeling of pain. It cannot work out the meaning of the NDE experience and is unable to explain it as an illusion or hallucination. If people enter into a different dimension in NDE how can they explain it to us? But Parnia has difficulty in explaining satisfactorily why some people who are not near death have such an experience. It has been suggested that the NDE occurs just before or just after an unconscious state.

Currently the best way of studying the association between brain and mind is when brain function is impaired. If mind is simply the product of the brain then why does it not stop? If I switch on a light and then switch it off again there are no problems but if the light remains on then it is coming from another source or something is wrong with the switch! Could consciousness be a subtle form of matter that we cannot measure similar to electromagnetic waves?[26]

Parnia is supported by Peter Fenwick. He points out that there has been a great interest regarding spirituality in medicine since 1995 and conferences have been held on prayer. Fenwick and his wife published a book, *The Truth in the Light* (1996), and received two thousand letters regarding NDE. Could it be due to lobe epilepsy? It is doubtful because no epileptic seizure has the clarity of an NDE. Cardiac arrest is the same as clinical death with no brainstem reflexes so science says that we cannot have experiences. How then is NDE to be explained? Does the soul temporarily detach itself from the body? Hallucinations are different from NDEs for those that have them are confused about what is going on in the ward and have weird ideas.[27] But the importance of the matter is now seen in the development of the International Association for Near Death Studies whose members are psychiatrists, psychologists and cardiologists.

ESP

We want to make a short comment on this since today it is being taken more seriously. It is an investigation of the power of the mind to communicate at a distance. But in the contact of two minds where is the physical cause? A psychological explanation postulates a common unconscious that connects yours with mine, which is telepathy. It leads to parapsychology where the medium goes into a trance and the consciousness of the dead person replaces her consciousness. Objectors point to fraud or that the medium can sense what is going on in the minds of those who attend the séance.

We are dealing with psychic forces that science does not recognize but the Society for Psychical research has piled up evidence, both experimental and anecdotal, over hundreds of years. William James, Henry Sidgwick, Frederick Myers, Sir Oliver Lodge, A. R. Wallace, Conan Doyle and other eminent people all believed that mind could affect matter. The opponents say it is based on our wishes, what we want to believe, but the response is that the need to disbelieve is so powerful that it stops us looking at evidence that contradicts our beliefs.

The University of Liverpool now has a research unit investigating telepathy. Experiments are being carried out to see if one mind can transmit a message to another who is in a different room. It is hoped to discover how some people have extra sensory perception.

CONCLUSION

We have noted throughout this book that there are the physical and spiritual factors. Some contend that the latter can be explained by the former with evolution as the key to the soul, mind, moral sense and conscience. The religions deny it, insisting that there must be the involvement of God. He is behind all things and uses evolution as the method of creation so the soul is indirectly given by Him. At death the spirit/soul takes a new body fitted for the new environment. The religions see the soul as "me," the person, and I pass over eventually into the new life.

Person is perhaps the best way of viewing continuity after death. But persons have bodies and they would appear essential in an after life for through them we express our personality. It will be a spiritual body and this was the message of Apostle Paul to the Corinthians who were apparently believers in the immortality of the soul. Our present bodies that are subject to morality, dishonor, and prone to temptation will be replaced by bodies that are incorruptible, immortal and full of glory.

We would appear to have a glimpse of what that body might be like in the resurrection of Christ. The body could be identified by the disciples in various ways. It was the same but it was different since it could appear and disappear and pass through doors. A clue to it is provided by Ramanuja the Indian philosopher who in his thinking about God argued that we are like Him yet unlike Him: identity-in-difference. The resurrected body of

Christ belonged to the divine dimension or order so unlike ours yet it was recognizable by the disciples hence remained human. There was identity-in-difference. The effect of the appearances on the disciples was devastating but it had some similarity to what they experienced when they saw the transformation of his body on the Mount of Transfiguration (Lk 9.28–36).

One thing seems sure that whether it is the resurrection of the body as hoped for in the Semitic religions or the immortality of the soul as portrayed in the Indian religions, we will be in the right condition to enjoy what God has prepared for us.

Notes

Introduction

1. Paul Heelas, "The Spiritual Revolution: From Religion to Spirituality," *Religions in the Modern World,* ed. Linda Woodhead, Paul Fletcher, Hiroko Kawanami, and David Smith. London and New York: Routledge, 2002, p. 366.

1 The Jewish Soul

1. C. M. Hoffman, *Judaism.* London: Hodder Headline, 2008, p. 13; Louis Jacobs, *We Have Reason to Believe.* London: Valentine Mitchell, 1962.
2. Ibid., p. 14.
3. R. J. Zwi Werblowsky, "Judaism or the Religion of Israel," 31ff. in *Concise Encyclopedia of Living Faiths,* ed. R. C. Zaehner. London: Hutchinson, 1977.
4. Glossary, A 213, *World Religions.* Milton Keynes: Open University, 1998, p. 29.
5. Hoffman, pp. 67–68.
6. Nicholas De Lange, *Penguin Dictionary of Judaism.* London: Penguin, 2008, p. 247.
7. Ian S. Markham, *World Religions Reader.* Oxford: Blackwell, 1996, p. 27.
8. Hoffman, pp. 149, 215.
9. Dave Tomlinson, *Re-enchanting Christianity.* Norwich: Canterbury Press, 2008, p. 39.
10. Hoffman, p. 35.
11. Jacobs, p. 22.
12. Ibid., p. 31.
13. Ibid., pp. 42–61.
14. H. W. Robinson, *Inspiration and Revelation in the Old Testament.* Oxford: Clarenden Press, 1946, pp. 52, 75, 95, 180.
15. Nancey Murphy, *Bodies and Souls or Spirit Bodies.* Cambridge: Cambridge University Press, 2006, pp. 8, 19, 76.

16. Jacobs, p. 54 and footnote p. 56.

17. D. S. Ariel, *What Do the Jews Believe?* London: Rider, 1996, p. 91.

18. Jonathan Sacks, *To Heal a Fractured World*. London: Continuum, 2005, passim.

19. Commentators make this point basing it on Isaiah, chap. 40.25 and other biblical passages.

20. Ariel, pp. 163, 167, 192.

21. Joseph Dan, *Kabbalah*. Oxford: Oxford University Press, 2006, pp. 4–10, 82.

22. A. Cohen, ed. *The Psalms, Soncing Books of the Bible*. London and Bournemouth: Soncino Press, 1950.

23. Ibid., p. 18.

24. Ibid., p. 39.

25. Ibid., p. 85.

26. Ibid., p. 161.

27. Markham, p. 531.

28. *The Authorised Daily Prayer Book*, S. Singer, trans. with notes by Israel Abrahams. London: 1922.

29. Hoffman, pp. 103–106.

30. John Bowker, *The Meanings of Death*. Cambridge: Cambridge University Press, 1991, p. 58.

31. Lavinia and Dan Cohn-Sherbok, *A Short Introduction to Judaism*. Oxford: One World, 1997, p. 50.

32. Bowker, p. 58–58.

33. Robinson, p. 101.

34. Ibid., pp. 181, 104.

35. Sacks, pp. 135–139.

36. David Goldstein, *Judaism: World Religions*. A 213, Units 1–2. Milton Keynes: Open University Press, 1998, p. 33.

37. Geza Vermes, *The Resurrection*. London: Penguin, 2008, p. 85.

38. Lavinia and Cohn-Sherbok, pp. 45ff., 230ff.

39. Nicholas De Lange, *Penguin Dictionary of Judaism*. London: Penguin, 2008, p. 250.

40. William Barclay, *Introducing the Bible*. London: Redhill Surrey, pp. 51, 57ff., 117, 122ff., 141 and St. Andrews Press Edinburgh, 1983, pp. 24ff. Compare W. O. E Oesterley, *Doctrine of Last Things*. London: John Murray, 1908.

41. Dan-Sherbok and Christopher Lewis, eds., "The Jewish Doctrine of Hell," *Religion*, pp. 54ff., 62, 75 (London: Elsevier, 1998).

42. E. P. Sanders, *Judaism: Practice and Belief*, 63 BCE–66 CE. London: SCM, 1992. See also De Lange.

43. John Bowker, *Worlds of Faith.* BBC London: Ariel Books, 1983, pp. 273–274.

2   THE CHRISTIAN EXPERIENCE
OF THE SOUL

1. John Bowker, *Worlds of Faith.* BBC London: Ariel Books, 1983, p. 270.
2. Louis Berkhof, *Systematic Theology.* Edinburgh: Banner of Truth Trust, 1981, pp. 161–162.
3. *Saint Augustine Confessions,* trans. Henry Chadwick. Oxford: Oxford University Press, 1998, pp. 285–286.
4. Berkhof, p. 129.
5. William Barclay, *The New Testament,* vol. 2: *The Letters and the Revelation* London: Collins, 1969, p. 328.
6. J. B. Green, "Bodies That Is Human Lives; A Re-examination of Human Nature in the Bible," ch. 7 in *Whatever Happened to the Soul,* ed. Warren S. Brown, Nancey Murphy and H. Newton Malony. Minneapolis: Fortress Press, 1998.
7. Julia Annas, *Plato.* Oxford: Oxford University Press, 2003, p. 73, 65–65.
8. Barclay, *The New Testament,* p. 304.
9. Geza Vermes, *The Resurrection.* London: Penguin, 2008, p. 71.
10. Barclay, *The New Testament,* p. 303.
11. William Barclay, *The Gospels and Letters of the Apostles.* London Collins, 1968, p. 335. See also John Polkinghorne, *God of Hope and the End of the World.* London: SPCK, 2002, pp. 72–74.
12. Ninian Smart, *Philosophers and Religious Truth.* London: SCM Press, 1969, p. 25–26.
13. Robert Crawford, *The Saga of God Incarnate,* 2nd ed. Pretoria: University of South Africa, 1988, p. 24–25, 72–73, 75
14. Anthony Flew, *There Is a God.* London: Harper Collins, 2008, p. 58.
15. Leslie Weatherhead, *Life Begins at Death.* Nutfield Redhill Surrey: Denhilm House Press, 1969, p. 77.
16. Barclay, *The Gospels and Letters of the Apostles,* p. 303. See also Christ Crucified and Crowned SCM 1971, London, p. 217.
17. James S. Stewart, *A Man in Christ.* London: Hodder and Stoughton, 1935 p. 16ff., 58
18. Ibid., p. 268.
19. C. K. Barrett, *I Corinthians.* London: Adam and Charles Black, 1968, pp. 373–377. See also John Parry, *Greek Testament I*

Corinthians. Cambridge: Cambridge University Press, 1957, ch. 15, p. 213ff.

20. James Moffatt, *Epistle of Paul to Corinthians.* London: Hodder and Stoughton, 1951, p. 72.

3   THE SOUL AND THE DEVELOPMENT OF CHRISTIAN BELIEF

1. Henry Chadwick, *Introduction to St Augustine Confessions.* Oxford: Oxford University Press, 1991, pp. 184–185, 105, 110, 178. See also James J. O'Donnell, *Sinner and Saint.* London: Profile Books, 2005.
2. John Hick, *Evil and the God of Love.* London: Collins, 1968, p. 295.
3. A. Pegis, *St Thomas and the Problem of the Soul in the 13th Century.* Basic Writings of St. Thomas Hackett. Cambridge, MA: Cambridge University Press, 1997, p. 372.
4. J. Calvin, *Institutes Bk 1 Henry Beveridge.* Edinburgh: T & T Clark, 1863, p. 165.
5. Francis Clark, *Reformation.* Units 20–27. Milton Keynes: Open University, 1972, passim.
6. Henry Bettenson, ed. *Documents of the Christian Church.* London: Oxford University Press, 1963, p. 262.
7. Nancey Murphy, *Bodies and Souls or Spirit Bodies.* Cambridge: Cambridge University Press, 2006, p. 16.
8. John Thompson, "The Formation of the General Assembly," in *Essays in Presbyterian History,* ed. J. L. M. Haire. Belfast: W & G Baird, 1981.
9. Walter Kasper, *Harvesting the Fruits, Basic Aspects of Christian Faith in Dialogue.* New York: Continnum, 2009, ch. 2, 3, 4. Chapter 1 has interesting reflections on the Trinity.
10. *The Book of Common Prayer.* Oxford: Oxford University Press, n.d., p. 395.
11. Ibid., p. 384.
12. Brother Ramson SSF (Society of St. Francis), *Franciscan Spirituality.* London: SPCK, 2008, p. 162–163.
13. Martin Forward, *The Nature and Name of Love.* London: Epworth Press, 2008, p. 131.
14. Paul Badham, *Christian Beliefs about Life after Death.* Basingstoke: Macmillan, 1976, pp. 69–81.
15. Ibid.
16. John Hick, *Death and Eternal Life.* London: Collins, 1976, pp. 385–397. See Leslie Weatherhead, *Christian Agnostic.*

London: Hodder and Stoughton, 1965 and *Life Begins at Death*. Nutfield Redhill Surrey: Denhilm House Press, 1969.

17. Society for Physical Research, vol. 26. New York: 1966. See John Hick, *Fifth Dimension*. Oxford: One World, 1999. David Millikan, "New Religious Movements," in *Christian Approaches to Other Faiths*, ed. Allan Race and Paul M. Hedges. London: SCM Reader, 2009, pp. 238–239.

18. Bruce M. Metzger and Michael D. Coogan, eds., *The Oxford Companion to Bible*. Oxford: Oxford University Press, 1993, p. 686.

19. Louis Berkhof, *Systematic Theology*. Edinburgh: Banner of Truth Trust, 1981, p. 696.

20. Ibid., p. 731.

21. Hick, pp. 399–425. Scott Hahn, *Signs of Life*. London: Darton Longman and Todd, 2009, pp. 256–257.

22. Allan D. Galloway, *Wolfhart Pannenberg*. London: George Allen and Unwin, 1973, pp. 23, 71.

23. *The Nature of Hell*, Report by Evangelical Alliance Commission. Carlisle, Cumbria: Paternoster Press, 2000.

24. C. S. Lewis, *The Great Divorce*. Glasgow: Collins, 1987, 30ff.

25. Metzger and Coogan, p. 270.

4   THE MUSLIM CLAIM

1. Most Translations of the Qur'an are by N. J. Dagwood, *The Koran*. Middlesex: Penguin Classic, 1997.

2. Kenneth Cragg, *The Religious Quest*. A 228, Units 14–15. Milton Keynes: Open University, 1987, p. 45.

3. Bruce Lawrence, *The Qur'an: A Biography*. London: Atlantic Books, 2006, p. 206.

4. Alfred T. Welch, "Islam," in *A Handbook of Living Religions*, ed. John R. Hinnells. London: Penguin, 1997, p. 274.

5. Michael Keene, *Islam*, rev. ed. Cheltenham: Stanley Thornes, 1999, pp. 61, 75ff.

6. Robert Crawford, *What Is Religion?* London: Routledge, 2002, p. 90–91.

7. Abded Haleem, "Life and Beyond in the Qur'an," in *Beyond Death*, ed. D. Cohn-Sherbok and C. Lewis. Basingstoke: Macmillan, 1995, pp. 64, 70–71.

8. W. C. Chittick, *Sufism*. Oxford: One World, 2000, pp. 16, 21–22, 26.

9. A. S. Tritton, *Islam*. London: Hutchinson, 1966, p. 108.

10. Majid Fakhry, *Islam Philosophy*. Oxford: One World, 2009, pp. 3, 36.
11. Ibid., pp. 38–43.
12. Ibid., p. 46.
13. Tritton, p. 55.
14. Fakhry, p. 89.
15. Ibid., p. 67.
16. Ibid., pp. 117ff., 123, 151.
17. John Bowker, *Worlds of Faith*. BBC, London: Ariel Books, 1983, pp. 247–248, 272, 275.
18. Keene, pp. 18, 271, 325.
19. Hadrat Ahmad, *Introduction to the Study of the Holy Qur'an*. Rabwah, Pakistan: Oriental and Religious Corporation, 1969, p. 253.
20. Lawrence, pp. 4–5.

5   THE HINDU AND THE IMMORTAL SOUL

1. C. Zaehner, ed. *The Concise Encyclopedia of Living Faiths*. London: Hutchinson, 1979, p. xii.
2. Gita, ch. 2, pp. 17–21 in *Man's Religious Quest,* ed. W. Foy. London: Croom Helm, 1978.
3. John Bowker, *Worlds of Faith*. BBC, London: Ariel Books, 1983, p. 251.
4. Zaehner, p. 243.
5. Chandogya Upanishad, Vl, p. xiii. Foy, pp. 92–93.
6. John Hick, *Fifth Dimension*, Oxford: One World, 1999, p. 248. Herbert Ellinger, *Hinduism*. London: SCM, 1995, p. 90, redefinition of jiva. R. C. Zaehner, *Hinduism*. Oxford: Oxford University Press, 1966, pp. 60–61.
7. Foy, Gita, ch. 2, p. 104
8. Zaehner, p. 244, article by A. L. Basham.
9. Paul Rowland, *Reincarnation*. London: Arcturus, 2008, pp. 9, 117.
10. Ibid.
11. Ninian Smart, *Hinduism in World Religions*. A 213, Units 7–10. Milton Keynes: Open University Press, 1998, p. 104.
12. Brian Hodgkinson, *The Essence of Vedanta*. London: Arcturus, 2000, pp. 7–10, 190.
13. Smart, p. 110.
14. Ibid., p. 108.
15. Zaehner, pp. 232–233, 257.

16. Robert Crawford, *Can We Ever Kill?*, 2nd ed. London: Darton Longman and Todd, 2000.

6 THE BUDDHIST DENIAL OF THE SOUL

1. P. Harvey, *An Introduction to Buddhist Teachings, History and Practices*. Cambridge: Cambridge University Press, 1990, p. 336.
2. Ian S. Markham, ed. *World Religious Reader*. Oxford: Blackwell, 1996, pp. 116–120.
3. Ibid.
4. Helen Waterhouse, *Buddhism*. A 213, Units 11–13. Milton Keynes: Open University, p. 25.
5. Paul Williams, *Buddhist Thought*. London: Routledge, 2000, pp. 27, 63.
6. Walpola Rahula, *What the Buddha Taught*. Oxford: One World, 1959, pp. 37, 47, 91.
7. I. B. Horner, "The Theravada" in *Concise Encyclopedia of Living Faiths*, ed. R. C. Zaehner. London: Hutchinson, 1979, pp. 263ff.
8. Ibid.
9. Gillian Stokes, *Buddha*. Oxford: Bookpoint, 2000, p. 49.
10. Williams, pp. 50–51.
11. Rupert Gethin, *The Foundations of Buddhism*. Oxford: Oxford University Press, 1998, p. 143.
12. Williams, p. 126.
13. Horner, p. 281.
14. Harvey, p. 40.
15. Dalai Lama, *Good Heart Rider*. London: Rider, 2002, p. 65.
16. Mel Thompson, *Eastern Philosophy*. London: Hodder Headline, pp. 169, pp 184–185, 192, 198.
17. Ibid., p.385.
18. Edward Conze, "Mahayana," in *Concise Encyclopedia of Living Faiths*, ed. R C Zaehner. London: Hutchinson, 1977, p. 305.
19. Ibid., p. 377.
20. Horner, p. 274.
21. R. F. Gombrich, *Theravada Buddhism*. London: Routledge and Kegan Paul, 1988, pp. 29–30.
22. Dalai Lama, p. 119.
23. Conze, p. 295.
24. Markham, p. 386.

25. Conze, pp. 305–306.
26. Stewart MacFarland, "Buddhism," in *Making Moral Decisions*, ed. Jean Holm and John Bowker. London: Pinter, 1998, p. 34.
27. Rupert Gettin, *The Foundations of Buddhism*. Oxford: Oxford University Press, 1998, pp. 228–229.
28. Thompson, pp. 184–185, 192, 198.
29. Dalai Lama, pp. 56, 65.
30. Denise Cush, *Buddhism*. London: Hodder and Stoughton, 1994, pp. 37–38.
31. Gethin, p. 217.
32. Bowker, pp. 329–230, 332–333.
33. E. Conze, *Buddhist Scriptures*. Penguin: Harmondsworth, pp. 103–116, 142.
34. Christmas Humphreys, *The Buddhist Way of Life*. London: George Allen and Unwin, 1969, p. 75.
35. Joseph Masson, *The Noble Path of Buddhism*. Units 5–7. Milton Keynes: Open University, 1987, pp. 32–33. See also Lawrence Freeman, *Introduction to Dala Lama's Good Heart*, p. 23 Father Laurence Freeman OSB is director of the World community for Christian mediation. He became a Benedictine monk and studied under the late John Main a Benedictine monk with whom he worked to teach the Christian tradition of meditation widely around the world, p. 205.
36. Waterhouse, p. 36.
37. Gettin, p. 210.
38. Waterhouse, p. 42.
39. Gettin, p. 210.
40. Ibid., p. 222.
41. Waterhouse, p. 59.
42. Ibid., 61.
43. Dalai Lama.
44. Conze, p. 312.
45. Gettin, p. 273.
46. Thompson, pp. 147, 213–214.
47. Dalai Lama, p. 52. Bassui sermon by Buddha. Whitfield Foy, *A Reader. The Religious Quest*, p. 201. Croom Helm, St. John's Road London: Open University 1978, SW11 5.5.6. p. 372
48. Gettin, p. 252
49. Williams, p. 55–55.
50. Udano. Translated by F L Woodward as verses of uplift 1948 p. 60

51. Keith Ward, *Images of Eternity*. London: Darton Longman and Todd, 1987, p. 66–67; Humphrey, p. 105.
52. Harvey, pp. 48, 104–105, 37.
53. Foy, p. 201.
54. Conze, p. 293.
55. T. R. V. Murti, *The Central Philosophy of Buddhism,* 2nd ed. London: George Allen and Unwin, 1960, p. 18.
56. C. S. Lewis, *Miracles*. London: Fount Collins, 1987, p. 136. See also *Problem of Pain*. London: Centenary Press, 1943.
57. Herbert Ellinger, *Hinduism*. London: SCM, p. 60.

7 THE SIKH PATH

1. Gurbachan Singh, *The Sikhs*. London: Tiger Books, 1998, pp. 81–88.
2. Ibid., pp. 13, 18.
3. H. W. McLeod, *Sikhism*. Harmondsworth: Penguin, 1997, p. 448.
4. Whitfield Foy, ed. *Man's Religious Quest, A Reader,* 4.1.6. London: Croom Helm 1978.
5. G. Beckerlegge, ed. *The World Religions Reader*. London and New York: Routledge, 2000, p. 420.
6. Foy, 4. 13.
7. John Parry, *The Word of God Is Not Bound*. Bangalore: Centre for Contemporary Christianity, 2009, p. 178.
8. Robert Crawford, *What Is Religion?* London: Routledge, 2002, p. 35.
9. Foy, 4.l.25.
10. Terry Thomas, *The Religion of the Sikhs*. A 228, Units 8–9. Milton Keynes: Open University Press, 1988, p. 29.
11. Ibid., p. 30.
12. Foy, 4.1.34.
13. W. Owen Cole and Piara Singh Sambhi, *The Sikhs*. London: Routledge and Kegan Paul, 1978, p. 90.
14. Thomas, pp. 24–25.
15. Foy, 4.1.27.
16. Ibid., 4.1.38.
17. McLeod, p. 86.
18. Foy, 4.1.5.
19. Thomas, pp. 39–45. Foy, 4.1.38.
20. Foy, 4.1.31.
21. Ibid., 4.1.27.

22. Ibid., 4.1.30.
23. Ibid., 4.1.31.
24. Singh, p. 50.
25. Ibid., p. 66.
26. Thomas, p. 28.
27. Foy, 4.1.29.
28. Thomas, p. 75.
29. McLeod, pp. 120–125, 143.
30. Ibid., p. 377.
31. Thomas, p. 34.
32. Khushwant Singh, *A History of Sikhism,* vol. 1. Delhi: Oxford University Press, pp. 39–40.
33. Crawford, p. 110.
34. Mcleod, p. 289.
35. H. W. Mcleod, *Guru Nanak and the Sikh Religion.* Oxford: Oxford University Press, 1968, p. 38. It is sometimes cited as "There Is Neither Hindu or Muslim..." p. 161. See also H. W. McLeod, *Who Is a Sikh? The Problem of Sikh Identity.* Oxford: Clarendon Press, 1989.
36. Parry, p. 243.

8   The Philosopher and the Soul

1. C. E. M. Joad, *Guide to Philosophy.* London: Victor Gollancz, 1946, p. 312.
2. S. E. Frost, *Basic Teachings of the Great Philosophers,* rev. ed. Garden City and New York: Dolphin Books and Doubleday, 1962, p. 104.
3. Anthony Flew, *There Is a God.* New York: Harper Collins, 2008, p. 164.
4. W. S. Brown and Nancey Murphy, eds. *Whatever Happened to the Soul?* Minneapolis: Fortress Press, 1998, p. 3.
5. Frost, p. 14.
6. Joad, p. 286.
7. Ibid., p. 502–503.
8. Richard L. Gregory, *Mind in Science.* London: Weidenfeld and Nicholson, 1981, p. 459.
9. Ibid., p. 489. See also Godfrey Vesey, *Personal Identity.* A 313, Units 7–8. Milton Keynes: Open University, 1980, pp. 7ff.
10. Ibid., p. 489. David Hume, *A Treatise of Human Nature,* 1888 ed. P. H. Nidditch. Oxford University Press, 1978, Book 1, Part 4, ch. 6.

11. Peter Cole, *Philosophy of Religion*, 2nd ed. London: Hodder and Stoughton, 2004.

12. Karl Popper and John Eccles, *The Self and Its Brain*. London: Springer International, 1977, pp. 7–15.

13. Ibid., pp. 20–25; Hume, Book 2, Part l, Sec. 40, 1888, p. 317.

14. Ibid., pp. 103–109.

15. Ibid., pp. 117–124, 144, 164.

16. Cole, pp. 464, 473–474, 485–486.

17. Ibid., 497.

18. Ibid., 555.

19. Richard Swinburne, *Evolution of the Soul,* rev. ed. Oxford: Clarenden Press, 1986, p. 21, New appendix D.

20. Ian Barbour, *Religion and Science*. San Francisco: Harper, 1990, pp. 270–271.

21. Raymond Martin and John Barrise, *Rise and Fall of the Soul*. New York: Columbia University Press, 2006, p. 3.

22. Ibid., pp. 381–388.

9   CAN WE AVOID THE DUALISM OF BODY AND SOUL?

1. Quoted by Roy Abraham Varghese in the preface to Anthony Flew, *There Is a God*. New York: Harper Collins, 2008, p. xvii.

2. Daniel C. Dennett, *Kinds of Minds, Towards an Understanding of Consciousness.* London: Weidenfeld, 1996; John Cornwall, "Conscious Raising." *The Sunday Times Bookshop,* August 11, 1996. The Nagel article is in *Philosophical Review* 83, October 4, 1974, pp. 435–50, Duke University, USA.

3. Godfrey Vesey, *Is Man a Machine?* Units 29–36. Humanities; A Foundation Course. Milton Keyes: Oxford University Press, 1975, p. 33.

4. John R. Searle, *Minds, Brains and Programs.* London: BBC, 1984, pp. 403ff., 412–417.

5. Paul Badham, *Christian Beliefs about Life after Death.* Basingstoke: Macmillan, 1976, pp. 105ff.

6. A. J. Ayer, *The National Review,* October 14, 1988, pp. 38ff.

7. J. Sartre, *Being and Nothingness.* London: Methuen, 1958, p. 59.

8. John Puddefoot, *God and the Time Machine*. London: SPCK, 1996, pp. 39–40.

9. Anthony Flew, ed. *Dictionary of Philosophy.* Basingstoke: Pan Books and Macmillan, p. 33. A. J. Ayer, *Central Questions of Philosophy,* 1973, p. 125.

10. John Hick, *Autobiography.* Oxford: One World, 2005, pp. 37, 126–127.
11. John Polkinghorne, *Scientists as Theologians.* London: SPCK, 1996, p. 29.

10   Did Darwin Kill the Soul?

1. Len Fisher, *Weighing the Soul: The Evolution of Scientific Beliefs.* London: Weidenfeld and Nicolson, 2004, p. 231.
2. Charles Darwin, *The Voyage of Charles Darwin: His Autobiographical Writings Selected by Christopher Ralling.* BBC, London: Ariel Books, 1982, p. 135. Missionaries commended in his letters xiv, p. 49. On finding strong feelings at Cape Town against missionaries, Fitzroy and Darwin published a defense of their work in the *South African Christian Recorder,* p. 213. *Charles Darwin's Letters: A Selection 1835–1859,* ed. Frederick Burkhardt. Cambridge: Cambridge University Press, 1998.
3. Ibid., pp. 18 and 141. Closing words of the *Origin of the Species.* London: Penguin Classics, 1859, p. 459. Intro. J. W. Burrow, 1985.
4. Howard E. Gruber and Paul Barrett, *Darwin on Man: A Psychological Study of Scientific Creativity.* London: Wildwood House, 1974, p. 209. This is a discussion of Darwin's private "M" and "N" notebooks on the use of evolution to explain mind and morality.
5. Darwin, pp. 81, 96.
6. Ibid., pp. 107–111.
7. Ibid., pp. 291ff.
8. Ibid., p. 133.
9. Ibid., pp. 156, 317, 323, 455.
10. B. S. Beckett, *Biology,* 2nd ed. Oxford: Oxford University Press, 1982. p. 235.
11. Darwin, pp. 173, 202.
12. Ibid., p. 189.
13. Gruber, p. 452.
14. Beckett, p. 238.
15. Darwin, p. 39.
16. Darwin, pp. 227–228, 237, 263.
17. Charles Darwin, *The Descent of Man and Selection in Relation to Sex.* London: John Murray, 1879. Intro. James Moore and Adrian Desmond. London: Penguin, 2004, p. 81.

18. Ibid., p. 116.

19. Ibid., pp. 120–121.

20. Ibid., pp. 134–138.

21. Ibid., pp. 150–157.

22. Ibid., pp. 672–682.

23. Ibid., p. 683.

24. Letter to Leonard Jenyns in 1860. Charles Darwin, The Expressions of the Emotions in Man and Animals 1890 ed. John Murray London ed by Joe Cain and Sharon Messenger Penguin London 2009 p. xviii

25. Ibid., p. xx.

26. Ibid., p. 332.

27. Ibid., xxxiv.

28. James Moore, *Humanities Block*. Milton Keyes: Oxford University Press, 1998, pp. 134, 143.

29. Ibid., p. 146.

30. Robert Crawford, *What Is Religion?* London: Routledge, 2002, p. 129.

31. Alister Hardy, *Darwin and the Spirit of Man*. London: Collins, 1984, p. 76.

32. Charles Darwin, *The Voyage of Charles Darwin: His Autobiographical Writings Selected by Christopher Ralling*. BBC, London: Ariel Books, 1982, p. 14.

33. Darwin, *The Descent of Man*, p. 107.

11   After Darwin

1. Robert Miller, *Arguments against Secular Culture*. London: SCM, 1995, pp. 187, 194–195; Cambridge, MA and London: Michael Ruse and Harvard University Press, 2003, pp. 252, 264, 266.

2. Ibid., pp. 288, 289, 297, 299.

3. Jacques Monod, *Chance and Necessity*. London: Fount Collins, 1977, p. 137. Mary Midgley, *Science as Salvation*. London: Routledge, 1992, p. 38. Mary Midgley, *Beast and Man*. Brighton: Harvester, 1979, ch 6, p. 231.

4. Paul Davies, *The Cosmic Blueprint*. London: George Allen and Unwin, 1989, p. 108.

5. Ibid., p. 96.

6. Ibid., p. 203.

7. Nora Barlow, ed. *Charles Darwin: The Autobiography*. London: Collins, 1958, pp. 87ff.

8. *New Scientist,* London, February 2000, p. 3.
9. Elving Anderson "A genetic view of human nature" in *Whatever happened to the soul?* ch 3 p. 57, ed by W. S. Brown. Minneapolis: Fortress Press, 1998.
10. Robert Crawford, *The God, Man, World Triangle,* Basingstoke, UK: Macmillan Press, 1997 (hardback), 2000 (paperback), pp. 39–40. This is a dialogue between science and religion.
11. Ibid., pp. 46–47.
12. *Charles Darwin's Letters: A Selection 1835–1859,* p. 203, ed. Frederick Burkhardt. Cambridge: Cambridge University Press, 1998.
13. David, Ian, John and Margaret Millar, *Dictionary of Scientists.* Cambridge: Cambridge University Press, 1996, p. 195.
14. Jane Goodall, *Daily Mail,* London, October 16, 2004.
15. Howard E. Gruber and Paul Barrett, *Darwin on Man: A Psychological Study of Scientific Creativity.* London: Wildwood House, 1974, pp. 316, 384, 390.
16. Charles Darwin, *The Descent of Man and Selection in Relation to Sex.* London: John Murray, 1879. Intro. James Moore and Adrian Desmond. London: Penguin, 2004, p. 124.
17. Ibid., p. 619; Gruber, pp. 241–242.
18. Ibid., p. 95–96; Gruber, p. 366.

12   THE DARWINIANS

1. David, Ian, John and Margaret Millar, *Dictionary of Scientists.* Cambridge: Cambridge University Press, 1996, p. 222.
2. Richard Dawkins, *The God Delusion.* London: Black Swan, 2007, pp. 143ff., 251–258, 268–269, 298, 324–330, 355ff., 383, 402ff.
3. Ibid., ITV Programme, October 4, 2009.
4. Kenneth Miller, Chris Stringer, Chris Wills and Stuart Kauffman, *New Scientist,* January 31, 2009, p. 43
5. Lawton, 38. "Uprooting Darwin's Tree," *Graham Lawton New Scientist,* January 24, 2009, p. 39.
6. Michael Brookes, "Natural Born Believers," New Scientist, February 7, 2009.
7. Bearing, p. 32.
8. Quoted by John Hick in *Frontier of Religion and Science,* p. 120.
9. Gregory, *Mind in Science,* p, 88; Davies, *Cosmic Blueprint,* p. 186

10. R. D. Holder, *Nothing but Atoms and Molecules?* Kent: Monarch Tunbridge Wells, 1993, pp. 81, 95.
11. Murphy, 77, 85–86. *Whatever Happened to the Soul.* See also Nancey Murphy and George F. R. Ellis, *On the Moral Nature of the Universe, Theology Cosmology and Ethics.* Minneapolis: Fortress Press, 1996. *Bodies and Souls or Spirit Bodies.* Cambridge: Cambridge University Press, 2006.
12. Michael Meredith, *The Thoughtful Guide to Science and Religion.* Hants: John Hunt, 2005, p. 78.
13. Richard Swinburne, *Evolution of the Soul.* Oxford: Clarendon Press, p. 127.
14. R. Crawford, *Is God a Scientist?* London: Palgrave, 2004, p. 92; Keith Ward, *In Defence of the Soul,* Oxford: One World, 1998.
15. Scientist correspondent, Hanlon, *Daily Mail,* London, August 22, 2003, p. 13
16. Crawford, p. 135.
17. John Polkinghorne, *God of Hope and the End of the World.* London: SPCK, 2002, pp. xiv, xxi.
18. John Hick, *Death and Eternal Life.* London: Collins, 1976, pp. 28, 40, 43–44, 47.
19. Alison Morgan, *What Happens When We Die?* Eastbourne: Kingsway, 1955, pp. 22, 235.

13 THE WAY FORWARD

1. Anthony Flew, ed. *A Dictionary of Philosophy.* London: Pan Books, 1979, p. 320.
2. Malcolm Jeeves and Warren S. Brown, *Neuroscience, Psychology, and Religion.* Pennsylvania: Templeton Foundation Press, 2009, p. 24.
3. Paul Davies, *God and the New Physics.* London: Penguin Books, 1990, p. 82.
4. Ibid., pp. 20–21.
5. Ibid., pp. 141.
6. Nancey Murphy, *Whatever Happened to the Soul,* ed. Warren S. Brown, Nancey Murphy and H. Newton Malony. Minneapolis: Fortress Press, 1998, p. 20.
7. Ibid., pp. 132–133.
8. Ibid., p. 135.
9. Brown, p. 223.
10. Davies, p. 82.

11. Russell Stannard, Letter of September 6, 2006.
12. Davies, p. 226.
13. Ibid., p. 98.
14. Ibid., p. 141.
15. John Polkinghorne, with comment by David Lawrence, *Reform*. London, November 1999, p. 15.
16. Robert Miller, *Arguments against Secular Culture*. London: SCM, 1995, p. 102.
17. Letter from Polkinghorne, July 17, 2009.
18. John Polkinghorne, *God Hope and the End of the World*. London: SPCK, 2002, pp. 106–107.
19. John Hick, *Reform*. London, July/August, 2009, pp. 22–23.
20. Stannard.
21. Robert Crawford, *The God Man World Triangle*. London: Palgrave, 2000, ch. 10.
22. P. F. Strawson, *Individuals*. London: Methuen, 1969, ch. 3.
23. Dave Tomlinson, *Reform*. London, May 9, 2010, p. 11.
24. Sam Parnia, *What Happens When We Die?* London: Hay House, 2007, pp. 49, 112–113.
25. Susan Blackmore, *Beyond the Body*, ed. Brain Inglis. London: Heinemann, 1982, pp. 73, 81, 149–150.
26. Parnia, refers to Eccles. pp. 142–143, 163ff., 177, 218.
27. Peter Fenwick, "Science and Spirituality, a Challenge for the 21st Century," the Bruce Greyson Lecture from the international association for near death studies, 2004. See also "Truth in the Light," an Investigation of over three hundred near death experiences. London: Headline Book, 1995.

INDEX